P9-DZN-557

AbL-5681

Please remember that this is a library book,
and that it belongs only temporarily to each
person who uses it. Be considerate. Do
not write in this, or any, library book.

WITHDRAWN

Group Work with Older Adults

Clinical Gerontology
GENERAL EDITOR: *Steven H. Zarit*

GROUP WORK WITH OLDER ADULTS

Ronald W. Toseland

WITHDRAWN

New York University Press
New York and London

Copyright © 1990 by New York University
All rights reserved
Manufactured in the United States of America

Library of Congress Cataloging-in-Publication Data
Toseland, Ronald W.
Group work with older adults / Ronald W. Toseland.
p.   cm. — (Clinical gerontology ; 3)
Includes bibliographical references (p.   ) and indexes.
ISBN 0-8147-8189-6 (alk. paper)
1. Social work with the aged—United States.   2. Social group
work—United States.   3. Social group work—Handbooks, manuals, etc.
I. Title.   II. Series.
HV1451.T67   1990
362.6—dc20   90-6338
CIP

New York University Press books are printed on acid-free paper,
and their binding materials are chosen for strength and durability.

To Sheryl Holland
for her enduring support through many
years with all my love

WITHDRAWN

Contents

Preface

This book is designed as a practical guide for students and practitioners who want to improve their skills in working with groups of older adults. It is divided into two parts. Part 1 provides an overview of group work with older adults and describes skills for working with all of the types of groups in which older adults participate. It contains four chapters. The first chapter presents an overview and an introduction to working with groups of older adults. The second chapter focuses on the skills necessary to facilitate therapeutic group dynamics. The third chapter examines leadership and coleadership skills, and the fourth describes the skills necessary to facilitate groups during the planning, beginning, middle, and ending phases of their development.

Part 2 focuses on methods and skills to facilitate specific types of groups for older persons. Part 2 contains five chapters: chapter 5 focuses on practice with support groups; chapter 6 on practice with therapy groups; chapter 7 on practice with social, recreational, and educational groups; chapter 8 on practice with service and advocacy groups; and chapter 9 on practice with groups for family caregivers of the frail elderly.

A number of individuals have assisted me in the preparation of this book. In particular, I would like to thank Margaret Hartford, Kitty Moore, Edmund Sherman, Sheldon Tobin, and Steve Zarit for their thoughtful suggestions. Their assistance is gratefully acknowledged.

I would also like to express my gratitude to the Andrus Foundation of the American Association of Retired Persons, the Health Services Research and Development Office of the United States Veteran's Administration, and the Prevention Research Branch of the National Institute of Mental Health. This book would not have been possible without the generous support that I received from these sources for my research on the effectiveness of group work practice with older adults.

Part I
FOUNDATION KNOWLEDGE

1

Working with Older Adults in Groups

The population of older persons in the United States is growing in the 1990s at a more rapid rate than other segments of society (U.S. Bureau of the Census 1989). This growth is expected to continue well into the twenty-first century. The "greying" of the American population has led to a dramatic increase in programs and services for older persons and their families.

Group work is used extensively as a service modality in a wide variety of community and institutional settings serving older persons and their families. Therefore, knowledge about how to work effectively with groups should be an important component of the expertise of any practitioner who works with older adults. Group work skills can be helpful both in formal group meetings and when working with cliques, small friendship groups, coalitions and other informal associations that form as older adults participate in service programs. Even in settings where services are delivered primarily on an individual or family basis, such as home-based health care programs, group work skills can help practitioners understand, participate in, and facilitate interdisciplinary teams that offer services in a comprehensive and coordinated fashion.

HISTORICAL FOUNDATIONS

Group work with older persons in the United States developed gradually in three distinct settings during the first three decades of the twentieth century. These settings were settlement houses and community centers, homes for the aged, and state mental institutions.

The first published reports of group work with older persons began to appear a few years after the end of World War II. Interest in group work with older adults increased during the 1950s for a variety of reasons, including an increase in the number of people who were living to old age; societal changes that led to a tremendous increase in the number of older people residing in homes for the aged and state mental institutions; an

3

increase in the number of professionals interested in aging; and the publication of books and articles incorporating the experiences of pioneers who had worked with older people in groups during the preceding decade.

Maurice Linden (1953) is often credited as being one of the early pioneers of group work with older adults because of his efforts to develop a group therapy program for "demented" residents of a state mental institution in Pennsylvania (see, for example, Burnside 1986; Shere 1964). However, it is clear from early reports that group work with older persons was being conducted in a variety of community settings in the 1930s. For example, James Woods (1953) described some of his pioneering efforts in the late 1930s to develop group work programs for the elderly in "golden age centers" in the Cleveland, Ohio, area with funding and support from the Benjamin Rose Institute and Case Western Reserve University. Other early pioneers who developed group work programs in settlement houses, public housing projects, churches, Jewish community centers, and institutional settings in Chicago, New York, and other urban areas include Jerome Kaplan (1953), Gisela Konopka (1954), Susan Kubie and Gertrude Landau (1953), Louis Lowy (1955), Jean Maxwell (1952), Sidney Shapiro (1954), Herbert Shore (1952), Gertrude Wilson and Gladys Ryland (1949), and Florence Vickery (1952).

Group work in settlement houses and community centers focused on helping older persons to engage in social and recreational activities with their peers. For example, in one of the earliest reports of group work with older persons appearing in the literature, Wilson and Ryland (1949) described methods for helping older people to develop a network of friends through a friendship club. In the same tradition, one of the first books to focus exclusively on group work with older persons examined how group methods were employed in a day center for the aged (Kubie and Landau 1953). Other reports of group work with older persons in community centers also began to appear at this time (see, for example, Hunter 1951; Kaplan 1953; Krasner 1952; Lowy 1955; Shapiro 1954; Vickery 1952).

The early literature also indicated that group work was practiced extensively in homes for the aged. The early writings of Herbert Shore (1952) and Gisela Konopka (1954) exemplify this tradition. Group work in homes for the aged focused on helping older residents to adjust to and become better integrated into the home, to maintain and increase feelings of well-being, to remain socially and physically active, and to stay in contact with reality. This was accomplished primarily through group discussion and participation in a wide variety of program activities.

During the early 1950s, group work for older persons was also being developed in state mental institutions. The population of state mental institutions in the United States reached its peak during this time, and many of the residents were elderly. Qualified staff were in short supply. Group work was viewed as an efficient method for serving the unmet needs of the neglected elderly residents.

Silver (1950) was the first to report on a program of group therapy with paranoid and senile psychotic female inpatients between the ages of seventy and eighty. However, it has been suggested that Linden's (1953) work had more impact, because it described a professional program of group therapy and clinical research with the very old, and because it reported the impact of the intervention program on the residents in a systematic and orderly fashion (Burnside 1986; Goldfarb 1971).

Contemporary writers such as Burnside (1986), Hartford (1985), and Lowy (1955) point out that group work practice with older persons continues unabated in a wide variety of settings today. If anything, the contemporary literature suggests that group work practice has expanded beyond the long-term social, recreational, and therapy group programs that made up the bulk of early practitioner efforts. Although these groups continue to account for the bulk of practice with older people, during the 1970s and 1980s there has been an increased interest in short-term educational and skills building groups, in reminiscence and life-review groups, and in self-help, support, and advocacy groups. In the 1980s there also has been an increased interest in support groups for caregivers of older persons.

THE AGING EXPERIENCE

To engage older persons in groups, to help them assess their needs, and to help them plan and implement effective intervention strategies, practitioners should recognize the strengths and capacities of older people and strive to understand the experience of aging. Understanding what it is like to be in the latter years of one's life helps practitioners to be empathic, realistic, and effective.

When working with individuals younger than themselves, practitioners have the advantage of having personally experienced the developmental issues faced by this age group. In fact, if they have children, practitioners experience these developmental issues again through parenting. They can use their experiences with these developmental issues as an aid when engaging younger clients and attempting to understand their subjective experiences of reality.

In contrast, relatively few practitioners have had personal experience with the developmental issues faced by older adults. They may be able to draw on experiences with aging parents and grandparents, but these experiences are not entirely the same as the personal understanding gained by living through an experience. Therefore, it can be more difficult for them to understand the life experiences and developmental tasks commonly experienced by older adults. It can also be difficult for them to respond to elderly group members who question whether the practitioner has the life experiences necessary to be helpful.

To minimize the impact of their lack of personal experience, it is essential for practitioners to sensitize themselves to the issues that older adults typically struggle with in the latter parts of their lives. Practitioners can begin this process by identifying their own feelings and attitudes toward the aging process. Like many young and middle-aged persons, practitioners' images of aging may be distorted by negative stereotypes. For example, there is some evidence to suggest that professional helpers are more likely to underestimate the capabilities of clients than are lay persons (Wills 1978). This may be because practitioners come into contact with many older individuals who are not functioning at optimal levels.

Whatever the reason, a negative image of aging interferes with effective helping, and sensitivity to one's own stereotypes about the aging process and about older adults promotes effective helping. Orr (1986), for example, has pointed out how a practitioner's sensitivity to ageism helped her to prevent individuals who were thirty years younger than other members of a group from treating the older members as invalids. Thus, practitioners should strive to understand as much as possible about the process of aging and about older adults.

Practitioners should be aware that there are both negative and positive aspects to growing old. In regard to physical aging, there is tremendous variability. In general, however, the young-old—those in their fifties, sixties, and early seventies—are not appreciably affected by age-related physical changes, whereas the old-old—those over seventy-five—experience increasing limitations of their everyday functioning.

What are the nature of these physical changes? There is a gradual decline in physical stamina and vitality with age. For example, the ability to get oxygen into the blood peaks at about age twenty, remains relatively high until age forty-five, and then gradually but steadily declines so that at age eighty the average individual can get only about half as much oxygen into the blood (Shock 1977). There is a slowing of reaction time and recall, and the speed and accuracy of movement declines with advanced age (Salthouse 1985). There are reductions in visual and auditory acuity, and the senses of taste and smell decline (see, for example, Kline and Schieber 1985; Olsho, Harkins, and Lenhardt 1985). As one ages, there is a greater number of, and greater susceptibility to, chronic and acute health problems (Shanas and Maddox 1985), and an increase in injury from falls and other accidents (Sterns, Barrett, and Alexander 1985).

Group work practitioners should be aware that the previously mentioned decrements in physical functioning do not become severe enough to appreciably affect the day-to-day functioning of most older adults until they reach advanced old age. They should also be aware that the great majority of older persons cope well with physical changes. For example, to compensate for slowed reaction time and reduced visual acuity, older adults may drive more slowly and cautiously, they may wear corrective lenses, and they may limit their driving to daytime hours.

In regard to psychological development, there is a high incidence of depression, dementia, and suicide in old age (La Rue, Dessonville, and Jarvik 1985). Yet the concept of self tends to solidify, and older adults use their personal history to maintain their self-concept. There is also a tendency among older adults to rely on well-practiced skills, which, in turn, provides them with a sense of mastery and competence (Atchley 1989). These positive psychological developments are reflected in empirical evidence concerning the way younger and older persons view themselves. For example, the self-esteem scores of older adults are at least as high as those of younger adults (Bengtson, Reedy, and Gordon 1985).

In the social arena, meaningful social roles are often lost. Family members and friends die more frequently as one ages, and widowhood is common. The negative effects of age on labor force participation and the negative effects of retirement are well documented (Robinson, Coberly, and Paul 1985). Retirement may create financial problems at a time when greater material resources may be needed to pay for medical care or to modify living arrangements to maintain independent living. However, identity crises resulting from retirement are relatively rare (Atchley 1983). Also, cultural and behavioral expectations are less clear than earlier in life, making it difficult for some older persons to define new roles and to use leisure time in a satisfying manner (Rosow 1974).

It should be emphasized, however, that the overwhelming majority of older people cope well with the loss of meaningful social roles. Lost roles are replaced with new ones, and new friendships are established. The widespread belief that older people become increasingly isolated with age is not supported by the available evidence (Antonucci 1985). Although some older people are socially isolated, these individuals may merely be continuing lifelong patterns (Cohen and Rajkowski 1982; Felton et al. 1977). The great majority of older people are surrounded by a support network of family and friends who do not abandon them in old age (Lebowitz 1978; Sussman 1979).

It should also be recognized that aging is often accompanied by freedom from some of the concerns of young adulthood and middle age. During the 1970s the economic status of older adults improved greatly (Chen 1985).

While there are still many older adults who live in poverty, for the great majority of older people who are financially secure, there is an independence from work-related roles and a freedom from striving to succeed in the workplace that was not possible in the earlier years of their lives. Older adults have time to pursue activities that they may not have had time for in the past.

Although it is helpful to understand as much as possible about the experience of old age, practitioners should avoid relying solely on generalizations, taking care to individualize each older person with whom they work by identifying unique characteristics, traits, and coping styles. There are two things that gerontologists have learned about development in later life that substantiate the validity of this practice principle. First, gerontologists have come to understand that, although it is possible to change dramatically in later years, there tends to be much continuity in development across the life span (Atchley 1989). Personality characteristics do not change significantly with age. Rather, they are elaborated, developed, and modified through a continual process of proactive and reactive interaction with the social and physical environment that surrounds them (Atchley 1989; Bengtson, Reedy, and Gordon 1985).

Older persons rely on the coping mechanisms they have developed over the years to help them adapt to the ever-changing world around them (Whitbourne 1985). Therefore, group workers should strive to identify and work with the unique and enduring coping mechanisms that each member has developed over his or her lifetime. It is these coping mechanisms that older individuals are likely to fall back on when they are faced with stress resulting from traumatic life events.

Gerontologists have also learned that chronological age, by itself, is a poor indicator of coping and adaptation in later life (see, for example, Hagestad and Neugarten 1985; Neugarten 1987). Unlike young children, who show many similarities in their development, aging people become more and more diverse and differentiated from one another. This occurs because of their unique physiologies and developmental histories, and as a result of their proactive efforts to create satisfying and meaningful lives for themselves. The interaction of their long developmental histories with their unique genetic predispositions is what makes older people different from one another as they age.

Practitioners who work with older persons quickly realize that some individuals are vigorous and vital in their seventies and eighties, while others have deteriorated before they reach sixty-five. They also realize that older adults are a diverse population and have developed a variety of creative mechanisms for adapting to life. In many respects, old age is the most diverse time of life. Although individuals experience similar developmental tasks as they age and rely on these experiences as an anchor for their self-identity, self-concept, and self-esteem, individuals have unique biological and familial heritages, and they experience unique sets of life events as they age. To cope with and adapt to the vicissitudes of life, older adults draw upon their unique backgrounds and the unique sets of coping strategies they have developed in response to the particular life events they have experienced.

A variety of qualities and characteristics of older group members are at least as important as chronological age. For example, groups will take on quite different dynamics if members are energetic and healthy, or if they are cognitively or physically impaired. Social class, ethnicity, education, sex, marital status, the timing of life events, and the specific types of problems experienced by older people all influence how they participate in groups. There is some evidence, for example, that gender differences are particularly important in later life development (Hagestad and Neugarten 1985; Bengtson, Reedy, and Gordon 1985).

Therefore, it is not appropriate for practitioners to stereotype individuals on the basis of their chronological age, a rigid set of behavioral expectations, or preconceived notions of what it means to grow old. Rather, practitioner should use their knowledge of development in later life as a reference point to guide their inquiry into the unique aspects of each group member's life. An understanding of development in later life can facilitate practitioners' ability to understand older adults' current life experiences, to engage those who are reluctant to participate in a group with their peers, and to develop and implement appropriate service plans.

Although there is relatively little information in the group work literature about the way age *per se* influences the forces that develop in groups, there are commonalities among different cohorts of older persons that are likely to affect group dynamics. For example, a group of seventy- and eighty-year-old individuals who had direct experience with the economic depression of the 1930s may place more emphasis on thrift and financial security than those in their fifties and sixties. In turn, those in their sixties are likely to be struggling with different developmental issues and tasks than those in their eighties. The young-old will more likely be dealing with issues of retirement, whereas the old-old are more likely to be concerned about maintaining functioning in the face of continual assaults on their person resulting from declines in their physical health and vitality. Therefore, although chronological age in the latter years may be a relatively unimportant variable as compared to health and financial status, it should not be overlooked.

COMMON THEMES

Within the diversity of the aging experience, there are some common issues and themes that typify the major concerns of older adults. These themes frequently arise when older persons come together in group meetings. It is helpful for practitioners to become familiar with some of these ubiquitous themes as they prepare to work with groups of older persons.

Continuity with the past. Clinical experience suggests that in peer groups, many older adults spend time talking about their past accomplishments and swapping stories about what life has been like for them. This is especially true if they are not engaged in activities that keep them involved and that help them to replace lost roles with new ones. Older adults often derive much satisfaction from recalling and reliving past experiences. Some, of course, have had painful life experiences, and reminiscing may cause them to recall unpleasant experiences. However, experience with older people suggests that many selectively remember those events that were particularly pleasurable and that give their life meaning (Atchley 1989; Tobin and Lieberman 1976).

It is also important for practitioners to understand that older adults are not preoccupied with the past merely for the sake of it. Rather, their sense of self was developed in earlier years, and they rely on their past to maintain a sense of self, to soothe them through difficult aspects of the transition to old age, and to give their life meaning.

Older adults actually make less of a distinction between the past and the present than do younger people. Tobin and Lieberman (1976) note, for example, that older adults who have retired from their jobs still think of themselves as carpenters, electricians, and school teachers. A focus on the past makes a great deal of sense for older persons because they have a longer history and a shorter future to look forward to than younger individuals.

Practitioners who are unaccustomed to working with older adults may be put off by their reliance on past experiences, interpreting it as a way to avoid dealing with the present and the future, or as a form of rigidity. This interpretation is often incorrect. Unless an older person constantly dwells on events in the past in a morbid fashion while actively avoiding the present, practitioners should not be concerned. Reminiscing is a way for older persons to socialize, to feel good about themselves and what they have to offer, to put their past in perspective, to come to terms with who they are, and to use their past experiences as a source of strength when coping with and adapting to changes resulting from the aging process.

Understanding the modern world. Older adults sometimes talk with peers to help themselves understand and adapt to the changing world in which they live. Practitioners must remember that older people were born into, and grew up in, a very different world than exists today. It is natural for all people to contrast their present and past experiences. In an attempt to conserve energy, to preserve their culture, their traditions, and their sense of self in a changing world, older persons tend to incorporate those aspects of the modern world that are consistent with their view of reality, and to gloss over those that are foreign until they are forced to do otherwise by the exigencies of life (Atchley 1989). Groups can be helpful by allowing older persons to interact with a peer group from a similar age cohort who share similar historical experiences and who confirm each others' world views. Groups are also helpful because they expand older adults' coping strategies by exposing them to others in similar situations who utilize different coping strategies.

Independence. Many older people are concerned about issues of dependence and independence. Chronic and acute disabilities make some older people more dependent on others even as they strive to be fiercely independent in order to maintain their own integrity and sense of self. Group time is frequently taken up by discussions of how they are able to manage their own affairs, how much they fear becoming dependent on their children, how they are sometimes treated as children by their own children or other family members, and how terrible it would be if they were forced to leave their home and relocate to an unfamiliar residence or a nursing facility. At these times, ventilation of feelings, support from the group for continuing to care for themselves, discussion of how to handle conflictual relationships with children, and the sharing of resources to help maintain independent living can be important benefits of group participation.

Physical and cognitive impairments. Just as adolescents become concerned with issues that are new for them, such as becoming sexually active, older people sometimes become concerned with the changes that they notice taking place in their physical stamina and vitality. Group time is often spent discussing concerns about recent illnesses, the lack of responsiveness of health care professionals, how best to be advocates for themselves with health care providers, the expense of medical care, and the sharing of information about medical resources to care for themselves or their spouses.

Older people also sometimes become concerned about occasional forgetfulness. They wonder if an occasional lapse of memory is an indication that they, or a beloved spouse, is developing Alzheimer's disease or some other equally dreaded brain dysfunction. The reassurance and support offered in a group can be particularly helpful for overcoming the anxiety that can result from preoccupation with physical ailments.

Loss of family members and friends. Loss is a theme that frequently emerges when older people gather together in groups (Burnside 1970). In no other age group are losses as common. It is, therefore, essential for practitioners who work with older adults to become thoroughly familiar with the process of grieving. For example, long after the death of a spouse, it is quite natural for a group member to want to discuss the impact that this event has had on his or her life, including how he or she is readjusting to life without the long-time partner. Similarly, it may take many months for the individual to reveal guilt feelings about his or her secret wish for the death of a spouse who was in constant pain, or to express relief over no longer having to provide 24-hour-a-day care for the spouse.

Older people experience the death of other family members and close friends more frequently than do younger persons. Thus, group time is often spent in supporting people who have had a recent loss and in discussing the impact that the death of family and friends have had on them. Group discussion and sharing about the loss of family members and friends also helps older adults to consider their own mortality and to prepare for their own death. Group workers should not assume, however, that all losses are devastating to older persons. Atchley (1989) points out, for example, that the widowhood of a person who hated her spouse may not be a devastating event. Similarly, experience in caregiver groups suggests that group members sometimes feel relief over the deaths of spouses who have suffered lengthy, painful illnesses. Group workers who assume that the event is devastating may prevent members from talking about feelings of relief that are not perceived as "socially acceptable."

Spouses and other family of origin relationships. Family relationships take on added importance in old age because of the loss of other social roles and relationships, the changes in marital relations brought on by retirement, and the increased dependence on family members for informal help when chronic health problems interfere with self-maintenance skills. Older adults often spend time discussing relationships with spouses and other family members when they participate in groups. For example, Waller and Griffin (1984) noted that depressed older women who met in a long-term group in a senior citizens center spent much time discussing changes in husband-wife relations due to retirement. In a similar vein, experience with older adult caregivers suggests that when they met together in support groups they frequently discuss the difficulties they have in relating to a spouse who has become severely impaired. Groups can be helpful by encouraging older adults to discuss family relationships, to examine historical patterns, to reflect on what they can realistically expect from spouses and other family members in the present and in the future, and to explore how relationships with these significant others might be improved.

Children and grandchildren. Children and grandchildren are a special source of pleasure, and of heartache, for older persons. In almost every group, older people find some time to talk with great pride about the accomplishments of their children, to share pictures, or to talk with animation about the activities of their grandchildren. At the same time, children and grandchildren can be problematic topics of discussion for older persons. Some older persons have not had children, and others have experienced the loss of a child. For these older persons, talk about children and grandchildren may not be a positive experience. Some older people have had lifelong conflictual relationships with children that have continued into old age. Others have not developed cordial relationships with sons-in-law and daughters-in-law. These relationships become even more problematic as they are forced to turn to their adult children for assistance as they become frail and dependent. Group participation provides older adults with an opportunity to share the accomplishments of children and grandchildren and to discuss problematic relationships and how to improve them.

Resources. Living on fixed incomes can make older persons concerned about their financial situations. The high cost of food, housing, and medical insurance and care is frequently a topic of discussion. Although pride sometimes interferes with discussions of food stamps, Supplementary Security Income (SSI), and other programs that they consider "welfare," older people readily share information with each other about medicare, nutrition, health screening, transportation, home care, and other programs for seniors. Groups can be helpful by making older people aware of resources and by helping them to overcome the stigma attached to "welfare" programs.

Environmental vulnerability and adjustment. As older people age, they may become more vulnerable to changes in their environment. Their experience of vulnerability is shown in their concern for safety, their fear of crime, and their responses to other changes in their community that threaten their sense of well-being. Their preception of vulnerability is also shown in their concern that their mobility may be curtailed by the loss of their ability to drive or to use public transportation, that they may no longer be able to maintain their own home or apartment, or that they may be forced to relocate to an institution. Support groups can provide a safe place for older people to talk with empathic listeners about their feelings of vulnerability and to get ideas about how to adjust to any recent changes in their lives. Groups also help older adults to sustain feelings of mastery by providing them with social support networks in which mutual aid is exchanged.

Religious and ethnic pride. Many members of the current cohort of older persons have strong religious and ethnic ties. Indeed, many live in community housing or institutional settings that are associated with particular religious and ethnic groups. It is not at all uncommon for group members to speak with great pride about their ethnic traditions or about the solace they obtain from firm religious convictions. In a similar vein, older people sometimes use group time to lament the changes they observe in younger people who do not seem to share the same commitment to religious values or an ethnic heritage. Groups provide an opportunity for older adults to come together and share their common religious and ethnic heritage.

Leisure pursuits. Leisure time is an inevitable by-product of work-related role losses that older adults experience as they age. Informal socializing before, during, or after group meetings often allows older adults to learn how their peers use their leisure time. In a subtle but very real way, discussions with group members about leisure time pursuits help older adults to gain insight into age-appropriate behavioral expectations and to consider becoming involved in new social roles. Participation with peers in social and recreational groups is also a way for older adults to spend their leisure time in a satisfying manner.

THE BENEFITS OF GROUP PARTICIPATION

In a well-functioning group, the ability to share common themes and individual diversity carries many benefits for older adults.

Belonging and affiliation. Groups offer a medium for human contact and human relatedness. The feelings of belonging and affiliation that come from participating in groups help older adults to counter the social isolation and loneliness that can accompany role losses that are frequently experienced in later life.

In groups, older adults can share their life experiences and learn about those of their peers. Well-functioning groups provide a warm, familiar, friendly, and supportive environment for mutual sharing and responsive social contact with peers.

Through group participation, older adults can expand their social networks. Old friendships are renewed and new ones are developed. Also, the common history and the emotionally charged, personal experiences shared by members can occasionally form the basis for enduring relationships that provide lasting support long after the demise of a group.

Consensual validation and affirmation. Group participation helps to validate and affirm the experiences of older adults. In groups, older adults hear others voice similar concerns and describe similar experiences. Sharing mutual experience helps older adults to feel that they are not alone with their concerns, that their thoughts, feelings, and experiences are not unusual or deviant. Also, older adults get recognition from each other for their talents, skills, and activities. They are encouraged by their fellow group members for their efforts to adapt to and cope with adverse life experiences. This, in turn, helps to build their feelings of competence, mastery, self-esteem, and self-confidence.

Ventilation and integration. Groups provide a place for older adults to share their life experiences and their emotional reactions with peers who are understanding and empathic. Unlike spouses, adult children, and other family members who are often emotionally involved in older adults' lives, peers can provide a more emotionally detached, objective perspective. Groups provide older adults with an opportunity to reflect on their life experiences and to come to terms with unresolved concerns and issues. Groups allow older persons to put problematic experiences in perspective. By selectively sharing positive and meaningful aspects of their lives with peers, older adults have the opportunity to develop a sense of ego integrity.

Satisfying and meaningful roles. Groups provide an opportunity for older adults to take on many different satisfying and meaningful roles and to expand their knowledge of the roles that are available to them outside of the group. In service and advocacy groups, older adults have the opportunity to make use of their expertise and their wisdom to accomplish particular tasks. In socialization and recreation groups, they can participate in enjoyable and stimulating activities, sharing with other group members their expertise in a particular program activity. In educational groups, they have the opportunity to pursue topics of interest and to share their knowledge, experience, and wisdom. They may also learn about social, recreational, and educational opportunities as well as about opportunities to volunteer or to engage in paid employment. In therapy groups, they can give help as well as receive it. For example, they can be supportive, they can offer other members their perspectives on the concerns and issues that are being described, and they can share what has worked for them in coping with stressful life events. All of these opportunities allow older people to demonstrate their capabilities, to exercise their talents, and to assure themselves and their significant others of their continued usefulness.

Interpersonal learning. Groups provide older adults with unique opportunities for interpersonal learning. They provide (1) multiple sources of feedback about here-and-now behavior in the group as well as about past situations that members share with the group, (2) role models who can be selectively imitated or rejected, (3) partners for role plays and other dramatic enactments, (4) opportunities for reality testing, (5) a range of alternative perspectives, creative ideas, and new insights, (6) a place to reflect on, discuss, and practice new behaviors in a safe, supportive environment before trying them out in other settings that are likely to be less receptive, and (7) help with the transition to new roles. For example, members learn about what behaviors are normative for grandparents by listening to what other group members do with their grandchildren. They are given feedback about appropriate and inappropriate behavior in their roles as grandparents, they are encouraged to try out new behaviors, and they are supported in their efforts to deal with any conflicts that may arise with adult children or grandchildren.

Information. Groups provide members with an excellent opportunity to share information. In groups, older adults learn about community resources and services as well as about recreational, social, and leisure activities. Perhaps more importantly, groups provide an opportunity for older adults to learn about what using a particular service or resource is like. Positive accounts help to overcome the reluctance and fear that some group members may have about using a service. Negative accounts help to make expectations realistic and enable older adults to prepare for obstacles.

Problem solving. Groups offer older adults the opportunity to resolve problems with the help and the support of fellow members and the leader. Objective input from other members helps to overcome blocks encountered when individuals attempt to resolve problems by relying solely on their own subjective perspectives. In groups, older adults identify and sort out their concerns in a more orderly, systematic, and concentrated fashion than when they solve problems in isolation. Group problem solving challenges older adults to be specific about priorities and goals. It helps members to examine factors that contribute to and exacerbate problems. It provides input from a variety of different sources, thereby exposing older adults to alternative perspectives and solutions. It motivates members to follow through on the implementation of action plans, and it provides a supportive environment when obstacles are encountered.

EFFECTIVENESS AND EFFICIENCY

How effective and efficient are groups in meeting the needs of older persons? Comprehensive reviews of the literature have uncovered over one hundred citations focused on group work with older persons scattered throughout a wide array of journals (see, for example, Burnside 1986; Tross and Blum 1988). The reviews suggest that there has been a consistent, albeit relatively small, interest in the use of groups with older adults by a number of different professional groups in the last several decades. Although it has been claimed that group work with older persons has been conducted primarily in institutional settings, the literature suggests that many group programs for older adults have also been developed in community settings (see, for example, Debor, Gallagher, and Lesher 1983; Ingersoll and Silverman 1978; Petty, Moeller, and Campbell 1976; Rosen and Rosen 1982; Steuer et al. 1984; Toseland and Rose 1978; Toseland, Sherman, and Bliven 1981).

Almost all of the reports of group programs for older persons extol the positive effects of group participation. Many of the reports, even those from the earlier years, include some evidence to support claims of program effectiveness. For example, Linden's (1953) early account of group therapy with inpatients indicated that 45 percent of the patients who received an average of 54 hours of group therapy had either left the hospital or were in the process of being discharged. The same article also gives figures on the "improvement status" of the group who remained in the hospital.

Unfortunately, many reports, including Linden's, do not include rigorous experimental designs, leaving one to wonder whether the positive results cited in the literature are too optimistic. In two excellent reviews of the literature about group psychotherapy for older persons, Goldfarb (1971) and Parham, Priddy, McGovern, and Richman (1982) have concluded that although the goals of the treatment programs were not always clear, and the designs sometimes flawed, group treatment programs appear to have many important benefits, only one of which is the direct effect of therapy for individuals with organic and functional mental disorders. The other beneficial effects that they mentioned include (1) the special status, recognition, and attention received from staff and other patients by participants identified for group programs, (2) the identification of previously neglected persons for therapeutic programming, (3) the increased observation and additional individual and pharmacological treatment given to participants as a result of being identified for a group program, (4) the increased staff morale resulting from the initiation of a new program, (5) the increased feelings of effectiveness experienced by staff who are provided with theories about participants' functioning and with group intervention techniques for how to help them improve, (6) the rise in participants' attention to personal hygiene, (7) the increase in staff's inclination to help participants, (8) the increase in family interest, sometimes leading to a trial at home and eventual discharge, and (9) the sense of community that group meetings give long-term residents of institutional settings.

Reviews of the empirical and clinical evidence concerning the efficacy of group work in relation to other service delivery modalities, though not directly focused on group work with older persons, are also encouraging. For example, a number of different reviews of the practice effectiveness literature have concluded that group treatment is more effective than no treatment and is as effective as other treatment modalities (Luborsky, Singer, and Luborsky 1975; Parloff and Dies 1977; Reid and Hanrahan 1982; Smith, Glass, and Miller 1980). However, these reviews summarize the therapeutic effects reported by studies not specifically designed to compare group work with other service modalities.

A review that used only rigorously controlled studies comparing group work to individual treatment found that it was the more effective modality in 25 percent of the studies (Toseland and Siporin 1986). In all of the remaining studies that were reviewed, no differences were found between individual and group treatment. Thus, the review suggested that group treatment is at least as effective as individual treatment.

A recent study by Toseland, Rossiter, Peak, and Smith (in press) that was not included in the review confirms the superiority of group treatment for increasing members' social support networks. However, it indicates that individual treatment may be better than group treatment for the amelioration of psychological problems. Thus, it appears that group work is the treatment of choice for those who are socially isolated and in need of support. For those who have psychological and social problems, a combination of individual and group treatment is likely to be more effective.

The review article by Toseland and Siporin (1986) also found that group treatment was associated with lower rates of discontinuance from treatment, and that it was more efficient than individual treatment. The studies that examined treatment discontinuance measured this concept by the number of dropouts from individual and group treatment. It was found that group treatment produced fewer dropouts than individual treatment in all of the studies that examined this question. The authors speculated that the mutual support, mutual aid, and cohesion found among group members tended to keep them participating longer than individuals who participated in individual treatment.

The review by Toseland and Siporin (1986) also lends some empirical support to the popular belief that group treatment is more efficient than individual treatment. Savings of between 15% and 40% of therapist time were reported. However, only a few studies addressed this question, and they were designed for other purposes. Therefore, despite the available findings, practitioners should be cautious about making assertions that group treatment is more efficient than individual treatment. It should be recognized that savings depend on a number of factors, including whether or not a cotherapist is used, the number of participants attending a group, the length of group meetings, how much preparation time is involved, and to what extent the content of meetings has to be individualized to meet the needs of members. For example, a group meeting for forty older adults focused on educating participants about community resources, with one well-prepared leader, is clearly more efficient than forty individual meetings designed to explain the same information. However, two practitioners coleading a ninety-minute group for six inpatients experiencing different mental health problems requiring individual treatment plans may not be any more efficient than two practitioners dividing the clients among themselves and seeing each individually for shorter time periods.

INDICATIONS AND CONTRAINDICATIONS FOR GROUP PARTICIPATION

Practitioners are often faced with the question of when they should recommend that older adults participate in a group rather than an alternative service modality. There are three categories of older adults for whom groups are particularly well suited. Older adults who are socially isolated, shy, and inhibited can benefit greatly from group participation. These individuals need accepting interpersonal relationships that groups can provide. Groups are well suited for older adults who have interpersonal problems. Groups provide opportunities for peer feedback and reality testing and for the acquisition of role models and partners to participate in role-playing exercises to increase interpersonal skills. Groups are also particularly appropriate for older adults who need assistance in identifying and participating in new social roles. Groups provide an opportunity for older adults to learn about new roles from peers, to stay active and involved, and to use the skills, expertise, and wisdom they have accumulated over a lifetime.

There are three broad categories of contraindications for group participation. These are (1) practical barriers, (2) particular therapeutic needs, and (3) certain personality attributes and capacities. Practical barriers constitute the primary reason why more group work is not done with older persons. They may preclude group participation in a number of ways. Some older persons are too frail to attend group meetings. In some settings, the number of older persons with similar concerns, problems, or needs may be too few to form a group. Transportation to and from group meetings may be unavailable or prohibitively expensive.

Factors such as fear of self-disclosure in a group situation, cultural norms discouraging group participation, and long-standing behavioral patterns of not being a "joiner" can also create practical barriers by causing older adults to avoid opportunities to participate in groups and to decline invitations that are offered. Concerns about health, weather conditions, safety, and the like deter some potential participants. Dislike for being with others whom they view as different or concerns about being forced into a social situation with others with whom they have long-standing conflictual relationships deter other potential participants. Experience suggests that the latter barrier arises most frequently in community settings where seniors live in the same highrise building, in the same scattered-site apartment complex, or on the same floor or wing in an institutional setting. Ways to overcome some of these practical barriers are described in chapter 4.

Particular therapeutic needs may also contraindicate group participation. For example, individuals who are experiencing acute crisis situations may be better served by individual treatment because they can receive concentrated help for their pressing needs. Individuals who have highly personal information to disclose may be better served individually. When the concerns of the older adult are primarily focused on relationships with a spouse or other family members, couple or family treatment may better meet the individual's needs.

Group participation may be contraindicated for older adults with certain personality attributes and certain mental health problems. Older adults who display very deviant or bizarre behavior patterns may elicit negative interactions in groups that may decrease their feelings of self-esteem and well-being. Older adults who are experiencing problems that are dissimilar from those of other members should also not be encouraged to attend groups if it is likely that other members will experience their behavior as alienating. For example, older individuals with dementia should not be encouraged to attend groups with others who are not experiencing this problem. Paranoid individuals may have their symptoms stimulated by being in a group. Depressed individuals with psychomotor retardation and difficulty in verbalization may not do well in groups (Horowitz 1976). However, some evidence suggests that groups designed specifically for depressed older adults can be effective (see, for example, Griffin and Waller 1985; Yost, Beutler, Corbishley, and Allender 1986). Also, severe pathology and low frustration tolerance may create too much stress in older adults, particularly when there is a high demand for responsive interactions, realistic relationships, or a great deal of competition for the attention and the time of the practitioner in a particular group.

When older adults are identified who have mental health problems or personality attributes that render them unfit for participation in a planned group, practitioners should consider developing specially designed group programs to meet their needs. If this is not possible, it is often helpful to begin services on a one-to-one basis, recommending group participation when they become ready and able to participate and are likely to benefit from their involvement. Concurrent individual and group service is often beneficial at first, to ease the transition from individual to group treatment and to monitor the individual's progress in the group.

SUMMARY

This chapter has presented an overview of group work with older adults. It began with a brief review of the history of group work with the elderly. Next, a description of the experience of aging and of the common themes that arise in groups of older persons were presented. The benefits of group participation for older people, and available evidence for the effectiveness and efficiency of group work was described. The chapter concluded with a section on indications and contraindications for group participation.

2

Facilitating Therapeutic Group Dynamics

The forces generated when individuals come together in a group are referred to as group dynamics. Over the past century, numerous studies have shown that these forces exert powerful influences on the behavior of group members. The purpose of this chapter is to help practitioners develop and sustain the group dynamics that enable older adults to achieve maximum benefit from their participation in a group.

THE GROUP-AS-A-WHOLE

A group is more than the sum of its individual members. When individuals meet together, they create forces that influence their subsequent interaction. These forces are dynamic, that is, they evolve as members continue to interact and as the group develops. As they take shape, group dynamic forces lend an identity to the group-as-a-whole. An understanding of group dynamic forces and an ability to utilize them to help individuals achieve maximum benefit from group participation is what distinguishes group workers from those who work exclusively with individuals.

The powerful influences exerted on members by the group dynamic forces that evolve in groups can be helpful or harmful. Many of the benefits of group participation mentioned in chapter 1 accrue to participants only when group dynamics develop that facilitate the growth and development of members and the group-as-a-whole. When group dynamics develop that inhibit the development of the group and its members, group participation is likely to be harmful rather than beneficial. It has been demonstrated, for example, that inattention to group dynamics can lead to individual casualties or the demise of the entire group (Bednar and Kaul 1978; Galinsky and Schopler 1977; Lieberman, Yalom, and Miles 1973). Therefore, attention to group dynamic forces is important if practitioners intend to be effective when working with groups of older adults.

Clinical experience suggests that to develop beneficial group dynamics, practitioners should focus on the process as well as the content of group meetings. Without neglecting content, effective group workers find that it is essential to pay close attention to the process of interaction among members and to the dynamics that arise from it. When focusing on group process, practitioners learn to examine the impact of group-as-a-whole processes on individual members and the contribution of individual members to the group-as-whole. They learn how to intervene to facilitate beneficial group dynamics, to prevent problematic dynamics from detracting from members' ability to benefit from the group, and to correct problems before they cause harm to individual members or the group-as-a-whole.

Group dynamics can be classified into four categories: (1) communication and interaction patterns, (2) cohesion, (3) social control mechanisms such as norms, roles, and status, and (4) the group culture (Toseland and Rivas 1984). Variations in these four categories of group dynamic forces give each group a distinct character.

COMMUNICATION AND INTERACTION PATTERNS

Communication is the process by which group members convey meanings to one another. Communication occurs both verbally and nonverbally. The communication process involves (1) putting the message a person wishes to convey into language and nonverbal gestures, (2) transmitting the verbal language and nonverbal gestures in a fashion that conveys the meaning intended, and (3) interpreting the message that has been sent by a group member.

Interaction patterns are established as members develop rhythms in the pace, duration, and frequency of their communications with each other throughout the life of a group. To be effective in facilitating groups of older adults, practitioners should pay attention to both communication processes and interaction patterns.

Improving Communication Processes

A number of steps can be taken to facilitate beneficial communications in groups of older adults. Become aware that members are continually communicating with each other, and watch for and tune in to members' verbal and nonverbal communications. Even when members are not talking, they continue to communicate on a nonverbal basis in the manner of their dress, their personal appearance, their posture, and their behavior. Practitioners should scan the group frequently to learn what members are communicating through their verbal and nonverbal behavior. They should tune into as many messages as possible by heightening their awareness of the behavior of each group member and by staying focused.

Become skillful at clarifying and highlighting members' communications. Effective leaders ask members to repeat unclear messages and to be specific about ambiguous ones. They check out the meaning of messages by repeating what they think they heard and what they think they saw, and by asking members if that was what they intended to communicate. They tone down judgmental, aggressive, or hostile messages, and they amplify ones that are likely to be beneficial. Also, they divert attention from messages that do not help the group or its members achieve the purposes and goals that have been agreed upon.

By highlighting certain aspects of members' communications, practitioners help members to stay focused on relevant themes and to explore them in greater depth than would be possible if the group conversation were allowed to drift. Highlighting particular portions of members' communications also helps to make connections among members. This is particularly important in groups of older people because those who are preoccupied with their own concerns have a tendency to share thoughts and feelings without any attempt to connect them to what has been said by the previous speaker. By modeling activities that clarify and highlight communications and by reinforcing members who engage in similar activities, the practitioner gradually shifts responsibility for the quality of the communication to the group-as-a-whole.

To facilitate beneficial communication in groups of older adults, it is also important to heighten members' awareness of the meaning of messages that are conveyed in the group. In some instances, members are not aware of the meaning of their communications. Practitioners help to enrich members' understanding of themselves by exploring the meaning that is implicit in their communications. They may ask members to be more explicit about what they mean or to reflect on the meaning of their communication. They may interpret the meaning underlying messages or they may help a member to get feedback from other members about what meaning was communicated by a message. In these ways the practitioner helps the group to serve as a mirror for each member, thus making the group a place for reality testing and for heightening self-awareness.

When attempting to deepen the level of communication in a group, practitioners should recognize that messages may convey many different meanings. Silence, for example, may communicate boredom, thoughtfulness, sorrow, or anger. Practitioners can be helpful by sorting out and clarifying the message being communicated. Nothing can be more frustrating for members than to have their messages interpreted incorrectly. A common tendency, for example, is for group members to offer immediate advice or solutions to individuals who risk sharing a problem or concern in the group. Members who share a concern may not want solutions, at least not initially. Rather, they may want to ventilate a thought or a feeling that they have not been able to share with others in order to obtain an empathic response, to feel that they are not alone with a particular concern, and to verify that they are not crazy or deviant for having such a thought or feeling. The practitioner can help by sorting out and clarifying the purpose of members' communications.

In deepening members' understanding and appreciation of the messages that are conveyed in a group, practitioners should remain aware of the impact of these activities on individual members and the group-as-a-whole. It is wise to assess the extent to which an individual member is ready to delve into the meaning of a message and whether or not a deeper analysis of the message will prove to be beneficial for the member. Many older adults, for example, are less interested than younger individuals in making deep-seated personality changes. They are more interested in learning how to adapt to and cope with stressful life events in ways that allow them to maintain a consistent identity. This makes sense because older adults have had many years to establish an identity. Their methods of coping have helped them get through stressful events in the past. Some evidence for this clinical observation is presented by Lakin, Oppenheimer, and Bremer (1982), who point out that older persons often prefer to dis-cuss concrete events from the recent past that threaten their established identity rather than to discuss here-and-now issues that are more likely to challenge them to reconsider their identity and their perceptions of themselves.

In assessing whether or not a deeper analysis of a communication will be helpful, several guidelines often prove useful. Check with the person to be sure the message was accurately understood. Ask the person what kind of feedback about the message he or she was expecting. Does the person want help exploring the meaning of the message, or did the person communicate with some other intention, such as to see if anyone else in the group experienced a similar feeling? Make sure that any interpretation of the meaning of a message is made tentatively so that the sender of the message can ignore or dismiss the interpretation without difficulty. When an interpretation is ignored or dismissed, it is often a signal to the practitioner that the interpretation was incorrect or poorly timed.

Do not try to force an older adult to accept an interpretation. Such an approach will lead to resistance. Clinical experience suggests that members who are not ready to discuss a particular issue when it is initially raised may return to it in a later group session. This may be because they have had time to consider the interpretation, to think about their response, and to assess whether the group is a safe place for them to discuss the issue. Members sometimes feel more in control when they raise a particular issue than when the practitioner or other members raise it. Also, watch closely for nonverbal cues. Facial expressions and body positions are often reliable cues about the impact of an interpretation on a member.

Practitioners should also assess the impact of deepening the level of communication on the group-as-a-whole. Consider the phase of a group's development. In the early phases, group members may not be ready for emotionally charged disclosures, whereas in later phases failing to help members deepen their level of communication may lead to superficiality, which may ultimately detract from the overall therapeutic benefit of the group. For example, a practitioner leading a first group meeting for widowed persons has to decide whether it is timely to focus on the anger that a group member experiences about becoming more dependent on a child, or whether such a focus is premature. The practitioner bases this decision on an assessment of whether exploring a different level of meaning in the message would be beneficial to the development of the group-as-a-whole. Being knowledgeable about group dynamics, the practitioner realizes that it is important to begin by building a supportive and empathic environment where members feel free to share their feelings. He or she may decide that exploring feelings of dependency this early in the group might do more harm than good; a high level of trust may not yet be built up in the group, and therefore, individual members or the group-as-a-whole may not yet be ready to function at the level of emotional intimacy that is likely to be required for a productive discussion of this emotionally charged issue.

To facilitate beneficial communications in groups of older people, it is also important to pay attention to those with special needs. Some older adults present special challenges for the practitioner. Health and mental health problems can make it more difficult to send clear messages and to interpret them. Sending a verbal message requires a group member to be able to use language effectively. Impairments caused by problems such as Alzheimer's Disease or a cerebral accident may interfere with older adults' ability to communicate. Also, transmitting subtle meanings can be difficult for older adults for whom English is a second language.

Physical disabilities, such as problems in speaking, hearing, and seeing can also interfere with members' abilities to encode and transmit verbal messages. Hearing loss is a common problem among older adults that increases with advanced age. For example, it has been estimated that approximately one third of all elderly men have some hearing impairment (Kart, Metress, and Metress 1978). For this reason, practitioners are encouraged to become familiar with techniques to communicate with the hearing impaired such as those presented in table 2.1.[1] Also, special procedures such as those presented in table 2.2 may be needed to help group members who have visual impairments to fully participate in the group. For additional ideas about these, call or write the American Foundation for the Blind.[2]

Nonverbal communication can also be impaired or distorted because of chronic physical disabilities that older adults sometimes experience. For example, they may have difficulty in moving about, or they may look awkward because of stiffness in joints caused by arthritis. Chronic mental impairments may also limit participation.

When practitioners anticipate that physically or mentally impaired older adults may participate in a group, they should consider coleading the group. A coleader can provide invaluable assistance in helping members get to and from the group and participate as fully as possible during meetings. For example, a coleader can be helpful by sharing responsibility for assisting individuals in wheelchairs or those using walkers, by keeping mildly demented individuals oriented, or by signing for hearing impaired members. Prevent distortions in communications from causing misunderstanding and conflict. Distortions are more likely to occur in groups of frail older people who have hearing losses or difficulty concentrating. Feedback can be used to check that messages are understood correctly. When attempting to clarify distortions, the practitioner should do so as soon as possible after the message has been communicated.

If you suspect that the content of a communication may not have been heard correctly by one or more members of the group, ask the members who may not have received the message as it was intended to verbalize their understanding of it. Ask the member who originally communicated if that is what he or she intended to communicate and, if necessary, to clarify what he or she meant. Make sure that all group members involved understand that feedback given in this manner is meant to prevent distortions or misunderstandings rather than to confront or attack group members who may have originally perceived a different meaning from the message.

Practitioners should use their knowledge of development in later life when making judgments about whether or not communications are distorted. For example, when using reminiscence as a therapeutic tool in groups, practitioners should be aware that some older adults benefit from a selective focus on past events, which allows them to place events in a positive framework, thereby helping them to put losses in perspective and

1. For additional ideas about communicating with the hearing impaired, see Blazer, D. 1978. Techniques for communicating with your elderly parent. *Geriatrics* 33 (11):79–84.

2. American Foundation for the Blind, 15 West 16th Street, New York, New York 10011. Telephone number 1-800-232-5463.

TABLE 2.1: Techniques for Communicating with Hearing Impaired
Older Adults in Groups

---

1. Position yourself so that you are in full view of the older person, and so that your face is illuminated.
2. Speak in a normal voice.
3. Speak slowly and clearly. Stress key words. Pause between sentences.
4. Make sure that no one else is talking when a group member is speaking to a hearing impaired person, and when a hearing impaired person is speaking to a group member.
5. Make sure the room is free of background noises and has good acoustics.
6. Look for cues such as facial expressions, or inappropriate responses, that indicate that the individual has misunderstood.
7. If you suspect that the individual has misunderstood, restate what has been said.
8. Speak to the individual, not about him or her.

---

to maintain a consistent sense of self. Therefore, practitioners should encourage members to be responsive to each others' reflections concerning the past, reinforcing selective views of past experiences as expressions of their own unique perception of events, rather than as distortions of true events.

To improve communication in groups it is also important to focus on strengths, positive experiences, and effective coping capacities. Too often, groups for older adults are focused on problems, concerns, and weaknesses. An exclusive focus on problems tends to affirm the negative stereotypes associated with old age, increase older adults' perception that the future is bleak, and inhibit the development of cohesion in the group-as-a-whole. For example, leaders of therapy groups in day treatment mental health settings sometimes spend too much time on lengthy descriptions of problems and on suggestions for changing long-standing behavior patterns, rather than helping members to identify and maintain strengths and to describe ways they have learned to cope with problems. By pointing out shortcomings about which they are vividly aware, the former approach demoralizes members and often leads to frustration as members fail to make suggested changes. In contrast, the latter approach encourages members to utilize and revitalize ego-syntonic coping skills that they are proud to share with the group.

Practitioners also should do all they can to counteract, not reinforce, negative stereotypes that can contribute to the high levels of depression and suicide found among the elderly. One way to accomplish this is to focus on older people's strengths. Like other age groups, older persons truly enjoy affirmations of the positive aspects of their life. They enjoy describing

TABLE 2.2: Techniques for Working with Visually Impaired
Group Members

1. Ask the individual if assistance is needed to get to the meeting room. If the reply is yes, offer your elbow. Walk a half step ahead so your body indicates a change in direction, when to stop, and so forth.
2. Introduce yourself and all group members when the meeting begins. Go around the group in a clockwise or counterclockwise fashion. This will help the group member get oriented to where each member is located.
3. When you accompany a visually impaired person into a new meeting room, describe the layout of the room, the furniture placement, and any obstacles. This will help orient the individual and reduce potential hazards.
4. Try not to disturb the placement of objects in the meeting room. If this is unavoidable, be sure to inform the visually impaired person about the changes. Similarly, let the individual know if someone leaves or enters the room.
5. When guiding visually impaired individuals to their seats, place their hands on the backs of chairs and allow them to seat themselves.
6. Speak directly to the visually impaired older adult, not through an intermediary.
7. Look at the visually impaired individual when you speak.
8. Don't be afraid to use words such as "look" and "see."
9. Speak in a normal voice. Do not shout.
10. Visually impaired older persons value independence just as sighted older persons do. Do not be overprotective.
11. Give explicit instructions to the visually impaired person about the location of coffee, snacks, and program activities. For example, state, "The coffee pot is ten feet to the left of your chair" rather than, "The coffee pot is right over there on your left."

These suggestions are adapted from a handout prepared by The Lighthouse, 111 East 59th Street, New York, NY, 10222.

strengths and building upon coping strategies that have been developed over a lifetime. A focus on positive experiences and strengths helps older adults to feel good about themselves. It encourages them to continue to make use of strengths and not to allow them to atrophy. It does not require them to mobilize scarce energy reserves to make changes. Instead, it frees up energy reserves that may be dissipated by an undue preoccupation with concerns and problems.

Therefore, throughout group meetings, members should be encouraged to share positive aspects of their present and past experiences. It is also helpful to set aside a specific time during each meeting for group go-rounds in which members are given time to share one pleasant memory or a recent incident in which they demonstrated a positive quality or skill. Group go-rounds that encourage members to describe skills they have used to cope effectively with difficult events in the past can do much to boost self-esteem. Experience suggests that when this is done on a routine basis at the beginning or end of a meeting, it often becomes a high point of the meeting for the members, something that they prepare for, look forward to, and enjoy. Practitioners will also find that the information that is shared during such a group go-round can be invaluable in helping members to cope with adverse experiences and setbacks and to avoid a morbid preoccupation with problems and concerns. As members bring up effective coping strategies and positive aspects of their situation, other members sometimes make comments that indicate that they would like to function as effectively. The skillful practitioner can use these opportunities to help these members to become motivated to work toward improving their own coping abilities.

Improving Interaction Patterns

At least four types of interaction patterns can exist in groups of older adults: (1) the maypole or closed interaction pattern, in which the leader is the central figure and communication occurs from member-to-leader and from leader-to-member, (2) the round robin pattern, in which each member takes a turn at talking, (3) the hot seat, in which there is an extended back and forth exchange between the leader and a member while the other members watch, and (4) the free-floating or open pattern, in which there is frequent member-to-member interaction that shifts among members as the content of a discussion changes (Middleman 1978).

Interaction patterns in groups for older adults who are energetic and healthy tend to be similar to patterns found in younger age groups. However, as age and physical disabilities increase, some distinctive interaction patterns, which are less common in groups of younger persons, begin to emerge. For example, the old-old exhibit less energy and activity in groups than do the young-old. The pace of the group process tends to be slower, and more methodical.

Member-to-member interactions can be more difficult to establish in groups of frail older persons, those who live alone, are isolated, and are out of the habit of being with, or talking to, others. Frail older adults may have less energy to invest in developing close relationships with fellow group members. There is more fear about losing close relationships through illness and death. Frail older adults also tend to be more reserved and more cautious about how they approach social interactions. They tend to spend time maintaining close relationships rather than developing new ones. Groups can provide frail older persons with an opportunity to talk about close relationships with empathic listeners, without necessarily developing close relationships with others in the group.

There is often more member-leader interaction in groups of older persons. Older adults tend to show respect for practitioners' education and training. As a result, communication may be directed to the practitioner rather than to peers. For example, a number of years ago I led a group for older people in a day treatment center, and also a group at a community center for young adults. I found that members of the group in the day treatment center were much more likely to turn to me for advice, suggestions, and support rather than to each other, whereas members of the group in the community center were much more likely to turn to each other for advice.

Leader-member communications also tend to occur more frequently because practitioners have a tendency to reach out to assist frail group members to fully participate. Practitioners should help groups of older adults to avoid the natural tendency to engage in leader-centered communication patterns. Practitioners should facilitate the development of open communication patterns that give all members an equal opportunity to interact. Members should be encouraged to communicate directly with each other, to share their wisdom and experience, and to rely less on the practitioner's counsel and more on their own adaptive capacities.

What can be done to improve interaction patterns in groups of older adults?

• Involve older adults in designing program activities and group exercises before implementing them. Older adults enjoy engaging in activities that are familiar to them and consistent with their former lifestyles. In contrast, they are somewhat less inclined than younger adults to engage in group programs that are unfamiliar to them.

• Share perceptions of interaction patterns. Practitioners should analyze patterns of interaction and share their observations with members. Spend a few minutes at the end of each group meeting reviewing the group process. Start by encouraging members to share their observations. Summarize these observations, amplify ones that are particularly salient, and add any that members have overlooked.

• Develop clear expectations. It is helpful for members and the practitioner to establish mutually agreed upon rules of group interaction. For example, members may agree to give each other the opportunity to participate by taking turns during group interaction, to avoid side conversations, to keep each communication fairly brief so as not to dominate group time, to allow each other to complete thoughts without interruption, and to limit interaction about sensitive issues to group meetings. It is also helpful to establish common purposes and goals and common expectations for how the group will accomplish its work.

• Encourage open interaction patterns. Older adults respond well to directions, praise, and nonverbal cues. Words or gestures can act as signals to talk more or less frequently. For example, practitioners can encourage members to respond to each other, ask each other specific questions, respond to each other's questions, or elaborate on a point that may be of interest to other members. Practitioners can also use gestures or other cues to signal members to talk to each other. As more appropriate interaction patterns are established, cues can be faded and the pleasure that older adults get from interacting freely with each other can be relied upon to maintain the new patterns that have been established (Toseland, Krebs, and Vahsen 1978).

• Change emotional bonds. Interpersonal attraction tends to increase interaction whereas negative emotional bonds tend to reduce solidarity and interpersonal interaction. Therefore, suggestions, made in the next section of this chapter, about increasing group cohesion can also be used to increase communication and member-member interaction.

• Avoid strengthening subgroups. Subgroups form from strong emotional bonds and interest alliances between two or more group members. Subgroups exist in all groups. They do not create problematic interaction patterns unless they are more attractive than the group-as-a-whole. However, when they become more attractive than the group-as-a-whole, they can distract members and create conflict that can reduce the group's overall cohesion. Help the group as a whole avoid the development of strong subgroups by suggesting program activities that get different members to interact with each other, by changing seating arrangements, and by pointing out commonalities and making connections between members who are not part of the same subgroup.

• Plan group size and physical arrangements carefully. Older people who have physical disabilities are particularly sensitive to the size and physical arrangement of groups. When groups are properly organized and arranged, positive interactions are encouraged. For example, large size allows less vocal members to be ignored. Extraneous noise, unattractive meeting rooms designed for other purposes, uncomfortable seating arrangements, lack of privacy, and inconvenient meeting locations and meeting times all detract from group interaction.

• Help members to understand the relevance and meaning of communications from other members. Some older adults are reticent to accept alternative viewpoints, especially those that are inconsistent with their extensive life experiences. The practitioner can be helpful by interpreting the relevance of alternative viewpoints within the context of older persons' lives.

• Change the structure of group meetings to accommodate those who are impaired. For group members who have visual or auditory impairments, a close circular seating arrangement can be helpful (Burnside 1969; Maisler and Solomon 1976). Do not sit around a table, for this may interfere with members getting close enough to communicate with each other. For severely impaired older persons, also consider shortening the usual length of group sessions. A decline in energy, chronic pain, and other physical problems tend to shorten attention spans and the duration of responses.

• Help group members to understand the relevance and meaning of communications from other members. Older adults have well-formed views about their life situations that have been established over many years. There is a tendency for them to be reticent to accept alternative viewpoints that are inconsistent with their life experiences. The practitioner can be helpful by interpreting the relevance of alternative viewpoints within the context of members' life experiences.

Burnside (1969) has pointed out that group members can assist the practitioner and other members to understand a particular group member. Older persons born in foreign countries may use unfamiliar terms or may have difficulty communicating in the English language. For example, in one group that I facilitated in a nursing home, several members were born in foreign countries. In particular, one individual was difficult to understand. She had come from Poland when she was fifty-seven. The member's roommate, who was also in the group, had lived in the United States since coming from Poland as teenager. She spoke English much more fluently. She occasionally helped her roommate to communicate when she had difficulty being understood by others in the group.

• Pay attention to the impact of norms, roles, and status on individual members. Norms, roles, and status have a marked influence on the way older adults interact in groups. By following the recommendations mentioned in a subsequent section of this chapter about developing beneficial norms, roles, and status associations in groups, practitioners can simultaneously alter detrimental interaction patterns. For example, dealing effectively with a dominant group member has implications for the interaction pattern of the group-as-a-whole.

COHESION

Cohesion is the force that binds members together, attracting individuals to each other and to the group-as-a-whole. According to Yalom (1985), as well as many other contemporary theorists, cohesion is absolutely essential for a successful group. Cohesion has many positive effects on the group and its members, including higher levels of participation, greater commitment to the work of the group, higher levels of satisfaction with the group experience, and improved treatment outcomes.

Cohesion helps to maintain a high level of participation throughout the life of a group. Believing that their participation is important and valued, members attend cohesive groups regularly and are more likely to notify the group leader or another member if they can't attend. Cohesive groups tend to have fewer dropouts and members tend to participate for longer time periods. Cohesion also helps to attract new members. Although new members may feel like outsiders when they attend a cohesive group for the first time, being invited to join a closely knit group is often perceived as a sign of recognition or favored status.

Cohesive groups influence their members more than groups that are less cohesive. Members of cohesive groups are more likely to listen to and respond favorably to each other's input. They are more likely to feel that they have had a say in the group's deliberations and, therefore, they are more likely to feel that they have a stake in the decisions made by the group. They are also more likely to agree with action plans and decisions made by the group, and they are more likely to implement these outside of the group. For example, Toseland, Rossiter, Peak, and Hill (in press) found that adult women who participated in caregivers support groups attributed the positive changes they experienced in caring for a frail parent to the understanding, support, empathy, and affirmation they received from fellow group members. These therapeutic elements are characteristic of cohesive groups.

Cohesive groups have been documented to have a positive effect on members' personal adjustment and satisfaction. Cohesion leads to increased feelings of self-confidence and self-esteem and to greater willingness to listen to and utilize feedback from others to try out new behaviors, to implement intervention strategies under adverse circumstances, and to share setbacks and continued difficulties with group members (Yalom 1985). Members of cohesive groups feel freer to make more assertive, confrontive, and probing remarks than do members of less cohesive groups. They report feeling more secure and less threatened when these remarks are addressed at them (see, for example, Pepitone and Reichling 1955). They also report feeling less psychologically distressed in cohesive groups (Seashore 1954) and more satisfied with their experience as participants (Toseland and Rose 1978; Toseland, Rossiter, Peak, and Hill in press).

Despite its many positive effects, cohesion has two potential negative effects that should be monitored as the group develops. First, highly cohesive groups tend to foster dependence. Members may be reluctant to act independently without first consulting with the group or its leader. They may continue their participation longer than necessary to receive the beneficial effects of group membership. This can be particularly problematic when a professional wishes to end work with a group. Experience suggests that older people who are unsure of their own skills are particularly vulnerable to become dependent on professional leaders for direction and for performing routine maintenance functions for the group. This dependence can be particularly problematic when a professional wishes to assist older adults to begin a self-help group or to develop a self-help group from an existing professionally led group. For example, Toseland, Decker, and Bliesner (1979) found that older adults who formed a support group that was facilitated by a professional leader resisted repeated attempts by the professional to turn the group's leadership over to them. Therefore, it is important for professionals to be clear from the beginning about what role they will play in supporting a group's development, how long they will play that role, and what expectations they have of members. Also, professionals should do all they can to foster leadership abilities in members.

A second potential problem with a high level of group cohesion is that it tends to foster conformity. Members may be less likely to express opinions that differ from the majority view because they fear causing disorder or being viewed as uncooperative. However, members of cohesive groups can be helped to express feelings, thoughts, or viewpoints that might be considered controversial by some group members. This can be done by praising and supporting members who share their feelings or who challenge the status quo, by using verbal and nonverbal prompts to encourage members to express divergent opinions, and by modeling these behavior patterns during group meetings.

Older adults present unique challenges for practitioners intent on developing cohesive groups. This is not meant to imply that cohesion is rare in groups for older persons, but rather that the potential obstacles are somewhat different than in groups for younger persons. Cohesive groups are generally characterized by a high level of enthusiastic interaction among members. Because of reduced energy levels, sensory impairments, a need to talk and to be listened to, and a high level of respect for professionals, member-to-member interaction is sometimes difficult to develop in groups of older adults, particularly in groups with physically or mentally frail members. When it does develop, it may appear somewhat blunted or dampened (Lakin, Oppenheimer, and Bremer 1982), and it may be difficult to sustain. For example, Toseland and Coppola (1985) observed that when isolated older adults from rural areas were brought together for a social support group, they needed much encouragement and support to begin the process of reaching out to each other rather than exclusively to the leader. Continued efforts were also needed to sustain the levels of support and mutual sharing that gradually developed in the group, and to extend the informal support that was achieved in the group outside of it. This was accomplished through the encouragement of telephone contacts and informal visiting between meetings.

Similarly, in attempting to empower clients in a board and care facility through a residents' council, Coppola and Rivas (1986) observed that many members feared group participation. Some feared speaking in large groups and others feared reprisals from administration if actions to change conditions were initiated. This latter fear was somewhat justified because previous "governance groups" had been run by the administrator largely to meet administrative and institutional needs rather than to foster democratic participation by residents in decisions about policies and practices that affected them directly. For others, participation was limited by lack of experience in groups, by a lack of assertiveness, and by implied intimidation from more sophisticated and assertive members. When members participated, they directed their comments and concerns to the leader rather than to each other. It took some time to develop enough cohesion in the group for members to feel comfortable discussing what actions they would like to see taken to improve the quality of life in the home.

Cohesive groups are often characterized by communications that go beyond superficial, topical discussions. Cohesion tends to open up older adults who may otherwise avoid expressing their feelings about each other. Some older adults have learned earlier in life that it is improper to share their innermost feelings, problems, or concerns with anyone other than close family members, or that such a disclosure implies that they have a mental health problem.

Cohesion may also be somewhat more difficult to develop in groups for older adults because some place a great deal of emphasis on maintaining old friendships and are less inclined to develop new ones. This may be because some lack the physical energy needed to establish new relationships, because inertia prevents some from reaching out to develop new friends, or because some who have experienced recent losses are reluctant to develop new friends. Also, because they have lived with their own ideas, habits, and beliefs for so long, it may be more difficult for some to accept and embrace others who may challenge their belief systems.

There are a variety of ways that practitioners can help to overcome obstacles to the development of cohesion in groups of older adults.

• Encourage interaction among members. Older adults are attracted to groups where they can freely interact with each other. They enjoy the give and take of interaction particularly when there is no demand to participate beyond their comfort level. Freedom to interact as desired also allows them to give and receive support and assistance based on their capacity and motivation.

Practitioners should aim to ensure that interaction is fairly evenly distributed, rather than centered among a few dominant members, or between a few members and the leader. Practitioners can contribute to group cohesion by tuning in to verbal and nonverbal cues that indicate members' desire to contribute to the group interaction, and by giving members the opportunity to participate. Whenever possible, solicit members' opinions and use go-rounds to guide group interaction so that meetings are not dominated by a vocal member or an assertive subgroup.

• Encourage members to value each others' opinions. In cohesive groups, the opinions, thoughts, and feelings that are expressed are respected and taken seriously by all members. When members communicate in cohesive groups they feel that they are being listened to and understood. Members may not always agree with each other, but they carefully consider what each other has to say. In cohesive groups, members believe that they can have an impact on decisions made by the group-as-a-whole. Practitioners can help promote this type of interaction by encouraging members to express their opinions, by preventing members from cutting each other off, discounting what each other says, or engaging in side conversations. They can help members to listen to, understand, and take seriously the messages that each member communicates. They can also emphasize the importance of communications that are being minimized, ignored, or distorted, and they can model respect and interest when responding to members' communications.

• Foster positive, noncompetitive, and nonthreatening intragroup relationships. Cohesion is promoted when members are encouraged to be as positive, optimistic, and hopeful as circumstances permit and to be as helpful and supportive toward each other as possible. When members express alternative viewpoints or give feedback to each other, they should be encouraged to do so in a thoughtful and helpful way without being critical or hostile, without belittling each other, and without being punitive or destructive. They should be encouraged to express how they are trying to be helpful by the message they are attempting to convey. In turn, members receiving feedback should be encouraged to listen without becoming defensive or threatened. The practitioner can help by periodically reminding members that feedback is intended to help them grow and develop and should be given in that spirit.

• Foster competitive intergroup relationships. Competition between groups tends to promote cohesion within the group. Members forget personal differences and work toward achieving a group goal to compete successfully with an opposing group. Thus, in senior centers, nursing homes, and other settings where more than one group can be developed at the same time, it can be beneficial to have different groups compete to achieve a desired outcome, for verbal recognition, or for a tangible reward. In a senior center, for example, groups might compete to see who can raise the most money for a worthy cause or to see which team can score the highest in a particular recreational activity. The resulting cohesion often makes the groups more satisfying for participating members. The one danger in this approach is that the competition between members from different groups spills over into other program activities. This can be minimized by changing the composition of groups when new program activities are planned, and by emphasizing the contribution that each individual, as well as each group, has made to the overall goal that all members were striving to accomplish.

• Help members to fulfill expectations and to achieve desired goals. When a group does not meet members' expectations or fulfill members' needs, it is not likely to continue to attract their participation. Members will either search elsewhere for fulfillment or will attempt to disrupt the work of the group. Similarly, members become frustrated when groups consistently fail to achieve stated goals. They begin to ask themselves if their efforts are worthwhile. For example, it may be better not to begin a patients' rights group in a nursing home when it is clear that the home's administration has no intention of responding in a sincere manner to the concerns that residents raise. Thus, when practitioners wish to create cohesion, they should elicit members' expectations, encourage members to have input into the objectives and goals of the group, guide the group toward meeting members' needs, help the group to select goals that are achievable, and encourage the group to partialize goals so that members can experience intermittent goal achievement without having to wait until the work of the group is completed.

• Form groups that increase members' prestige and status or give members access to resources they would have difficulty obtaining by themselves. Groups that are selective, that enhance members' standing in the community, or that provide members with resources that they need or desire tend to be attractive and cohesive. In the early phases of group development, practitioners can promote cohesion by screening members for appropriateness, limiting membership, conveying the benefits of participation to members, and consulting with members before adding new participants. During later phases of the group, cohesion can be promoted by being responsive to members' needs, providing them with access to resources that may be difficult or impossible for them to obtain without the help of the practitioner, helping members to be responsive to one another, and reinforcing, highlighting, and making explicit the implicit feelings of connectedness, mutual support, and *esprit de corps* that arise as the group develops.

NORMS, ROLES, AND STATUS

Norms, roles, and status are group dynamic properties that govern how individuals behave in the group. For this reason, these properties have been referred to as social control mechanisms (Toseland and Rivas 1984). By defining the behavior of individuals in the group-as-a-whole, norms, roles, and status help to make group interaction predictable and orderly.

The effective practitioner should strive for a balance between highly constrictive, stringent social control mechanisms and those that are diffuse. A degree of order, predictability, and stability are prerequisites for effective and efficient group functioning. Without some social control mechanisms, group interaction would be stressful and threatening because members would be uncertain about what to expect during their interaction with each other. However, social controls that are too stringent can lead to member dissatisfaction and intragroup conflict. In the most extreme cases, when members feel that their freedom is severely and unduly curtailed and their input unwanted and unheeded, they are likely to sabotage group functioning or opt to discontinue their participation.

In groups where members are clear about the norms, roles, and status that operate, they take comfort in knowing what to expect, and they understand how social control mechanisms contribute to the achievement of group goals. At the same time, it is important for them to feel that there is a certain amount of freedom and latitude within established patterns to express their own individuality. In general, practitioners should balance the needs of individuals and the group-as-a-whole, avoiding excessive conformity or deviance and ensuring that social control mechanisms are working to benefit rather than to hinder the performance of individual members and the group as a whole. For example, when members of a support group sponsored by a Catholic family service agency expressed their strong religious beliefs, the leader actively facilitated the discussion. However, when one member made a statement about Afro-Americans that was offensive, the leader encouraged a discussion of feelings about the matter.

Norms

Norms are shared beliefs and expectations about the proper and appropriate way to behave in a group. By providing guidelines for acceptable and unacceptable behavior, norms increase the predictability of interaction and, in turn, members' feelings of security, comfort, and familiarity. Norms help to avoid a capricious use of power by one group member or the need for excessive external controls to control the actions of the entire group.

Although norms stabilize and regulate behavior, normative constraints have a paradoxical effect in that they free members to take some risks by defining and making concrete the limits and boundaries of acceptable behavior.

Norms result from what is valued, preferred, and accepted in a particular group. They develop gradually as the group develops. Often they are manifested as tacit, implicit, covert understandings that are not articulated or made explicit unless a special effort is made to do so by the practitioner. Norms become clarified as members observe that positive consequences, social approval, and praise result from certain behaviors and that negative consequences, social disapproval, and sanctions result from others.

The types of norms that are beneficial to effective group functioning vary from group to group depending on a particular group's functions and goals. However, in general, beneficial norms are those that encourage members to respect each other's right to participate, to value each other's input, to be supportive and helpful to each other, and to become involved and invested in the work of the group. Typical dysfunctional norms found in groups of older persons are those that encourage members to interrupt speakers, to engage in side conversations, to become late to meetings, and to sidetrack the group from discussing emotionally charged issues. When working with groups of older adults, practitioners can do the following things to help develop beneficial group norms and to prevent the development of dysfunctional norms.

• Establish norms early in the group's development. Because they have a pervasive, powerful, and subtle effect on members' behavior, norms are difficult to change once they are established. Therefore, it is helpful for practitioners to be as clear as possible about the basic assumptions, expectations, and rules that they would like to see operate in the group. Solicit members' input and feedback so they feel involved in shaping the norms that will operate in their group.

• Make norms explicit. Too often norms are left unstated and unchallenged. It is a good practice to spend a few minutes at the beginning or end of each group meeting discussing normative expectations and other group dynamic properties that are likely to enhance members' satisfaction with their participation in the group. Experience suggests that it is helpful for practitioners to take the initiative, spending only a few minutes talking about their impressions of the group process so as to stimulate members' own reactions and comments. Sharing perceptions in this way has many beneficial effects. It helps to make members aware of beneficial norms, and it increases the likelihood that they will behave in accordance with them. Sharing perceptions of norms that detract from the group process helps to confirm the perceptions of members who might have been vaguely aware of problems in group functioning without being able to clearly articulate them. It also serves as a catalyst for a discussion of needed changes and how to accomplish them.

• Restate norms periodically. Practitioners have a tendency to pay less attention to the functioning of the group-as-a-whole than they do to the functioning of individual group members. Restating norms periodically throughout the life of the group demonstrates to members that the practitioner is concerned about overall group functioning and dedicated to ensuring that the group functions at the highest possible level. Restating beneficial norms helps to reinforce their use and to deepen members' commitment to them. Making norms explicit also helps to reinforce feelings of comradery and *esprit de corps* among members.

• Hold members to agreed-upon norms. Initially, the practitioner should take responsibility for holding individual members to norms agreed upon by the membership. This can be done by restating agreements and by asking for members' cooperation. Gradually, as members feel more comfortable with each other, they can be encouraged to take responsibility for reminding each other of the agreements they have made with each other.

• Solicit members' opinions when attempting to change a norm. When practitioners believe that a dysfunctional norm is operating in the group, they should share their perceptions with the group-as-a-whole. Group members should be encouraged to comment on a practitioner's perception and together decide on what changes, if any, they would like to make in the way the group functions.

Roles

Roles are shared expectations about the way members should behave in relation to the work of the group. They define the specific functions and tasks members should undertake as the work of the group is conducted.

Roles can be functional or dysfunctional for the group as a whole. Roles that are functional allow for a division of labor in the group. When roles are clear, they help to define members' responsibilities and areas of expertise, thereby promoting harmonious, conflict-free group interaction. Roles that are dysfunctional interrupt or detract from the work of the group. Common dysfunctional roles in groups of older adults include:

• The monopolizing member. The monopolizing member dominates group interaction by engaging in lengthy monologues that are often repetitive and not germane to the task at hand. The monopolizer interrupts other members who are engaging in productive interactions. Complicating intervention strategies, the monopolizer is frequently insensitive to subtle nonverbal and verbal cues indicating other members' annoyance.

Whenever possible, the practitioner should screen members carefully to avoid including monopolizers. Background information on each participant can also be helpful in this regard. Frequently, however, screening interviews fail to detect monopolizers. This may occur because most screening interviews are conducted on a one-to-one basis, or because the monopolizer does not exhibit these tendencies in initial interactions with others.

When a monopolizer is included in a group, either inadvertently or with a planned therapeutic purpose, the practitioner can successfully intervene by suggesting that the group establish norms about participation in the first group meeting. These norms can include limiting input to brief communications, respecting other members' rights to participate, allowing members to complete thoughts without interrupting, listening intently, asking for feedback about communications, and not engaging in side conversations. Once these norms are agreed upon, the practitioner can call attention to the monopolizer's behavior in a caring, concerned manner, and ask the monopolizer to comply with the established norms.

Experience suggests that most monopolizers will agree to cooperate but have difficulty following through on their commitment. When this is the case, the practitioner can remind the monopolizer of his or her commitment to the norms and ask other members to help the monopolizer fulfill his or her commitment. The practitioner can ask another member or a coleader to sit next to the member and give the monopolizer a physical cue, such as a touch on the hand, when a norm is violated. In groups with members who have memory impairments, it can also be effective to pass a symbolic item, such as a ball or a baton, around the group to signify who has "the floor."

• The silent member. When asked, most quiet members indicate that they are comfortable with their role in groups and get much out of listening to and reflecting on the group's discussion. Therefore, practitioners should be cautious about screening out shy members. Also, practitioners should be cautious about singling out and drawing attention to silent group members. Such an approach may intimidate them. However, silence can become problematic when it is prolonged over many group meetings or when several members appear to be reluctant to contribute to group interaction.

The practitioner should check to make sure that physical disabilities, language barriers, or similar problems are not interfering with members' ability to communicate. Also, the practitioner should check to make sure that silent members are invested in the goals of the group and clearly understand the connection between group process and goal achievement. If silent members indicate that they would like the opportunity to participate, practitioners can help by being alert to nonverbal cues that suggest silent members would like to contribute, and by mentioning that talkative members should give less talkative members the opportunity to share their thoughts.

Group go-rounds and other exercises that encourage each member to contribute can also be helpful. For example, each member can be asked to take a turn at completing a sentence such as, "When I feel happy I . . . ," or members can be asked to describe one event that was the highlight of their week since the last group meeting. Group go-rounds such as these avoid singling out individual members who tend to be silent, and they have the added benefit of reducing the dominance of talkative members.

Other techniques to help shy members communicate include reducing the size of a group or breaking the group into subgroups. Shy members often feel more comfortable sharing with a single individual than with a whole group. It can also be helpful to ask silent members to share their knowledge about topics in which they have a particular interest or expertise. Older adults respond well to this latter technique because they are eager to share their knowledge, wisdom, and experience with others who may benefit from it.

• The inappropriate member. The inappropriate member is one who is not functioning at a similar level to other members. Such a member may become a target for scapegoating, and may impede the level of group process that could be achieved by higher functioning members. Practitioners should avoid mixing members who are functioning at widely different levels. For example, avoid mixing older adults with cognitive impairments with those without such impairments.

• Gatekeepers and rescuers. The gatekeeper is a group member who tries to control what is expressed during group meetings. If the gatekeeper is uncomfortable with conflict, for example, he or she attempts to smooth over the conflict. Similarly, if the gatekeeper is uncomfortable with a group discussion of loss, he or she tries to divert the group's attention by changing the topic of discussion. The gatekeeper's role can be particularly insidious because members of the group may be seduced into the mistaken belief that the member is performing a helpful function by rescuing a fellow group member who is distressed by an interaction or by relieving the stress associated with discussing a difficult topic.

To deal effectively with gatekeepers and rescuers, practitioners must first become aware of their own reluctance and inhibitions about discussing emotionally charged issues. Many practitioners, for example, have difficulty allowing conflict to be expressed in groups. They fear that it will lead to the demise of the group, and therefore conflict is avoided rather than resolved. Often, this prevents a group from achieving the level of intimacy and the cooperative, trusting relationships that are essential for effective work. Once practitioners have come to terms with their own feelings about the expression of emotionally charged issues, they can then point out gatekeeping and rescuing activities, praising the member for being sensitive to the needs of a particular member or the group as a whole, but suggesting that diverting the groups' attention or preventing a discussion and resolution of an emotionally charged issue may not be helpful.

Status

Status refers to an evaluation and ranking of group members in relation to each other. Evaluation and ranking varies from group to group so that the same individual may have a different status in two separate groups. In general, members' status is determined by their prestige, position, and expertise outside of the group as well as their ability to contribute within a particular group.

Status is important in groups of older adults because of the way it affects group interaction. High status members feel freer to express their opinions in the group, and their contributions are often given greater consideration. Status differentials are sometimes greater in groups of older adults than in groups of younger adults because the elderly have had many years to establish themselves in their communities and in the work force. This is particularly true in groups of the young-old who are still working. To avoid problems resulting from status differentials, practitioners should emphasize the strengths that each member brings to the group experience, the contribution that each member can make, and the important role that each member plays in the work of the group. Effective ways to change status hierarchies include placing lower status members in leadership positions during a program activity and actively seeking out the opinions of lower status members whose opinions have not been fully considered by the group.

GROUP CULTURE

Group culture arises from the values, beliefs, customs, and traditions that members bring to the group from their familial, ethnic, cultural, and racial heritage. It is also the result of the group's interaction with the larger environment in which it operates (Olmsted 1959). In the early phase of a group's development, members explore each other's value orientations to find a common ground on which to relate to each other. They also experience external pressures to conform to certain organizational, community, and societal norms. As the group develops, these influences are blended together to form a unique group culture.

A group's culture has a powerful but subtle effect on its ability to achieve goals and satisfy members' socio-emotional needs. A culture that supports a diversity of opinion, that encourages respect, fairness, and equality of participation, and that promotes members' views of themselves as proactive, self-determining agents can do much to enhance effective group functioning. Older adults sometimes bring to groups ethnic, cultural, religious, or social stereotypes that inhibit the development of a positive group culture. For example, some older adults have been encouraged all their lives not to share problems of concerns outside of the family context. Others have been told that members of other cultural or racial groups are not to be trusted. Through guided group discussion and interaction as well as participation in program activities, practitioners can help members to broaden their perspectives and to appreciate different value orientations and the cultural heritages on which they are based.

SUMMARY

This chapter has focused on strategies to facilitate therapeutic dynamics in groups of older adults. It was divided into four sections. The first section of the chapter focused on facilitating effective communication and interaction patterns. Techniques for increasing understanding and reducing distortions were presented. The second section of the chapter focused on helping groups of older people to become cohesive. Techniques to reduce interpersonal conflict and promote harmonious functioning were presented. The third section of the chapter focused on social control mechanisms and presented techniques to facilitate the development of therapeutic norms and roles and to prevent status hierarchies from interfering with the development of the group. The chapter concluded with a brief discussion of methods to facilitate the development of a therapeutic group culture in groups of older persons.

3

Leadership Skills

This chapter focuses on the skills, procedures, and methods necessary for working with groups of older persons. Leadership is the process of guiding the development of the group through all stages of its life, from planning to termination. Leadership is a shared function that is best understood as a sequence of actions rather than as a quality lodged in a single individual. This conceptualization of leadership helps group workers to distinguish between the practitioner as "designated" leader and the members as "indigenous" leaders. A practitioner acts as a designated leader by helping the group and its members to achieve the goals that they have agreed to accomplish. Indigenous leadership emerges as members take increasing responsibility for guiding the group as it develops.

Leadership is not lodged solely in the designated leader but instead is shared, to a certain extent, by all group members. The designated leader takes primary responsibility for organizing the group but encourages members to exercise their leadership capacities as fully as possible. Effective practitioners realize that it is important for members to take as much responsibility as possible for their own actions and for the development of the group-as-a-whole. Therefore, they encourage members to exercise power, influence, and leadership over the direction of the group by involving them in goal setting and in the development and implementation of effective action plans.

How much leadership responsibility can members be expected to assume? Almost all older people have had leadership experiences over the years in their roles as workers, family members, and members of community groups. It is important for practitioners to keep in mind that older people continue to look for leadership roles in voluntary associations, and that many are capable of being effective leaders with little or no assistance from practitioners. Practitioners should ensure that neither they nor the agency for whom they work subverts these individuals' leadership abilities.

In contrast, some older people who are very capable have been so undermined by ageism that they accept dependency rather than assume active leadership roles. Others who have lost some of their energy and vitality as a result of chronic disabilities are also more willing to accept practitioners' leadership. Therefore, to determine their role in the leadership of a group, practitioners have to assess the capacities of the older people with whom they are working and their willingness to assume leadership responsibilities.

LEADERSHIP AND OLDER ADULTS

What makes leadership different when working with older adults? Although many of the unique aspects of working with older adults in groups have already been mentioned in the first two chapters, three particularly important factors to keep in mind when reading this chapter are the heterogeneity of older people's backgrounds, the way they relate to practitioners, and the way practitioners relate to them.

The heterogeneity of the older population requires group workers to have a broad range of skills. Contrast, for example, the types of skills that are needed to work with older adults who are demented with those needed to facilitate a group of vigorous and active older adults who wish to establish a volunteer services program in their community. Because of the capacities of members and the purpose of the group, in the former group the practitioner would use a much more structured and procedurally specific approach to organizing the content of group meetings than in the latter group. Also, the practitioner would give more verbal and physical directions to members and would assume much less member autonomy.

The way older adults relate to practitioners also has an important impact on group leadership. Many pay a great deal of attention to the leader. This may occur because their needs and their opinions are not given the attention they deserve by the larger society, or because of their respect for the leader's education and position. As Poggi and Berland (1985) found in their experience in working with older people in a nursing home, older people want to be valued for what they have accomplished in their life. They also found that "another older person's opinion is the opinion of someone in the same boat and is likely to be dismissed as biased" (511). Thus, practitioners are in a unique position to affirm older people's self-esteem and self-worth.

Although the attention paid to practitioners by older adults tends to make group facilitation gratifying, practitioners must take care not to foster older adults' dependence by doing too much for them. Such a response can foster dependence and increase self-perceptions of helplessness.

Practitioners may notice also that some older adults are particularly candid and direct in their communications in groups. Having had years to live with the choices they have made and the directions they have taken in their lives, most have established firm identities and have well-formed ideas about how to live. Some are not hesitant to express their views, and may

surprise inexperienced practitioners with the directness of their statements. For example, Burnside (1969) states that "elderly patients are so
absolutely direct in their comments that they sometimes stagger one." She
goes on to point out that such directness can be positive or negative. She
gives an example of a stately old man who attempts to dismiss the input of
a younger practitioner by stating, "She is only forty-five years old and I am
eighty-two, and she is trying to teach us something about living" (127).

Practitioners should strive to help the group understand the meaning of
members' candid comments so that they become opportunities for growth
rather than opportunities to dismiss input from members and to disengage
from the group. For example, an individual who appears to be dismissing
the input of the practitioner might be questioning whether the leader is
skilled enough to be helpful or, alternatively, suggesting that the leader
encourage members to share their own wisdom and discover their own
"truths." Practitioners can be helpful by pointing out how a candid comment
can contribute to the growth and development of the entire group. For
example, the practitioner might explore with the group how she could be
helpful, or mention how she will need the assistance of the group to fully
understand each member. Therefore, when candid comments are made,
the practitioner should not hesitate to explore their meaning and to have
members elaborate on them.

Just as sometimes it is helpful to clarify and amplify feelings that may not
be forcefully presented, it may also be necessary to tone down strong
messages or to refocus the group on issues and concerns that are more
central (Shulman 1984). For example, when one individual in a preretirement planning group mentioned that they did not approve of "those who
left their roots, traditions, and children to live with other old folks in a hot
weather community," the leader pointed out how the comment illustrated
the different ways that members planned to use their retirement.

On other occasions, it may be helpful to reframe a message so that it is
more easily accepted and integrated by other members of the group. For
example, when one member of an advocacy group in a nursing home stated,
"What's the use, we're all just here waiting to die," several members
reacted negatively, denying the validity of the member's statement. The
leader pointed out that the member's comment helped to point the group in
the direction of examining barriers to change and determining what could
be realistically accomplished in the home. The leader also interjected that
the member was expressing a feeling that is common in advocacy groups
no matter what the setting or the age of members, that is, that change
rarely comes easily and that it often feels as though it takes a great deal of
effort to make even a small change. The practitioner used as an example
the history of the women's right movement. This, in turn, led to a lively

discussion as both male and female members of the group recounted their perceptions of the changes in women's roles over the years. Gradually, the practitioner guided the discussion back to an appraisal of what changes the advocacy group would like to promote within the nursing home and what barriers would likely be encountered.

Many older persons have a strong desire to share their knowledge, wisdom, and experience in groups. However, some do so without attempting to connect their thoughts to what others have been expressing. The self-focus of these older adults may occur because they become preoccupied with their own health and their own efforts to adapt and to cope with the changing world around them. Encouraging older people to ventilate their idiosyncratic thoughts and feelings is important. It helps to overcome isolation and to affirm and validate older persons' experiences. However, it is also beneficial to help members connect with fellow group members by encouraging them to listen to and react to what others are expressing. Lakin, Oppenheimer, and Bremer (1982), for example, have pointed out that a useful technique is for leaders to facilitate members' sharing and comparing of their positive and negative experiences. This encourages vicarious identification with the joys and problems of their fellow group members, and can also help members learn about effective coping mechanisms that others have found to be helpful in their lives.

Except for those with behavioral problems resulting from dementia, older people in therapy groups are somewhat less likely than younger age groups to act out or to become aggressive. They are, for example, less inclined than children or adolescents to challenge the basic normative structure of the group, the practitioner's authority, or group rules. Compared to those in their earlier years, they are less likely to jockey for status and position. Therefore, unlike in group work with children or adolescents, practitioners spend less time helping members to avoid allowing their activity level, their striving for independence, or their tendency to test the normative structure of the group from undermining the cohesion of the group-as-a-whole. Instead, the practitioner may need to be more active with some older adults, helping them to stay engaged in the work of the group. Steuer et al. (1984), for example, pointed out that one of the few differences they found in cognitive-behavior group therapy with older as compared to younger people was older persons' passivity. They speculate that years of prior medical and psychotherapy experiences among the group of older adults with whom they worked may have engendered expectations of passive receptiveness to expert help. They suggested that older group members needed to be encouraged to actively generate and enact new behaviors and new coping strategies for themselves rather than asking therapists for suggestions and recommendations about how to proceed.

Gerontologists have also pointed out that working with older persons fosters certain characteristic responses in practitioners (see, for example, Eissler 1977; Ford and Sbordone 1980; Group for the Advancement of Psychiatry 1971; Kastenbaum 1963; Katz and Genevay 1987; Kosberg and Audrey 1978; Poggi and Berland 1985; Ray, Raciti, and Ford 1985; Sprung 1989; Tobin and Gustafson 1987; Wolk and Wolk 1971). The most common type of reaction mentioned in the literature is death anxiety. Work with older group members can stimulate practitioners' fears concerning their own aging, dependence, and death.

Work with older people can also cause some practitioners to feel unskilled. This occurs, in some instances, when practitioners feel that older people are rigid and will not change. These practitioners feel that their skills and efforts are being wasted. Feelings of being unskilled are also engendered when older people relate to practitioners as if they were children. For example, Poggi and Berland (1985) report feeling angry, emasculated, and unskilled because they were repeatedly referred to by members of their group as the "boys." Practitioners are also commonly referred to as "honey" or "dear" in a maternalistic or paternalistic fashion by some older adults.

Older group members' need to feel valued can also create pressures on the practitioner to react in certain ways. For example, Poggi and Berland (1985) speculate that older group members' wishes to be valued are so important to them that the only response they will tolerate is one that affirms their value. Anxiety about what type of response they are likely to get from the practitioner is sometimes manifested in controlling and intolerant interactions with the practitioner or with other group members. Older group members' need to be valued can also foster feelings of omnipotence in the practitioner.

Practitioners also need to be aware of, and grapple with, their own reactions to and stereotypes about the older adults with whom they work. There is a tendency among some practitioners to deny their feelings, particularly when they are not socially acceptable. For example, inexperienced practitioners sometimes cover up feelings they have about frail, deteriorating, or cantankerous older people. They may experience these individuals as not being very pleasant to see, smell, or be with for an entire group meeting. Experience working with older adults suggests that it is better to confront these feelings and to work them through in supervision than to deny that they exist.

There is also a tendency for practitioners to relate to older group members as they would to their own parents. This may cause them to hold certain expectations or preconceived notions about older group members that are based on their experience with their own parents and grandparents. One such response that is frequently mentioned in the literature is the lack of any attention to, or discussion of, the sexual needs of the elderly. Reacting to elderly group members as they would to their own parents can also stimulate practitioners to reexperience unresolved issues and conflicts with their own parents. For example, some practitioners attempt to resolve the guilt they feel about how they related to their own parents by giving to, or doing for, elderly members of their group even when that may not be therapeutically warranted.

Although strong emotional reactions to particular group members can make practitioners feel uncomfortable or confused, clinical experience suggests that these feelings should not be denied or repressed. Instead, they should be actively explored as valuable clinical information that can tell us much about ourselves and our clients. Therefore, when strong emotional reactions are experienced, it is a good practice to assess your relationship with the group member who is engendering these feelings, carefully considering the dynamics underlying your reaction as well as the dynamics of the individual's reaction to you. Ask yourself such questions as these: "What do I feel before, during, and after interacting with the member?" "What is the member doing to activate these feelings in me?" "What do I do or say to bring out these feelings?" "Who do I remind the member of?" "Who does the member remind me of?" "What role am I playing in the member's fantasies about me?" "What role is the member playing in my fantasies about him or her?" Often, clinical supervision can be a useful place to explore the nature of your reactions to the member and the member's reaction to you.

MODELS FOR EFFECTIVE LEADERSHIP

Because of the heterogeneity of the older population, and the many different kinds of groups that practitioners may be expected to facilitate, practitioners should be conversant with a variety of therapeutic approaches. Toward this end, it is important to be familiar with different styles of leadership. Three broad models of leadership are the reciprocal, remedial, and social goals models (Pappell and Rothman 1980). These can be used differentially, depending upon the needs and capacities of members and the goals that have been established for individual members and the group-as-a-whole.

The aim of the reciprocal model is to form a mutual aid system among group members that will, in turn, help members to achieve an optimum level of adaptation and socialization (Pappell and Rothman 1980). In the reciprocal model, the practitioner shares leadership functions, helping members to describe their concerns and to share their hopes for what the group might accomplish. Members are seen as partners working together to support one another through difficult times, to resolve shared concerns, and to accomplish mutually agreed upon goals. The practitioner may act as a resource person and as an enabler, contributing information and providing access to resources. The practitioner may also act as a mediator between society's demands and group members' needs.

Although the reciprocal model has wide applicability, it is especially appropriate for facilitating groups whose primary purpose is to support older adults through stressful life events and stressful life transitions. Using a reciprocal approach, the practitioner can help members who are in different phases of coping with a similar life transition to share their experiences with each other. Members learn that they are not alone with their concerns and that others have experienced similar reactions. The practitioner helps members to develop a mutual aid system to overcome obstacles to coping with difficult life transitions and the stress that results from them. For example, a practitioner encouraged one member of a group for widows to recount how guilty she felt about wishing that her terminally ill husband, who was in much pain, would die. Because of the group norm of mutual aid that the practitioner's leadership helped to develop, another member of the group shared the similar experiences and feelings she had had when she had been caring for her husband who died. Other members of the group mentioned how difficult it was to provide long-term care at home while watching a loved one gradually deteriorate. Others expressed their amazement that the member had coped so well with the unrelenting demands of caregiving that she had experienced over the past seven years. For more information about the reciprocal model of group work see Shulman (1984), Shulman and Gitterman (1986), and chapter 5 of this text.

The aim of the remedial model is to restore and rehabilitate the adaptive capacities of older adults who are socially withdrawn and those who suffer from debilitating chronic illnesses. It is also useful for those who want to learn something new because they expect the leader to be a guide, a teacher, and a content expert. Therefore, this model is especially useful when working with frail older adults in therapy groups and for working with a broad spectrum of older adults in educational groups.

The remedial model assumes that group members are not functioning at optimum levels. It also assumes that impairments interfere with members' abilities to establish mutually agreed upon goals without support and guidance from the practitioner. Therefore, the reliance on mutual goal setting and mutual aid is often less pronounced than in groups emphasizing a reciprocal approach. Instead, the practitioner takes more responsibility for establishing and implementing a structure for group interaction and for preparing and developing group content that will help members to function at optimum levels.

In general, groups using a remedial approach focus less on process and more on content than groups using a reciprocal approach. Practitioners are less interested in helping members to develop their own approaches to the work of the group than they are in helping members to follow through on intervention strategies that have proven to be effective with others in similar situations. For example, a practitioner decides to begin a community living skills group to help inpatients living in a geriatric ward of a state mental institution to make the transition to community living. After a careful assessment of the skills of those selected for the group, the practitioner decides to focus on money management and housekeeping. The practitioner employs role playing, modeling, rehearsal, and guided practice to prepare members for community living because she is aware of literature that suggests that these techniques are effective for teaching psychiatric patients independent community living skills. The practitioner welcomes suggestions about the focus of the group from members, but her experience suggests that members have lived for so long in an institutional environment that it is difficult, at least initially, for them to take a great deal of responsibility for planning the direction of the group. Therefore, the practitioner takes the lead in structuring the agenda for group meetings.

As the group continues to develop, the practitioner remains responsive to input from members, encouraging members to assume whatever leadership they are capable of taking. Thus, groups that are initially based on a remedial model of leadership may slowly evolve into ones that are based on a reciprocal model. For additional information about the remedial model of group leadership, see Rose (1989) and chapter 6 of this text.

The aim of the social goals model is twofold: to help older adults engage in informed political and social action and to raise their social identity, social consciousness, and social responsibility. The social goals model is an early group work model that began in settlement houses, community centers, and youth organizations.

In relation to political and social action, the social goals model is designed to help empower older persons so that they can engage in informed and responsible citizenship. The practitioner acts as an enabler by facilitating members' efforts to identify important social concerns, by helping members to actively participate in groups designed to discuss and grapple with these issues, and by assisting members to develop effective action plans and to devise methods to carry them out and evaluate their impact.

The social goals model focuses on members' social identity, their social consciousness, and their social rights and responsibilities. As a group, older persons often encounter negative stereotypes and age-based discrimination. In addition, the dependence of some older persons on community and institutional care makes them particularly vulnerable to exploitation and to a compromising of their rights as citizens. The social goals model is particularly useful for addressing these concerns.

The social goals model is used extensively for facilitating service groups, advocacy groups, and social and recreational groups. Senior centers, community centers, civic and religious associations, and other community-based and institutional settings sponsor many different kinds of social, recreational, and cultural activities for older adults. They also sponsor numerous service and advocacy groups. On a national level, the National Council on Aging, the American Association of Retired Persons, the Alzheimer's Disease and Related Disorders Association, the Grey Panthers, and similar organizations make extensive use of this leadership model in the local groups that they sponsor.

When working with frail older persons, and those without the inclination to take on active leadership roles, practitioners use the social goals model to plan group experiences to enhance members' self-esteem and social identity, to increase members' social support networks, to help members utilize their talents in socially beneficial ways, to help members better understand and live with each other and with other age groups in society, and to ensure that the rights of members, and any larger constituency represented by members, are not being violated.

With vigorous and active older adults who have leadership capacities, the practitioner is well advised to assume more of a staff role, helping older adults to assume leadership roles, respecting their abilities to organize and facilitate their own groups, and following through on requests for assistance and support in whatever ways members deem necessary to maintain and enhance the functioning of their group. For more information about how the social goals model is used in leading groups of older persons, see Coppola and Rivas (1986), Pernell (1986), and chapters 7 and 8 of this text.

SELECTING AN APPROPRIATE LEADERSHIP MODEL

In practice, most group workers blend aspects of different leadership models to serve the needs of older adults in the most effective manner possible. Practice wisdom and research findings indicate that a single practice model is not effective in all situations and that effective leadership should be tailored to the particular situation. Given the evidence, Toseland and Rivas (1984) have concluded that approaches that suggest that a single leadership model is effective in all situations are overly simplistic. To be maximally effective, leadership methods should reflect the results of a comprehensive assessment of the group and its members.

What factors should a group worker consider when attempting to use leadership skills differentially to meet the needs of diverse groups of older adults? Clinical and empirical evidence suggests that, at a minimum, practitioners should consider (1) the purpose and goals of the group, (2) the capabilities of members and the leader, (3) the environment in which the group operates, and (4) the phase of a group's development.

Purposes and goals give groups their direction. To a large extent, they determine the skills a practitioner uses to facilitate the work of a group. For example, a practitioner would use quite different leadership skills in a residents' council in a nursing home than in a support group for caregivers. The residents' council might benefit from some help with developing an agenda and organizing and conducting meetings, whereas the support group is more likely to need educational information and assistance about how to cope with emotional reactions to the stress of caregiving.

The capacities that members bring to a group are also a very important factor to consider when selecting an appropriate leadership model. The extent of members' interpersonal skills, the amount of information they possess or have access to, their motivation to work on individual and group goals, and their expectations about the process and outcome of the work of the group should all be considered as the practitioner decides how to facilitate a group.

According to Heap (1979), the degree of activity of the leader should be directly related to the social health of group members. In developing her broad-range model of leadership, Lang (1972) also suggested that practitioners vary their leadership style based on the extent to which group members and the group-as-a-whole can function autonomously. In groups with members who have limited ability to function autonomously, practitioners should consider taking a central role, whereas in groups of older adults who are more autonomous, practitioners should rely more extensively on members' initiative and their indigenous leadership abilities. For example, a practitioner in a psychogeriatric day care center takes a very active role when facilitating a group of individuals with Alzheimer's disease. In contrast, the same worker may be better advised to take a less active enabler role in a group of older adults who are meeting to plan an ethnic food festival to benefit an emergency food bank. Similarly, a less active stance would probably be warranted when acting as a consultant to a group of older adults who serve as an advisory group for a senior center.

Practitioners should also examine their own capacities when deciding on how to facilitate groups of older persons. They should examine their experience with the problems and concerns expressed by the group, their comfort in dealing with these issues, and their expertise in helping the group to cope with and resolve them. As pointed out earlier in this chapter, practitioners should also be cognizant of their own reactions to working with older persons and of older persons' reactions to them.

The environment in which a group operates can also have an important impact on leadership. Environmental influences come primarily from the immediate physical setting, the sponsoring organization, and the larger social system in which the group operates.

Practitioners should strive to ensure that the physical setting facilitates the work of the group. For example, Toseland and Coppola (1985) have suggested modifying the environment to accommodate the needs of older adults by using straight-back chairs that provide support for the back and are easier to get in and out of, a room with easy access for the kind of chronic disabilities commonly experienced by members of the group being served, and a relatively small, private meeting room to capture voices and to avoid distractions.

The sponsoring agency and the larger society have an important influence on the leadership of a group. Boards and other administrative groups set overall policies for agencies that can encourage the development of certain types of groups and discourage the development of others. The practitioner should be aware of how the sponsoring agencies' policies, rules, and regulations affect the development of group programs. When policies interfere with effective group functioning, the practitioner should lobby for changes that promote older persons' welfare.

Practitioners' leadership efforts are also influenced by the resources and the supportive services that are available through the agency and the larger social service delivery system. For example, a practitioner working with a group of terminally ill older people in a hospital setting can do better work when adequate home care and home-based hospice care programs are available. Practitioners should possess up-to-date information on existing community resources and services and should utilize their leadership role to help older persons to make effective use of them. When appropriate resources are not available, practitioners should advocate for their development.

The phase of a group's development also has an enormous impact on the way practitioners facilitate groups. Theoreticians have consistently pointed out that groups go through distinct phases of development that have important implications for leadership (see, for example, Garland, Jones, and Kolodny 1976). Each phase requires a different combination of skills to facilitate a group's continued development. For example, in the beginning phase practitioners are generally more active in structuring the work of a group than in middle or ending phases. Group development will be discussed in detail in chapter 4.

COLEADERSHIP

A chapter about leadership would not be complete without a discussion of the advantages and disadvantages of two leaders working together. Many groups of older persons are co-led. Although there is little empirical evidence for the effectiveness of coleadership (Yalom 1985), the group work literature contains many clinical reports about its effectiveness.[1]

Coleadership has a number of potential advantages.

• Assistance when working with frail older persons and during demanding program activities. The more physically or cognitively impaired group members are, the more the group will benefit from coleadership. Coleaders can sit next to impaired members, assisting them in whatever way that is needed. For example, a coleader can sign to a deaf member, keep a cognitively impaired member oriented, or assist a physically impaired member in a program activity.

• Support when obstacles and impediments are encountered. Burnside (1986) has pointed out that work with older persons can be physically and emotionally draining. Because they share in the group experience, coleaders are in a good position to support each other through difficult times.

• A catalyst for professional development. Coleaders share their perceptions of the group and their roles in it. Alternate frames of reference and feedback can help practitioners improve their group leadership skills.

• An additional model for effective group participation. Through their interactions, coleaders can be models for appropriate group participation. They can facilitate members' participation by tuning into their needs and by helping them to overcome obstacles to goal attainment. They can assist in role plays and dramatic enactments of problematic situations and help members to rehearse more effective coping strategies.

• An educational tool. A novice group leader can learn much about how to be an effective leader by working with an experienced leader. The experienced leader can provide support for the novice leader in difficult situations and can point out strengths and weaknesses in the novice leader's skills.

The potential benefits of coleadership should be weighted against its potential disadvantages. Coleadership is expensive and time-consuming. It more than doubles the amount of professional time taken to serve the same number of individuals because, to work effectively together, coleaders need to spend time between meetings coordinating and harmonizing their efforts on behalf of group members. Also, coleaders may not work well together.

---

1. See, for example, a special issue of *Social Work with Groups* 3, no. 4 (1985) on coleadership, and earlier articles by Davis and Lohr (1971) and Levine (1980).

If differences are not skillfully resolved, the ensuing tension and conflict can detract from a group's optimal development or, in extreme situations, lead to its demise. Therefore, when considering whether or not to colead a group of older persons, the potential benefits and drawbacks of having two leaders should be carefully weighed.

SUMMARY

This chapter has focused on the effective leadership of groups of older persons. It began with a discussion of some of the unique features of leading groups of older adults. The essential features of three distinct models of group leadership were presented. This was followed by a discussion of the selection of the most appropriate leadership model for particular groups of older adults and an examination of some of the factors that influence choice of a leadership model. The chapter concluded with a brief review of the benefits and drawbacks of coleadership.

4

Phases of Group Development

When older adults connect with each other in a group, they begin to develop a group identity. The development of this identity evolves as the group continues to meet. This chapter reviews each phase of group development, delineating procedures and skills that practitioners should be familiar with when facilitating groups of older persons.

There are many models of group development. For example, Garland, Jones, and Kolodny (1976) have developed a five-stage model: (1) pre-affiliation, (2) power and control, (3) intimacy, (4) differentiation, and (5) separation. In contrast, Tuckman (1965) has developed a four-stage model: (1) forming, (2) storming, (3) norming, and (4) performing. This chapter uses a four-stage model of group development: (1) planning, (2) beginning, (3) middle, and (4) ending. This model is derived from the commonalities among many of the better-known models of group development.[1]

When considering phases of group development, practitioners should remain aware that a variety of factors influence the way groups develop. For example, healthy older adults who come together with a clear purpose in mind may coalesce quickly, whereas the frail elderly, those who have been socially isolated, or those with hearing impairments, may take longer to develop into a cohesive group.

LEADERSHIP DURING THE PLANNING PHASE

Those who have written about group work with older persons have suggested that a well-planned group is likely to be more effective in achieving its purposes and goals than one that has been formed haphazardly (see, for example, Hartford 1985). To plan an effective group, practitioners should (1) establish the group's purpose, (2) publicize the group, (3) compose the group, (4) prepare and orient members, and (5) prepare the group's environment.

1. For a description of some of the better-known models of group development see Toseland and Rivas (1984).

Establishing the Group's Purpose

The process of clarifying and specifying the purposes and goals of the groups should begin as early as possible in the planning process. Initial attempts to specify the purpose for a group should be tentative and open ended to encourage input from all interested parties. For example, when making initial contact with potential members of a group for recent widows, the practitioner might mention that one of the purposes of the group would be to provide a place where members could describe what they are going through, and to get feedback and support from others in similar situations.

Potential members should be encouraged to participate in the process to the extent that they are willing and able. For example, the leader should encourage potential members of a widow's group to talk about what they want to get out of the group. The inclusion of potential members in the development of group purposes promotes cohesion and contributes to effective group functioning by developing a consensus about what the group is attempting to accomplish.

Sponsors should also be included in the development of group purposes. In many settings, the cooperation of staff members is essential for the smooth operation of the group. For example, coordination and cooperation with other staff are essential for avoiding bureaucratic miscommunication that can lead to absences and late arrivals in groups conducted in nursing home settings (Maisler and Solomon 1976).

To establish a group's purpose, practitioners should conduct a needs assessment and assess the potential sponsorship for the group. Generally, this process begins with the practitioner perceiving an unmet need in previous work with older persons. The practitioner should avoid relying solely on personal perceptions of need as the basis for establishing a group service. A needs assessment can help to verify a practitioner's perception.

A needs assessment can take many forms. At a minimum, practitioners should collect information to confirm their perceptions from a representative sample of colleagues who are in a position to assess whether an unmet need exists. Team meetings are often an effective forum for an exchange of information and ideas. It is also useful, though not always essential, to survey the population that practitioners intend to serve. This can be accomplished by asking existing clients to fill out a questionnaire or by asking some other convenient sample of older adults to respond to questions about their needs.

When larger program developments efforts are planned, the investment in time and resources may warrant a community survey that is designed to more accurately estimate the extent of a need. Indeed, a well-executed needs assessment can be very useful in helping the practitioner to develop an effective publicity campaign, to determine how potential participants are likely to respond to a group experience, and to assess what intervention strategies are likely to be most effective.

The practitioner should also be sensitive to the potential sponsorship for the group. Groups rely on organizational sponsorship for their professional sanction and mandate, for their financial resources, for some or all of their membership, and for the physical facilities necessary to plan and conduct meetings. The practitioner should consider the reputation of the sponsor of the group among potential members. Some older persons may be attracted by the sponsorship of particular religious organizations, whereas others may be attracted by the sponsor's ethnic identification or location in the community. For example, many more Hispanic elderly attended the first meeting of an Alzheimer's support group when it was held in a neighborhood community center than when it was held in a hospital in a predominately non-Hispanic community. For additional information and illustrations concerning the importance of sponsorship for effective service delivery to older persons see Tobin, Ellor, and Anderson-Ray (1986).

When assessing sponsorship, the practitioner's goal is to determine the level of support that the group can anticipate. To the extent possible, the group's purpose and goals should be conceptualized within the mission of the sponsoring agency. The practitioner should examine whether or not there is a goodness-of-fit between an organization's policies and goals and the purposes of the proposed group. Any policies and procedures of the agency that conflict with the tentative purposes of the proposed group should be reconciled. When practitioners encounter a lack of support or outright resistance to a new group service, it can be helpful to demonstrate to administrative and line staff how the proposed group will help to achieve the agency's mission. In rare situations, when differences cannot be reconciled, a different sponsoring agency should be sought.

Publicizing the Group

Practitioners should ensure that there is enough interest to begin a new group and to maintain ongoing membership. Practitioners can use several strategies to publicize a group, including (1) informing colleagues within their own agency, (2) publicizing the group in settings where potential participants are likely to congregate, and (3) publicizing the group in the larger community.

The most common form of recruitment occurs when practitioners publicize a group within their own agency. For example, fellow workers at a senior center can be asked to identify potential members whom they think would be interested, or potential members may be identified from agency records or mailing lists. Depending on the nature of the group, experience suggests that anywhere from two to five times the amount of members needed for a viable group may have to be identified in order to ensure sufficient participation after screening, because many who say they will attend will not show up at the first group meeting. Also, some may come to the first meeting, discover that the group is either not what they expected or not to their liking, and fail to return to subsequent meetings.

When a sufficient pool of potential members is unavailable or when wider participation is desired, the practitioner should consider recruiting members from likely sources outside of the agency. Congregate meal sites, senior centers, age-segregated housing, churches, and adult education programs are examples of places where it is often possible to contact large numbers of older adults.

In certain situations, practitioners may want to reach out beyond the circle of older persons known to social service agencies to recruit those who need services but are not as readily identifiable. The practitioner can do this by locating concentrations of potential participants in the community, by gathering information about likely gathering places of older persons from knowledgeable community leaders, by going to gatherings of older people, and by sponsoring community events that encourage older persons to attend (Toseland 1981).

Practitioners can choose from several methods to inform potential participants about a group experience, including making direct contact, posting announcements, preparing press releases and radio and television announcements, arranging for feature newspaper stories, and appearing on radio or television shows. Direct contact is probably the most effective means of informing potential participants about a group. This method, however, often requires much effort and may not be as cost effective as alternative methods. In contrast, preparing and posting announcements requires much less effort, but may not be effective by itself. Brief announcements in newspapers, on radio, or on television are generally more effective than posted announcements and cost nothing when they are provided as a public service. If this method is selected, be sure to examine what radio and television stations target older adults as a major audience and whether any local agencies prepare newsletters specifically for older adults.

Publicizing a group by arranging for a feature newspaper article or for an appearance on a radio or television talk show can also be a very effective strategy for recruiting members. Just one newspaper article or one appearance on a popular radio or television show is sometimes all that is needed to recruit a sufficient number of participants for a group. Although sometimes feature newspaper articles and radio and television appearances can be difficult to arrange, experience indicates that they are an effective means of reaching a broad segment of older adults.

Generally, newspapers try to ensure that a description of the group experience will have a wide appeal for the newspaper's readership. Be prepared with written material explaining the group as well as a clear verbal description of the importance of the group as a community service. The written material can be used later by the reporter when preparing the story. Experience suggests that giving reporters a written as well as a verbal description of the group helps to ensure the accuracy of the feature story they prepare.

Reporters and radio and television talk show hosts may ask to interview older persons who have participated in previous groups or, if that is not possible, to interview older persons who are in need of the group service. It can be difficult to find a willing participant for an interview, especially when he or she suffers from a problem or a concern that is socially stigmatizing. Experience suggests that this obstacle can frequently be overcome if the purpose for the interview is carefully explained to a committed individual.

Composing the Group

After publicizing the group and obtaining a sufficient number of applicants, the practitioner screens potential members and composes the group. This process begins with the practitioner deciding on the size of the group and whether its membership will be open or closed.

There is no optimum size for a group. According to Bertcher and Maple (1974), the size of a group depends on its purposes and goals and the attributes of its members. Generally, in larger groups, members have less opportunity to interact with each other, whereas in smaller groups, more demands are placed on each member for active participation.

Support groups and therapy groups are often conducted with between six and ten members. This size allows each member sufficient time to participate, without putting undue pressure on any one member to participate at a given time. In contrast, other types of groups for older adults can accommodate a larger membership. For example, advocacy groups may benefit from having a larger membership that can be drawn upon for expertise and person power for selected projects and tasks.

Before composing the group, the practitioner should also consider whether the membership will be open or closed to new members. Closed groups accept no new members after the first few sessions. Frequently, members of closed groups meet for a predetermined number of sessions and then terminate together as a group. In open groups, members enter and terminate throughout the life of the group. Open groups can maintain a relatively constant size by replacing terminating members with members who are awaiting admission.

In many situations, the nature of the group and the sponsoring organization determine whether the group will be open or closed. For example, it makes a great deal of sense for a resident's council to have an open membership policy so that new residents can be included as others leave a facility. In contrast, it may be disruptive to add new members to an outpatient therapy group when members share common understandings and experiences based on earlier sessions.

In general, practitioners should consider the advantages and disadvantages of open and closed membership when opting for either alternative in a particular situation. Closed membership generally allows for a greater sense of cohesion and comradery. There tends to be greater stability of roles and norms. Closed groups proceed through the stages of group development in a more orderly and predictable fashion. When members drop out or are absent, however, closed groups run the risk of having their membership fall below the number of individuals needed for meaningful interaction. Also, without the benefit of new members and their ideas, closed membership groups run the risk of becoming stale or of engaging in "group think," which is the avoidance of minority opinions.

Open membership allows new ideas and new resources to be brought to the group. It helps to ensure sufficient participation over the life of a group. On the negative side, adding new members can be disruptive, particularly when previous experience in the group is important. Open groups generally do not experience phases of group development in the same manner as closed groups, because members are in different stages of initiation and termination. Instability resulting from changes in leadership and membership can interfere with the development of cohesion and group identity among members.

Some open groups combat these problems by limiting the number of new members added at any time or by adding new members only when the remaining group members are prepared and when the new members can be educated about the norms and procedures of the group. Adhering to a routinized agenda that all members can become easily engaged in, no matter how sporadic or short-term their attendance, is another technique that is frequently used to maintain a sense of continuity and stability in open membership groups. For example, two-hour monthly meetings of a support group for caregivers of frail elderly with Alzheimer's disease that was open to the public began with a one-hour guest presentation on such topics as the latest research findings on Alzheimer's disease, guardianship and other legal issues, memory aids, management of behavior problems, and so forth.

The presentation was always followed by a coffee break that lasted about fifteen minutes, and then the meeting concluded with a question-and-answer period and discussion of the presentation by those who were present.

Once tentative decisions about size and open or closed membership have been made, practitioners can compose a group using the following practice principles: 1) a homogeneity of member purposes and characteristics, 2) a heterogeneity of coping skills and expertise, 3) an overall balance of member qualities in relation to the purpose and goals of the group.

The principle of homogeneity suggests that members should identify with the purpose and goals of the group. This helps members to function in harmony with other members and to maximize their achievements within the group. Without a common purpose, members have little basis for interacting or working cooperatively together. The principle also suggests that members should share some similar personal characteristics such as their physical and emotional stamina, communication abilities, social skills levels, and types of problems or concerns. For example, Feil (1982; 1983) has pointed out that mixing mildly disoriented residents with severely confused residents of nursing homes was not helpful. She suggests that mildly disoriented residents responded well to remotivation techniques (described in chapter 6) whereas severely confused residents did not respond well to these techniques. Similarly, recreational groups may be able to function more effectively when the very old, who have less physical stamina, are encouraged to participate in certain activities and the young-old are encouraged to participate in others.

The practitioner should also try to ensure that members have enough personal characteristics in common to facilitate their work on a particular task. For example, support groups for caregivers function optimally when their membership is limited to adult children or to spouses because adult children and spouses react quite differently to providing care (see, for example, Horowitz 1985; Montgomery and Borgotta 1989).

The principle of heterogeneity suggests that members should be selected for the diversity they exhibit in coping skills and expertise. Including members who utilize different coping strategies and who bring different perspectives, information, and life experiences to the group experience expose all members to a variety of options, choices, and alternatives for accomplishing individual and group goals, thereby helping members to learn from each other. For example, in an advocacy group it may be useful to have members with expertise in law, in public relations, in the media, and in different technical areas. Thus, the steering committee of a chapter of the Grey Panthers included a retired lawyer, a bookkeeper, two retired teachers with excellent speaking abilities, and an individual who had been a legislative aide.

The principle of balance suggests that practitioners should select group members who complement one another. For example, when composing a therapy group in an inpatient setting, the practitioner avoided placing all of the most severely withdrawn older adults in the same group. Similarly, in another group the same practitioner decided to include some members who were almost ready for discharge and others who were just beginning to consider making the transition to community living.

Preparing and Orienting Members

It is good practice to prepare members for the group experience by orienting them during a screening or intake interview. The orientation process includes (1) explaining the purpose and benefits of the group, (2) familiarizing members with group procedures, clarifying expectations, and responding to questions and concerns, and (3) contracting for group procedures and individual and group goals.

A practitioner's explanation of the purpose of the group should be clear and concise. It should be specific enough to allow potential members to get a clear sense of the focus of the group but broad enough to encourage their input. Frail older people and the old-old may be slower to process what you say and slower to recall what they have heard. Take extra time to make sure they understand. Invite feedback about your explanation of the group. Respond to any questions, and check to be sure that potential members have a clear understanding of the nature of the group and their participation in it.

Familiarizing potential members with procedures for participation and for how the group will conduct its work helps to clarify what the experience will be like and to overcome the fears of older adults who may be insecure about what they have to contribute. It also helps to induct members into appropriate roles in the group and to overcome the self-centeredness of those who have difficulty reaching out and responding to others because of preoccupation with their own concerns and problems or because of the effects of disengagement from their former roles. For example, Yost, Beutler, Corbishley, and Allender (1986) report that one step in their process of orienting depressed older members to groups is to explain the major tenets of group cognitive therapy for depression. The leader explains that cognitive therapy focuses primarily on the negative thoughts that increase dysphoric feelings associated with depression. The leader also briefly explains the type of exercises and activities that are used in the group to combat the typical downward cycle of depression.

Orientation interviews should clarify members' expectations. Clinical experience and research evidence suggests that congruent expectations among members and leaders helps groups to function smoothly and to avoid conflict and dissatisfaction in later meetings (Toseland and Rivas 1984; Yalom 1985). Expectations that are not congruent with those of the other members and the leader can lead to premature dropouts (Yalom 1985). For example, the practitioner leading a group for widows explained to potential new members that current members had decided on a group format that included taking a few minutes to summarize and highlight what occurred during the last meeting, allotting time for individual members to share their experiences and concerns in coping with the deaths of their spouses, and spending a few minutes at the end of each group meeting summarizing insights gained during the meeting. The leader explained that members had decided on this format because that they were interested in participating in a support group rather than a social group that focused on doing activities together.

It is useful to end an orientation interview by contracting for group procedures and by beginning the process of contracting for individual and group goals. Contracting for group procedures can be an informal process in which the length, frequency, and duration of meetings are discussed, any fees for participation are explained, and any special rights, privileges, or access to resources that result from committing oneself to participation are described. Some practitioners prefer a more formal process wherein applicants are asked to sign a group contract such as the one shown in table 4.1.

The practitioner can begin the process of contracting for individual and group goals by asking members what they would like to accomplish and what role they see themselves playing in the group. In many situations, practitioners will find that members do not have well-formed plans. Discussion of goals during an intake interview can start members thinking about the work of the group and how they will participate in it. The process of contracting for individual and group goals should continue, in a more focused way, as goals become clarified during the beginning and middle phases of the group.

Preparing the Group's Environment

When preparing the group's environment, the practitioner should consider (1) the setting where the group will be held, (2) the resources necessary for the group to accomplish its work, and (3) the integration of the group program into the sponsoring agency and the larger community. Because some older people are likely to have chronic disabilities, the setting for group meetings is especially important. A comfortable and intimate setting facilitates communication and interaction. For older persons, a comfortable setting is one where there are few if any stairs to climb, handrails to aid in

TABLE 4.1: An Example of a Group Contract

As a group member I agree to:
1. Attend all group sessions.
2. Arrive on time for each group session.
3. Keep the proceedings of each group meeting confidential.
4. Participate fully in the group interaction.
5. Allow other members to finish a thought when they are speaking.
6. Not dominate the group discussion.
7. Pay for each group session in a timely fashion.

As the group leader I agree to:
1. Be prepared for each group meeting.
2. Begin and end all group sessions on time.
3. Be respectful of each member's unique contribution to the group.
4. Keep the proceedings of each meeting confidential.
5. Help members to get the most out of their participation in the group.

Group Member's Signature	Date
Group Leader's Signature	Date

walking, non-skid carpeting rather than scatter rugs, a relatively warm temperature, good ventilation, plenty of light, high-back armchairs, a size that is about half again as big as the circle formed by the seated group, and few distractions.

The level of noise is a particularly important consideration because of the incidence of hearing impairments among older persons. The setting should be as free as possible of background noises. It is also often handy to have a blackboard, newsprint, and other learning aids to convey ideas visually as well as verbally. The practitioner should try to anticipate the resources that will be needed by the group. Being prepared can mean different things depending on the group. For a caregiver's support group it might mean preparing a community resource directory, recruiting volunteers, or finding resources to pay for respite care while a participant is attending meetings. For a "Try Out a New Exercise" recreational group it might mean securing arrangements for visits by the group to local golf courses, tennis courts, swimming pools, and bowling alleys.

The practitioner should also pay attention to how the group is integrated into the sponsoring agency and the larger community. In particular, the practitioner should focus on how the sponsoring agency and larger community can support and enhance the work of the group and how members can be enabled to continue their work after a group ends. Knowing what resources exist in the agency and the community helps the practitioner to connect members to appropriate sources of support while they are in the group and after it ends. Access to services or resources can enhance the effect of the group experience. For example, members of a short-term, professionally led group for caregivers of the elderly can be encouraged to hire a sitter, to use respite services offered by a local residential care facility, and to begin attending meetings of a self-help support group as the group nears termination.

LEADERSHIP DURING THE BEGINNING PHASE

The beginning of a group can be a stressful time for those who have decided to participate. Beginnings are characterized by caution and tentativeness as members attempt to find their places within the group while at the same time maintaining their own identities. Group members look to each other for clues as to how to behave. Through their initial interactions, they begin to find a comfortable niche within the group.

It is good practice to support and validate older persons' positive views of themselves from the beginning of the group. There is some clinical evidence to suggest that older persons may be more sensitive to practitioners' empathy and support than younger people (Lazarus 1984). One study of the process of therapy, for example, revealed that older people sought approval and help to restore self-esteem, to view themselves as competent, masterful, and psychologically healthy, and to reestablish continuity with their previously positive senses of self (Lazarus et al. 1984). In a similar manner, older adults who do not have mental health problems may use groups to validate their existing feelings of competence and self-esteem. For example, in comparing groups of younger and older persons, Lakin, Oppenheimer, and Bremer (1982) point out that group interventions with the elderly should emphasize an "acceptant, encouraging, supportive, and nonconfrontational mode, concretized in clarification and mild amplification of feelings" (452).

In the beginning phase, it is often helpful for the leader to involve group members as fully as possible in deciding on the work to be done in the group and on the structure to be used for accomplishing it. This can be done by soliciting input from all group members and involving them in the process of evaluating alternatives and arriving at a consensus about how to proceed. Involving older persons in this process in the first few meetings takes skill because some may have difficulty articulating what they would like to accomplish and others may have difficulty seeing what they have in common with their fellow group members. Concerns about the quality of their participation is sometimes heightened by the presence of other members. A supportive, patient, and relaxed leader can contribute to members' satisfaction with the group experience.

The beginning phase of group work can be challenging for the leader because members seek direction and structure but guard their privacy and their freedom to participate at their own discretion. There is frequently an approach-avoidance conflict as members alternate between striving to connect with each other in order to be accepted and validated and keeping their distance in order to avoid the emotional ties and vulnerability that accompany intimacy. Although need for affiliation draws members together, life experiences, certain established ways of behaving, and inertia may interfere with the development of trust and intimacy in a group. As the group unfolds, the practitioner uncovers obstacles to closeness and helps members to achieve deeper levels of trust and intimacy than they felt comfortable with initially.

Practitioners can take the following steps to help ensure a group's proper development in the beginning phase: (1) help members to feel at ease with themselves and their fellow group members, (2) describe the purpose and function of the group as clearly as possible, (3) provide the opportunity and the climate for members to describe the fit between their needs, the practitioners' view of their needs, and the function of the group as specified by the sponsoring agency, (4) balance task and socio-emotional aspects of the group process, (5) determine goals and a working agreement or contract with the fullest possible participation of members, and (6) facilitate members' motivation and abilities for accomplishing the goals of the group.

Help Members to Feel at Ease

When members arrive and the group is ready to begin, the practitioner's first task is to introduce members to each other. Introductions should allow members to share who they are and to begin the process of connecting with other members about mutual interests and concerns. The practitioner can facilitate this process by deciding on a uniform process for introductions, by suggesting to members what information they might want to share, and by modeling appropriate self-disclosure. For example, in a caregiver's group, while introducing themselves members were also asked to describe the person for whom they were caring, what kinds of illnesses the person had, what they did for the person, and how long they had been caring for the person.

There are many methods for facilitating introductions. The most common method, the "round robin," occurs when members introduce themselves one after the other. Another method is to have members divide into pairs, interview each other for five minutes, reconvene, and introduce their partner to the group. This method is used most effectively in groups for the well elderly who are not cognitively, emotionally, or physically impaired. It helps group members to develop a relationship with their partners and tends to reduce the tension that arises when members are asked to speak about themselves to a group of individuals with whom they are not familiar. It also tends to lead to greater levels of self-disclosure because individuals are likely to reveal more about themselves on a one-on-one basis than when they are asked to introduce themselves to the group.

Depending on the nature of the group and the members' needs, other introductory exercises can be useful in the first session, or as "ice breakers" in later sessions. Each member may be asked to select an animal that they believe represents their own personality characteristics and then describe their feelings about the animal. Members may be asked to describe how they feel about their surname. Members may be asked to go on a "treasure hunt," finding out one or two new facts about every other group member. The informal milling about and interaction that results from this exercise can often reduce initial tensions and anxieties and can reveal important new information that, in turn, can deepen and expand group interaction. Another useful opening exercise is "problem swapping," where members take turns describing a problem or concern they had between group meetings. This opening is useful to encourage the emergence of shared problems and concerns. A variation on this exercise, called "sharing positive experiences," encourages members to describe the coping skills they used to overcome adversities between meetings. For additional ideas about opening exercises see Middleman (1968) or Pfeiffer and Jones (1972–1981).

The kinds of introductory exercises to employ are limited only by a group worker's creativity and the needs and capacities of members. Practitioners should keep in mind the following principles when developing their own exercises:

1. Model desired levels of self-disclosure by fully engaging in introductory exercises and modeling appropriate responses. It is rare for members to disclose more than the practitioner discloses.
2. Enhance "universality" (Yalom 1985), that is, the feeling that members are not alone with their concerns, by highlighting and underscoring any commonalities revealed during introductions.
3. Make sure that members do not reveal anything that is too threatening or too personal, that they may later regret, or that other group

members do not yet feel safe and secure enough to benefit from. Praising a member for taking a risk but suggesting that discussion of the issue be postponed to a later group session can be an effective strategy to constrain revelations that may be too threatening at a particular time in the group's development.

4. Enhance comfort and support by acknowledging tension, by pointing out that it is a normal experience early in groups, and by mentioning to members that it will gradually dissipate as they get to know one another and develop a sense of shared purpose.

5. Acknowledge members' contributions and their attentiveness to others.

6. Invite members' participation. Provide opportunities for less assertive members to speak up.

Describe Purposes and Functions

After introductions have been completed, the practitioner should make a clear, concise statement about the purpose of the group, the practitioner's role, and the group's function in relation to the sponsoring agency. Members' anxieties are heightened in the beginning phase when they are not clear about the purpose of the group, the role of the practitioner, or their own roles.

The statement of a group's purpose should be presented in as positive terms as possible. Practitioners should avoid a focus on the negative aspects of problems and concerns and instead should make statements such as, "Through this group experience we can become more. . . ," "Together we can. . . ," "We can help each other to. . . ," "We can learn to. . . ." The description should contain an upbeat, enthusiastic, hopeful, but realistic presentation of what the group is capable of accomplishing.

When practitioners have had previous experiences with similar groups, it is helpful to discuss briefly what was accomplished and any beneficial effects that resulted from previous members' participation. It can be effective to have a former group member share what it was like to be in a previous group and what positive impact the group experience had on his or her life.

After discussing the purpose and function of the group, the practitioner may wish to discuss issues of confidentiality, record-keeping, and release of information. Practitioners should be clear about with whom and under what circumstances they are required to share information about the group. Beyond this, group members should be encouraged to develop a consensus about the level of confidentiality they would like to operate in their group.

Provide Feedback

It is important for the practitioner to solicit members' feedback to opening statements of purpose. It can sometimes be difficult to achieve open communication early in a group, particularly when a member's opinions differ from those of the practitioner or other members. However, to avoid hidden agendas and premature terminations, as well as to help ensure members' active participation in the work of the group, it is essential for the practitioner to encourage candid expressions of alternative viewpoints. Therefore, practitioners should reach out for feedback from reticent members and demonstrate their receptivity to feedback by taking actions that are responsive to members' input.

Balance Task and Socio-Emotional Needs

No matter what type of group older people belong to, clinical experience indicates that they try to turn them into social, personally satisfying occasions. Most older people, whether frail or vigorous and active, seek places to connect with other people. They enjoy talking and socializing with each other and the practitioner, as well as working to accomplish meaningful tasks.

When older adults decide to accomplish a task, it is important to encourage them to go at their own pace. Repeat concepts as needed and, whenever possible, connect new ideas to previous life experiences. In general, older adults do not do well in pressured situations requiring rapid responses. Instead, they prefer a relaxed, easygoing focus on task accomplishment.

Robert Bales (1950; 1955) was the first to emphasize that all groups have both instrumental and socio-emotional needs and that members' needs in both of these areas must be met for a group to maintain itself. His research suggests that about two thirds of the average administrative group's time was spent on task accomplishment and one-third was spent on meeting members' socio-emotional needs (Bales 1955). Treatment groups spend more time than administrative groups on meeting members' socio-emotional needs (see, for example, Hill 1977; Munzer and Greenwald 1957).

Research and clinical experience suggests that older adults generally value groups in which a great deal of attention is paid to their socio-emotional needs, even at the expense of task accomplishment. For example, Toseland, Sherman, and Bliven (1981) found that members of two senior centers who participated in an experiment to test two methods for developing social support preferred a relatively unstructured approach that emphasized informal social interaction to one that encouraged role playing and the learning of interpersonal skills. Similarly, when comparing three different methods of social skills training in groups, Toseland and Rose (1978) found that older adults expressed somewhat more satisfaction and enjoyment with a format that emphasized mutual sharing and discussion rather than a structured problem-solving format or a behavioral skills training format.

It is clear from these and other studies that an exclusive focus on task or socio-emotional needs can lead to the demise of the group. Besides being exhausting, focusing exclusively on tasks can lead to competitiveness and conflict because members are expected to relate to each other solely on an instrumental level. This, in turn, can lead to feelings that the group is a cold, unsupportive, and pressured place. Conversely, focusing exclusively on members' socio-emotional needs can lead to dissatisfaction with the group's ability to accomplish a task in an efficient manner.

Develop Goals and a Structure for Work

The process of goal setting begins with practitioners' statements about the purpose and function of the group. Goals are formulated through a process of exploration and negotiation as members and the worker share their perspectives. As the group continues to develop and members become more comfortable with each other, goals are clarified and elaborated upon.

Developing clear goals is a prerequisite for successful group development during the middle phase. The practitioner can help to guide and clarify the process of goal formulation by focusing on three sets of interrelated goals: (1) group-centered goals that focus on the proper functioning and maintenance of the group, (2) shared goals that focus on the needs of all members, and (3) individual goals that focus on the particular concerns of a group member.

Experts disagree about how much responsibility the practitioner should take for developing goals and for structuring the way the group accomplishes them. Some, who are associated with the remedial model of group work described in the preceding chapter, suggest that responsibility for goal setting and for structuring the work of the group should be taken by the leader (see, for example, Feldman and Wodarski 1975; Rose 1989). Others, who are associated with the reciprocal model described in chapter 3, suggest that the leader's function is to facilitate group members' goal-setting efforts (see, for example, Klein 1970, 1972; Shulman 1984; Tropp 1976).

Practitioners who decide to take the lead in goal setting and providing a structure for the group can do so by reviewing the guidelines for group participation that are presented in table 4.1, by summarizing and highlighting the goals that are shared by members, and by working with members to help them focus on individual goals. They may also use written agendas such as the one shown in table 4.2, developed for the weekly meeting of a group of wives caring for aging veterans, sponsored by the social services department of a veteran's administration medical center.

There is no magic formula for making decisions about the proper balance between members' autonomy and leader-imposed structure. It depends to a great extent on the capacity of older adults who are members of the group, the nature of the setting, and the purpose of the group. Generally, however, leaders will find that more assistance with goal formulation and structure are needed in early group sessions than in later group sessions. As members become more comfortable with their abilities in later group

---

TABLE 4.2: An Example of a Written Agenda

Date _____

Session One

Goals
By the end of this group meeting each member will become acquainted with:
1. The purpose and goals of the group.
2. The names and life situations of their fellow group members.
3. Guidelines for group participation.
4. A ten-step problem solving method.
5. A deep-breathing relaxation procedure.

Agenda
1. Welcome to participants
      Distribution of name tags and notebooks
      Outline of the group sessions
      Description of purposes and goals of the group
      Description of guidelines for group participation
      Feedback from group members
2. Introduction of the facilitator
3. Introduction of group members
4. Coffee break
5. Introduction of a ten-step problem solving method
6. Deep breathing exercise
7. Closing summary and evaluation

---

sessions, they tend to take more responsibility for the direction and leadership of the group.

Facilitate Members' Goal Attainment Efforts

Throughout the beginning phase, practitioners should help members to increase their motivation for accomplishing the purposes and goals that have been established during the goal-setting process. Motivation is enhanced when members have participated to the fullest extent possible in the development of individual and group goals. Motivation is also enhanced when there is congruence between members' and workers' expectations about how the group will function to achieve the goals that have been mutually agreed upon.

In the beginning phase, it is helpful to continue the process that was begun during the intake interview of clarifying members' expectations and goals. The practitioner can do this by asking members directly about their expectations about group functioning and what they hope to accomplish through group participation. Frequently, older persons have difficulty articulating their needs, expectations, and personal goals. When this situation arises, the practitioner is well advised to reiterate the purpose and function of the group, to reach out for members' reactions, and to explore with members how they would like to use the group. In some groups, such as those aimed at remotivating and rehabilitating long-term residents of psychiatric facilities, one of the primary purposes of a group may be to help members formulate goals to help them cope with the transition to community living.

When goals have been agreed upon, a structure for working on them should be developed. Contracts, which are mutual agreements that specify expectations, obligations, and duties, are useful for this purpose. Most contracts are informal verbal agreements between a member and the leader or between all members and the leader, but occasionally members make formal written contracts with the leader, with other members, or with someone outside of the group.

Contracts are useful because they help the group to focus on goal achievement. They provide continuity across meetings because they help members to keep track of what was agreed upon in previous meetings and because they serve as a focal point for discussion of future progress. By providing a means of measuring what the group has accomplished, they can also serve as an evaluation and accountability device.

Contracts may require older adults to make changes in established patterns. Older adults surviving today have had much experience with economic, social, and cultural changes. They have survived changes for decades. At the same time, there is much comfort and security in doing things in familiar ways, and there is a natural tendency for older people to utilize familiar coping methods that have worked in previous situations. With many years of experience, increasingly frequent threats to their ego integrity from physical and social losses, and an uncertain future, it is no wonder that older adults are sometimes ambivalent about changes, particularly large ones, resisting them in favor of the familiar.

Practitioners can be helpful by encouraging members to share their ambivalent feelings. Experience suggests that sharing ambivalent feelings is the first step in overcoming them. Sharing ambivalent feelings also frequently stimulates other members to do the same. This results in feelings of comradery, supportive interactions, and new ideas and suggestions for overcoming obstacles. The support and encouragement that develops among members for identifying particular problems and accomplishing particular goals is one of the primary benefits of group work.

A realistic appraisal of members' ability to reach a particular goal is much preferred to glossing over barriers and impediments that will arise, in any case, as members attempt to work on agreed upon goals. One technique for accomplishing this is to ask members to list their motivations for reaching a particular goal and the impediments and obstacles that are likely to be encountered. To promote feelings of active engagement in the helping process, the practitioner should encourage all members to examine how goal attainment is likely to be facilitated or impeded. After the items on a particular list have been thoroughly discussed and clarified, the group can suggest alternative ways of overcoming obstacles and impediments. Alternatives can then be evaluated and the best one selected and, if appropriate, practiced within the group prior to implementing it in "the real world."

Table 4.3 is an example of a list of facilitating and impeding forces made by a group in a senior center who were helping a couple decide whether or not they should move to a retirement community in the South. A visual display of facilitating and impeding forces on newsprint or a blackboard can often help members to get an overall picture of the difficulty of reaching a particular goal. In general, the use of visual and audio aids is helpful for presenting new ideas or concepts to the healthy aged, and for facilitating learning in groups where members suffer from mild or moderate cognitive impairments.

LEADERSHIP DURING THE MIDDLE PHASE

The middle phase of group work is characterized by an initial period of assessment, testing, and accommodation as members get to know each

TABLE 4.3: An Example of an Analysis of Facilitating and Impeding
Factors Developed by a Group in a Senior Center

Problem: Should Mr. and Mrs. J. move to a retirement community in the South-
west?

Facilitating Factors	*Impeding Factors*
The nice weather	The cost of the move
The beneficial effect of the low humidity on Mr. J.'s arthritis	The children live in this area
Both children may move soon	The cost of housing in the retirement community
Ability to golf (Mr. J.) and to swim (Mrs. J.) year round	The move will necessitate Mrs. J. giving up a part-time job
Adequate income to make the move	The soft housing market in this part of the country
The life style of the retirement community	
The lower costs for heat and clothing	

other and begin to assume predictable roles in the group. As members
become adjusted to each other and the leader, their energy is freed to work
on group and individual goals. During the middle phase, practitioners fine-
tune their work by engaging in a continuous cycle of assessment, intervention, and reassessment as the group and its members develop.

During the middle phase of group work with older persons, practitioners
help members to accomplish specific purposes and goals by using a variety
of specialized skills and procedures. These specialized skills and procedures
are described in chapters 5–9. Many skills that practitioners use during the
middle phase of group work, however, are applicable to a wide range of
groups. For example, during the middle phase of group work with older
persons, practitioners are commonly called upon to prepare and lead meetings, to make assessments of the group and its members, to facilitate
effective group functioning, and to help members achieve goals. Skills to
accomplish these generic tasks are described in the next section of this
chapter.

Preparing and Leading Group Meetings

When preparing for upcoming meetings, it is often helpful to develop an
outline or an agenda that highlights the major content areas to be covered.

For service, advocacy, and educational groups, a formal written agenda may be prepared. An agenda lends structure and direction to the work of the group. Members of service, advocacy, and educational groups appreciate being presented with an agenda because it helps to avoid confusion about role expectations and about how the group will function. It also gives members something to react to when voicing their opinions about the way work should be accomplished in the group.

It is helpful to begin meetings with a brief review of the previous meeting, highlighting important aspects of the work that was accomplished in relationship to the ongoing goals of the group and the processes that have contributed to effective group functioning. This contributes to the group's sense of identity and continuity and helps to prevent content that is repetitious or irrelevant from diverting the group from its purposes.

However, avoid dwelling on previous meetings. Instead, move smoothly to reviewing the agenda for the current meeting, asking members for their reactions and suggestions. Once an agenda has been agreed upon, it is the practitioner's responsibility to help the group work through it in an expeditious fashion, keeping in mind members' socio-emotional needs. To facilitate movement through an agenda, the leader may find it helpful to summarize and highlight important points frequently, and to seek closure before moving to a new item or, in the case of support groups and therapy groups, a new member's concern. In general, the leader's control of the agenda should be limited to helping the group and its members overcome obstacles to the work they have decided to accomplish. Members are not likely to be interested in an agenda that has been imposed on them.

The leader should ensure that the pace of the meeting leaves sufficient time to attend to all agenda items. Inexperienced leaders sometimes plan too many agenda items, which the group could not possibly accomplish in the time available to it. To avoid this, the leader should help members to prioritize their work and to budget sufficient time for each item. Allowing sufficient time avoids the pressure to rush through an agenda, giving members a chance to deepen their relationships with each other in the process of working together. A flexible, relaxed approach to the agenda is essential because it is not possible to anticipate members' emergent needs, nor the obstacles and impediments that arise as the group continues its work.

At the end of a meeting, practitioners should summarize the work that has been accomplished. A summary helps to clarify and highlight what was accomplished and to promote common understandings among members. Summaries should include a review of any assignments that were agreed to during the meeting. Reviewing assignments helps to clarify and reaffirm commitments and to avoid confusion in later meetings. The closing minutes of a meeting can be used to evaluate the group's progress, to examine group dynamics, and to compliment members for their contributions. It is not a time to introduce new agenda items. Whenever possible, the work implicit in "door knob" communications[2] should be deferred to the next meeting. Such communications often convey important information that cannot be fully discussed or acted upon in the remaining minutes of a meeting.

The time between group meetings can be used to carry out any assignments that were agreed to at a previous meeting and to prepare for upcoming meetings. In some groups, much of the work is conducted by individuals or in committees between formal group meetings. Such is the case, for example, in many service and advocacy groups.

Assessing Members' Needs

The assessment process can be viewed as a continuous intricate spiral, where data gathering leads to greater understanding, and greater understanding leads to additional, more accurate data gathering. Assessments are made in all phases of a group's development, but they are particularly pronounced at the end of the beginning phase and at the beginning of the middle phase. Practitioners make assessments to help the group and its members function more effectively.

When assessing members, practitioners should inquire about their capacities, abilities, and talents as well as their needs, problems, and concerns. Avoid focusing exclusively on problems. Overlooking older persons' strengths gives the practitioner little indication of how to proceed to help older persons cope more effectively with problematic life events.

In therapy groups and support groups, practitioners make thorough assessments of members. To understand members as fully as possible, practitioners are encouraged to ground their assessments of current functioning in the developmental history of the member. Respect and appreciation for what older adults have learned over a lifetime is an important device for tuning in to them. It helps to convey the feeling that the practitioner is working with them rather than doing something to them.

At a minimum, a developmental assessment should focus on (1) the meaning of important events for the individual, (2) uncovering patterns of behavior, their intensity, duration, and scope, and (3) adaptive and maladaptive coping mechanisms that the individual commonly relies upon in stressful situations. A developmental assessment can help practitioners to avoid

2. A term that is frequently used to refer to important communications that occur just prior to members leaving a meeting room.

suggesting coping strategies that members have used without success. It also enables practitioners to help members utilize adaptive capacities and resources that are lying dormant.

When making assessments of individuals in therapy and support groups, practitioners may find it useful to help members examine their (1) intrapersonal functioning, that is, the physical, emotional, and cognitive domains of their functioning, (2) interpersonal functioning, that is, the quality and the structure of familial, informal, and formal social networks, and (3) environmental functioning, that is, their ability to take care of themselves, the adequacy of their home and their neighborhood, and their ability to utilize community services and resources.

Expectations, motivations, feelings about oneself and about one's world, memories of stressful events, and other components of individuals' intrapersonal lives are not open to public view. When assessing this dimension, practitioners rely to a large extent on the self-reports of the individual and those who know him or her well. The reliability, accuracy, and depth of self-reports are affected by the mental health of the reporting individuals and the nature of the relationship the practitioner and the group members have with each other. Members are more likely to be open when they have developed trust in the practitioner and the other members of the group. Therefore, it is important for practitioners to help members develop trusting relationships with each other and the leader as early as possible in the group experience.

The group context is a natural laboratory for assessing the interpersonal relationships of members. In their interactions during meetings, members display the interpersonal skills they use to relate to each other. As they share who they are with the group, members also describe their roles in specific interactions and important interpersonal relationships outside the group. Gradually, practitioners get a clear picture of members' interpersonal skills, coping strategies, and the history and current status of the important interpersonal relationships they have with family, friends, and other acquaintances.

Asking members about the environment in which they live helps practitioners to understand what members' lives are like when they leave the supportive environment of the group. This understanding leads to greater sensitivity regarding the concerns and issues raised by members. It can also help to identify resources that are available to help members achieve desired goals, factors that maintain or exacerbate maladaptive behavior patterns, and obstacles and impediments that hinder goal achievement.

With advanced age, many older people become increasingly reliant on a supportive environment to help them function independently. Improvements in older persons' living situations often depend on interventions that have a direct impact upon the social and physical systems that support their lifestyles outside of the group. Pinkston and Linsk (1984), for example, found that a careful assessment of the environment in which participants lived was an important component of an effective home-based intervention program for frail older persons.

Sources of Information

Practitioners are well advised to seek a variety of sources of information about members' functioning because many perspectives help to provide as complete and accurate a picture of members' situations as possible. Probably the most common source of information is members' self-reports. Practitioners may find it useful to help members improve the accuracy of their reports by keeping logs, diaries, or journals of their experiences between meetings.

Experience suggests that, unlike young people, who are used to homework assignments, older persons are not accustomed to between-session assignments. To avoid problems with follow-through, practitioners should be sure to include older persons in the process of planning between-session assignments. Check to make sure that physical impairments such as poor eyesight or inability to write will not interfere with members' ability to complete assignments. Review the benefits that are likely to accrue to group members as a result of collecting additional information about a situation. Even with such preparation, clinical experience suggests that practitioners should encourage older members to undertake between-session assignments only when they are highly motivated.

Observations by practitioners and reports by others are also common sources of information about members. Practitioners may find it helpful to design exercises and program activities that allow older persons to demonstrate their abilities to function in particular situations.

Information obtained through observation is often thought to be more reliable than self-report data, which may be distorted by members' subjective views of their own situations. However, observers are also subject to bias and distortions. Therefore, it is a good practice to assess the context in which information is collected, to consider the motivations and intentions of the person reporting the information, and to be aware of any other potential sources of bias that may influence how information is collected, reported, and assessed.

Standardized and nonstandardized assessment instruments are used less frequently to collect information about older group members, but they have been gaining in popularity in recent years as helpful sources of information. Standardized instruments can yield high quality, uniform information in relatively short time periods. For example, when members of an outpatient therapy group who expressed symptoms of depression were asked to fill out a Beck Depression Inventory, the practitioner was assured that many different depressive symptoms were assessed and that all members had the same type of information available to them when they continued their discussion of the particular symptoms that they were experiencing.

There are many different kinds of standardized instruments available to assess a wide variety of physical, social, psychological, and cognitive dimensions of functioning, but relatively few have been standardized on older populations.[3] Despite this shortcoming, there is some evidence that suggests that the use of standardized and nonstandardized measures can serve as a catalyst for discussion of sensitive, previously unspoken issues (Toseland and Reid 1985). For example, a social network chart such as that shown in figure 4.1 can be used to stimulate a discussion of members' satisfactions and dissatisfactions with the support they receive from family members. The same chart can also be used to stimulate discussion about how inactive social relationships with particular family members and friends can be revitalized.

The Group-as-a-Whole

Throughout the middle phase, practitioners should maintain a dual focus on individual group members and the group-as-a-whole. Too often, workers fail to pay attention to group processes until problems arise. Besides not being a sensible stance, the practice of waiting for problems to develop fails to take full advantage of the powerful effects that group dynamics have on all group members. Therefore, practitioners are well advised to pay careful attention to group dynamics from the very first meeting, taking time to promote cohesion and to develop shared norms that foster goal attainment as the group develops.

To assess group-as-a-whole functioning, practitioners may find it helpful to use the framework presented in chapter 2. For example, practitioners might begin by assessing a group's communication processes and interaction patterns. Next, practitioners might focus on the development of cohesion and the development of norms, roles, and status hierarchies. The practitioner could end by examining the overall development of the group's culture.

When assessing group-as-a-whole dynamics, workers generally rely on their own observations, coupled with feedback from the group. Older group

3. For some notable exceptions see, for example, Kane and Kane 1981; Mangen and Peterson 1982.

FIGURE 4.1: A Social Support Network Chart

Outside the Social Support Network

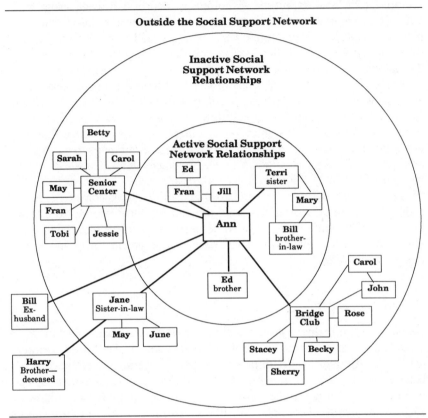

members can be reluctant to express candid opinions about group functioning because they fear offending the leader. To avoid this, reach out for members' feedback at opportune times during the group's work, and save a few minutes at the beginning or the end of group meetings for feedback about the functioning of the group. Such an approach helps to fine-tune group functioning before problems arise.

Facilitating Group Functioning

During the middle phase, practitioners use a variety of skills to help the group-as-a-whole function effectively. A few of the most important include attending skills, focusing skills, and guiding the group interaction skills.

Attending skills refer to verbal and nonverbal behaviors that convey empathy, respect, warmth, genuineness and trust. According to Egan

(1982), good attending skills include nonverbal body positions, eye contact, and gestures, as well as verbal statements that indicate that a practitioner has heard and understood what a member has said. Good attending skills also include what Middleman (1978) refers to as "scanning"—a procedure whereby leaders periodically make eye contact with members, acknowledging their presence and letting them know that the worker is concerned about how the group is affecting them. Good attending skills help practitioners to establish rapport with members and a climate of acceptance in the group-as-a-whole.

Focusing skills help members to avoid losing sight of the purposes and goals for meeting together. Focusing can be done by highlighting themes, by drawing members' attention to particular communications, and by pointing out when members appear to be straying from the agenda. Shulman (1984) has suggested other useful focusing skills such as helping members to move from the general to the specific, reaching for individual communications and for the group response to the individual, pointing out obstacles, helping members to discuss taboo subjects, and making a clear demand for work.

Practitioners guide group interaction by providing members who have something to contribute with the opportunity to do so, by limiting or blocking the communication of members who are dominating the group's limited meeting time, by encouraging members to elaborate on statements, by linking one member's communications to others, by realigning subgroups, and by encouraging group members to speak directly to each other. The purpose for taking an active role in guiding the group's interaction should be to help members maximize their contributions to the work of the group-as-a-whole, rather than to demonstrate a worker's authority or leadership abilities. Depending on the particular agenda item, this may mean encouraging some members to be more active and other members to be less active.

Helping Members to Achieve Goals

Because the middle phase of the group is focused primarily on the work to be accomplished, an important task for practitioners during this phase is to help members and the group-as-a-whole achieve the goals that have been agreed upon. This can be accomplished by enhancing members' awareness of and commitment to specific goals, helping members to develop sound action plans, and facilitating members' ability to implement plans of action.

Helping members to develop goals and to commit themselves to the work necessary to accomplish them is a process that continues throughout the middle phase. Tentative agreement about individual and group goals may be reached early in the group's life, but, over the course of weeks and months, members can lose track of what they are working on. To help members remain aware of group and individual goals throughout the middle phase, review goals frequently, summarize and highlight how the group has been working to achieve them, check periodically to ensure that all members share a common understanding of evolving goals, and encourage members to consider how they have been contributing to goal attainment.

Motivation to work on goals wanes and waxes as the group develops. Practitioners can make a conscious effort to help members maintain their commitment by being positive and optimistic about their abilities and capacities to accomplish goals, by pointing to progress toward goals, by praising members for their accomplishments and their sustained commitment, by acknowledging obstacles and impediments, and by supporting members' efforts to cope with obstacles rather than abandoning their efforts.

Practitioners can assist members to develop sound action plans during the middle phase by helping them to gather all relevant data, consider a variety of perspectives and alternative action plans, examine the merits and potential drawbacks of each alternative before one is selected for implementation, and prepare carefully for the implementation of the most promising alternative.

Members should be encouraged to examine a situation carefully before implementing a plan. Early failure experiences that are the result of hastily prepared, ill-conceived plans of action can be avoided by thoroughly evaluating relevant data. For example, older adult women who came together as a group to consider ways to increase their level of exercise began by exploring information about the benefits and drawbacks of different exercises. They decided to accomplish this by inviting experts in recreational and physical therapy for older adults to speak at upcoming meetings.

One of the potential benefits of meeting together as a group is that members are able to share alternative frames of reference, different perspectives, and creative solutions that they can adapt to their own life situations. Practitioners can utilize this inherent strength of the group modality by encouraging members to share alternative perspectives and discouraging them from making valuative judgments about alternatives until all members have had a chance to contribute. There is evidence to suggest that inhibiting members' tendency to make evaluative judgments based on limited information is essential for arriving at well-conceived action plans (Bloom and Broder 1950; Delbecq, Van de Ven, and Gustafson 1975; Maier 1963). For example, each member of the previously mentioned exercise group was asked to share her opinions and thoughts about the effects of the different exercises reviewed by the guest speakers. As members spoke, the leader summarized, on newsprint, the major points that were made. After all members had a chance to speak, they compared and commented on each other's thoughts about alternative ways to exercise.

Once all alternative action plans have been considered, carefully examine the merits and potential drawbacks of each one, considering how obstacles and impediments might be overcome. For example, members of the previously mentioned exercise group considered the potential merits and drawbacks of each of the five exercises that were favored by a majority of the members. Because they lived in a rural area without access to an indoor pool during inclement weather, they ruled out swimming despite its many benefits.

Plans sometimes fail because members are not prepared to implement them. Practitioners should avoid assuming that members know how to implement plans. For example, the leader of the exercise group insisted that each member consult with her family physician and, if recommended, obtain a stress test before beginning the activity. The leader also helped the group to consider how they would obtain the necessary facilities and equipment to engage in the activity.

To help members achieve individual and group goals, it is also important to assist them in implementing the action plan they have developed. Practitioners may find it is useful to play a dual role, helping members to understand and be prepared for the demands placed on them when they implement a plan, and helping members to utilize their own resources and those of the practitioner to ensure that the plan will be successfully implemented.

When the entire group is responsible for implementing a plan to achieve a goal, the practitioner can be helpful by suggesting a division of labor based on members' expertise. The practitioner can continue to be helpful by coordinating the work of the different subcommittees, and by working with individuals and organizations outside of the group who may be in a position to assist the group in accomplishing its goal.

To help individuals achieve particular goals, practitioners can spend some group time focusing on helping individual members implement a plan. However, try to avoid spending a great deal of time with any one individual. To maintain the interest and the active participation of all members, it is necessary to universalize issues that one individual is struggling with. Make as many connections as possible between members by pointing out shared concerns. Sometimes, it is also possible to interest other members by getting them to consider what resources a member might draw upon to overcome obstacles and impediments to goal achievement.

Before implementing an action plan, it is often helpful to rehearse what actions will be taken. Make sure it is clear how the resources of the member and the practitioner will be combined to overcome any obstacles or impediments to goal achievement that are anticipated.

LEADERSHIP DURING THE ENDING PHASE

The ending phase is a time to consolidate the work that has been accomplished in the beginning and middle phases of the group. It is also a time to help members look forward to the future, assisting them to use what they have learned in the group in new situations they are likely to encounter after the group ends.

Members' Reactions to Ending

Members' reactions to ending their participation in a group vary according to a number of factors, including the relationships they have developed with other members, their satisfaction with the group experience, and their psychological makeup. When members have formed close interpersonal relationships in which intimate, emotionally charged life events have been shared, terminating is likely to be an emotional experience. This is frequently the case in long-term therapy groups and in long-term support groups. In contrast, in educational and recreational groups, members typically share little of themselves, and therefore, endings rarely stir strong emotional reactions. Similarly, when members are dissatisfied with the group experience, the only reaction they may have to ending is one of relief. For example, because of previous losses, a history of deprivation, or unresolved separation issues, some members may have stronger reactions to endings than others. Feelings of rejection, of being abandoned, can be heard when members make statements such as, "Why are we stopping?" "Can't we continue to meet?" "Are you too busy for us?" "I wish we could continue, but I guess you're tired of listening to us."

Members may vacillate between feeling sad that the group is ending and feeling good about the experience. Statements such as "I really got a lot out of this; maybe we could get together occasionally to catch up with each other," and "I'm gonna miss our weekly meetings" indicate the mixed emotions that older adults may experience during endings.

Endings can also engender positive feelings and reactions in members. For example, members may feel a renewed sense of hope about the future and a renewed feeling that they can connect with others and that they are valued by others. They may feel a sense of accomplishment as a result of successfully completing their participation. They may feel potent and in better control of their life situations because they have worked productively in the group to accomplish particular goals. They may feel a sense of satisfaction, pride, and usefulness because they have contributed to the goal attainment of other group members and the group-as-a-whole. They may also feel a sense of security knowing that they are able to turn to the worker or their fellow group members for assistance after the group ends.

No matter what members' reactions are to ending, practitioners can take the following steps to ensure effective group functioning during the ending phase: (1) help members with their feelings about endings, (2) help members to maintain and generalize the changes that have resulted from their participation in a group, (3) plan for the future, and (4) evaluate the accomplishments of the group and its members.

Helping Members with Their Feelings

When the ending phase engenders negative feelings and reactions in members, the practitioner should be prepared to help members work through them. Sometimes, members become dependent on the group and regress or act out to avoid ending their participation. Such reactions are more common in therapy groups than in other groups because members are more likely to feel insecure about their coping abilities. For example, when a 78-year-old member of a long-term outpatient therapy group sponsored by a geriatric day treatment program in a state psychiatric facility learned that the group leader believed she no longer needed to participate in the group, she stopped taking Lithium, which has stabilized her manic depressive episodes. The worker, who had not anticipated this reaction, postponed termination until the member was again stabilized on Lithium and had worked through her feelings about how she would cope with daily life without the support of the group. The leader helped the member to successfully end her participation three months later by encouraging her to express and work through her feelings of abandonment and by helping her to develop and implement an aftercare plan that helped her to feel secure about leaving the group.

Feelings of sadness and loss, and other less extreme reactions, are more common. However, although it might be thought that older group members would be particularly vulnerable to feelings of loss because of social isolation and previous losses, clinical experience suggests that most have learned to accept endings, and their reactions often appear to be milder than those of children, adolescents, and young adults. Even when reactions are mild, however, practitioners should help older group members with feelings of sadness and loss by preparing them for endings gradually, by highlighting how much they have accomplished during their participation in the group, by expressing confidence in their abilities to function independently, by helping them to utilize their coping capacities outside of the group, and by helping them to anticipate and plan for their future needs.

Preparing for Endings

Members should be prepared for endings gradually. It is helpful to make the duration of short-term, time-limited, closed-membership groups clear from the outset. In longer-term groups, and those with open membership, leaders should introduce the subject of termination gradually, beginning five or six weeks prior to the planned termination date. Sometimes, scheduling meetings less frequently or for shorter time periods can help prepare members for termination.

Program activities can also be helpful in preparing members for ending. Appropriate program activities for ending a group include those that encourage members to (1) summarize and reflect upon what they have learned through their participation in the group, (2) express their feelings about the group and its members, (3) work on individual rather than group-oriented tasks, (4) become involved in activities outside the group that will compete for the members' time, (5) consider how they will cope with obstacles and impediments that they are likely to encounter in future situations, and (6) discuss why they no longer need the group.

Ceremonies are also commonly used to mark the ending of a group. Particularly effective for helping members prepare for endings are ceremonial activities such as going to a restaurant, having a party, organizing a potluck dinner, giving out certificates of merit, or having each member prepare a written or verbal statement about what he or she appreciated most about other members' participation.

Maintaining and Generalizing Changes

The positive changes that result from group participation will fade gradually unless careful attention is paid to how they will be maintained and generalized in the new situations that members are likely to encounter when the group ends. Unfortunately, group workers sometimes fail to prepare older persons for the challenges that they are likely to encounter in the "real world."

To maintain and generalize the positive changes that are achieved while participating in a group, practitioners should help members to

• Work on issues and situations that are relevant to all members. Concerns and issues should be relevant to the majority of older persons who participate in a group. For example, a member of a support group discussed a particular problem she was having in her relationship with her daughter.

Although it was important to discuss the specifics of the situation and to help the particular member improve it, it was also important to identify an underlying theme that had broad implications for all group members. Therefore, the leader asked the other members, who all had adult children, to describe their relationships with them. Later, the leader asked members to describe how they tried to promote good relationships with their adult children.

• Anticipate changing conditions and plan for them. Members should be helped to anticipate changing conditions and to plan for them. This can be done by encouraging members to identify problematic situations they might encounter in the future and to consider how they will respond to them. For example, in a preretirement planning group, the leader emphasized the importance of both marital partners understanding household finances in case one partner should die. Similarly, in a support group for caregivers, members were asked to consider what would happen to the person for whom they were caring if the member suddenly became incapacitated.

• Build supportive social and physical environments. Changes achieved through group participation can upset the adaptive balance that older persons had achieved with their physical and social environment. To help ensure that changes achieved through group participation will persist after the group ends, members should be assisted to develop and utilize informal support systems. For example, members of a twelve-week "Swimnastics" group were asked to consider how they would continue to exercise consistently after the group ended. Members decided to form a walking club. The informal support network that developed among members of the walking club was relied on by them long after the original group ended. Similarly, it proved helpful for the members of a weight reduction group to invite their spouse or a family member to the next-to-last meeting of the group for a discussion of how these individuals could support members' efforts to maintain their weight loss once the group ended.

• Develop confidence in themselves. Groups sometimes spend too much time focusing on members' problems, concerns, issues, and inadequacies and insufficient time on members' strengths, capacities, and coping abilities. Because older adults enjoy identifying their strengths and describing their accomplishments, exercises, program activities, and role plays that encourage members to utilize and display their skills and to become more confident in their use are at least as helpful as discussions that focus on problematic aspects of members' functioning. For example, the new leader of a resident's council of a seniors-only housing project helped members to reduce the amount of time they spent complaining to each other about problems in the facility and more time focusing on how they could work together and, with administrative staff, to have their complaints addressed.

• Utilize follow-up services. One important way to ensure that changes made in the group are maintained and generalized is to help members use appropriate follow-up services. In some situations, the worker may find that it is useful or essential to gradually terminate service or to plan specific follow-up meetings. For example, members of a widow-to-widow self-help program were encouraged to gradually reduce their participation as they felt better able to cope with the loss of their spouses. As they reduced their participation, members were encouraged to attend whenever they felt the need for support. In addition, special meetings of the group were planned twice each year and former members were invited to attend.

Planning for the Future

Another important task of the practitioner in the ending phase is to help members plan for their future needs. One strategy that has proven to be effective is to teach members generalized coping skills. For example, members of an outpatient therapy group in a mental health clinic were taught how to identify when their medication needed adjustment, how to solve problems more effectively by using the ten-step problem-solving model outlined in chapter 6, and how to reduce their anxiety by using progressive muscle relaxation techniques (see, for example, Bernstein and Borkovec 1973).

Sometimes, members may wish to continue to meet beyond the number of sessions that were originally planned. Leaders who consent to continue should help members to clarify their continuing needs and the goals they hope to achieve. Together, the practitioner and the members should plan for the duration of continued group service and for any modifications in group functioning by revising the original contract for their work together.

In some situations, workers may want to encourage members to form a self-help group that continues to meet without the practitioner. For example, initially the leader of a health education group took responsibility for planning lecture and discussion materials and for bringing in outside speakers. Gradually, the leader helped members to plan their own meetings and to develop their own indigenous leadership. The leader continued to reduce her participation after ensuring that the sponsoring agency would continue to provide space and support services. The practitioner maintained limited contact with the group by consulting with the new leadership about ongoing problems in group functioning and by suggesting the names of speakers for upcoming meetings.

Planning for the future may also entail helping members to connect with additional community resources. Workers should be knowledgeable about available community services that are frequently used by older persons. Members should be referred to appropriate services well before the last meeting so that the worker can follow up to be sure that members have received what they needed.

When a case manager or another practitioner is involved with a member, the leader should seek the member's permission for contacting this person. When making the contact discuss the member's progress in the group, the member's current life situation, and the member's additional service needs.

Evaluating Accomplishments

Although evaluations of a practitioner's work with a group take time to prepare and to implement, they are valuable from a number of perspectives. Clinically, evaluations can serve to review, summarize, and highlight what was accomplished in a group. They give members a concrete sense of accomplishments and of areas that need continued work. They give practitioners feedback about their work and an opportunity to examine their own strengths and weaknesses. Administratively, evaluations can be used to justify a group service, to account for how funds were expended, or to seek additional funding.

Evaluations do not have to be viewed as an onerous responsibility that is best left to researchers. Rose (1989) and Yalom (1985) both recommend frequent, but brief, evaluations. For example, Yalom (1985) recommends taking five minutes at the end of a group for leaders to discuss group process, and five minutes for members to react. Rose (1989) recommends asking members to respond in writing and anonymously to a few brief questions about what they liked most and least about the group meeting, what they learned during the meeting, and what they would like to see covered in future meetings. Workers should be cautious about written evaluations, however, making sure that members are able to read the material and to respond in writing in the time allotted.

SUMMARY

This chapter has focused on the skills that are necessary to facilitate groups of older adults during each phase of their development. The first portion of the chapter focused on planning issues such as the composition of the group, the importance of screening interviews, and preparation of the group's environment. The second portion of the chapter focused on beginning issues such as using introductory exercises and developing group purposes and working agreements. The third portion of the chapter focused on preparing and leading meetings, making assessments, facilitating effective group functioning, and helping members to achieve agreed-upon goals. The last portion of the chapter focused on helping members to cope with their feelings about ending, to maintain the changes they have made as a result of participating in the groups, to plan for the future, and to evaluate their participation.

Part II
LEADING SPECIALIZED GROUPS

The remaining chapters of this book focus on the skills and procedures that can be used to facilitate different types of groups for older persons. Table 4.4 summarizes selected characteristics of the five types of groups that are included in part 2: (1) support, (2) therapy, (3) social, recreational, and educational, (4) service and advocacy, and (5) groups for family caregivers.

For uniformity of presentation, each chapter in part 2 begins with a description of the distinguishing characteristics and features of the type of group being described. Then, the roles of practitioners and members and the specialized skills and procedures needed to facilitate each type of group are presented. Each chapter concludes with a case example illustrating a group in action.

There are many possible ways to categorize groups for older adults. Categorization schemes based on the disability level of group members, the setting where the group is held, or the purpose of the group all have merit. For example, a practitioner who works in a senior center or a nursing home would be likely to find chapters on groups in these settings particularly appealing. Similarly, a practitioner who works exclusively with the well elderly or the frail elderly might find chapters focused on these individuals particularly useful.

Why were these categorization schemes not selected for the presentation of the material in part 2 of this book? Although disability level and setting are important variables to consider when leading groups of older people, there is much overlap in these factors among the types of groups. Also, the skills and procedures group workers use when conducting groups in different settings and for members with different disability levels overlap. For example, social, recreational, and educational groups are led in senior centers as well as nursing homes. Similarly, the life review technique can be used with the well elderly as well as the frail elderly. Purpose is also an important distinguishing feature of different types of groups for older adults, but many groups have multiple purposes, and frequently, similar procedures can be used in groups with different purposes.

TABLE 4.4: Selected Characteristics of Five Types of Groups for Older Adults

Selected Characteristics	Type of Group				
	Support	Therapy	Social/ Recreational/ Educational	Service/Advocacy	Family/ Caregiver
Goal	To help members cope with stressful life events	To help members change their behavior and to rehabilitate themselves	To help members become actively engaged with peers in activities that promote enjoyment and stimulate learning, growth, and development	To help members join together to accomplish a task for the benefit of others	To help family members function in their roles as caregivers
Leadership	Facilitator of mutual support and mutual aid	Expert, authority figure, change agent, or facilitator, depending on theoretical orientation	Facilitator of program activity, provider of structure	Coordinator, staff, or chair who helps organize and facilitate the actions of members	Educator, supporter, enabler, broker, and advocate
Focus	The shared concerns of the members	Members' problems, concerns, and goals	Group program as a medium for activity, participation, learning, and involvement	The task to be accomplished	The needs of the caregiver and the care receiver and the stress encountered in caregiving

Bond	Shared problems, common goals based on a similar traumatic event	The relationship of members to the group as a whole	Common interest in an activity, in learning, and in skills development	Sameness of purpose, larger concern	The caregiving role
Composition	Members who experience a similar traumatic event	Can be diverse or composed of members with similar concerns	Diverse membership, similar skill level, and ability to engage in the program activity	Large, diverse membership to provide diverse knowledge and skills, representative viewpoints, and alternative perspectives and to encourage a division of labor	Diverse but homogenous groups based on relationship to care receiver, care receiver's illness, and gender often develop cohesion more quickly than heterogeneous groups
Communication	Highly interactive, open, member-to-member	Leader-to-member or member-to-member, depending on the approach	Instrumental member-to-member, member-to-leader, and leader-to-member communication characterized by verbal and nonverbal behavior in regard to the program activity	Relative to task or role	Member-to-member and leader-to-member interaction

TABLE 4.4: Continued

Selected Characteristics	Type of Group				
	Support	*Therapy*	*Social/ Recreational/ Educational*	*Service/Advocacy*	*Family/ Caregiver*
Level of Self-Disclosure	Moderate to high self-disclosure, mutual sharing of coping skills	High self-disclosure	Low self-disclosure	Low self-disclosure	Moderate to high self-disclosure and mutual sharing of coping skills
Operation	Informal, equality of participation around a traumatic event	Members help each other to cope with and solve problems and concerns with the help of the leader	Governed by the rules of the program activity, characterized by active verbal and nonverbal participation and team spirit	Formalized procedures based on by-laws	Often informal, with equality of participation, but can include lectures and other more formal presentations by the leader or by guest speakers

The categorization scheme that was selected for part 2 of this book is a pragmatic one that focuses on the types of groups that are commonly described in the literature and that are commonly found in practice settings. For example, although groups for family caregivers have many supportive features, and although chapter 5 focuses on support groups, groups for family caregivers were deemed sufficiently different from other groups to warrant a separate chapter. Similarly, one could argue that social, recreational, and educational groups are conceptually different from each other and should not be described in a single chapter. However, from a pragmatic point of view, these groups are linked together by their emphasis on program activities and by the similarities in the roles of the facilitators. Thus, it was decided that they could be described in a single chapter rather than in three separate chapters that would have a great deal of overlapping material.

A categorization scheme such as the one presented in table 4.4 can serve as a useful guide for practitioners as they conceptualize and develop specific groups to meet the needs of particular older adults. However, in practice, workers may often wish to combine features of two or more of the types of groups that are described in the remainder of this book. For example, a practitioner who is planning a group for older adults who have been recently discharged from an inpatient psychiatric facility might wish to combine features of a support group and an educational group. Using table 4.4 and the following chapters as a guide, the practitioner recognizes that there may be some conflict among the types of interventions used to achieve both purposes. For example, making a formal presentation on a particular topic may inhibit the mutual sharing found in a support group. The practitioner decides to make support the primary purpose of the group, and to include the educational component by suggesting themes that members could discuss each week. The practitioner prepares by becoming familiar with each topic and by being prepared to answer specific questions about resources and services. After assessing the needs of members in an intake interview, the practitioner decides that it would be best to cover specific topics in a flexible manner depending on group members' needs for support in coping with stressful events that emerge as the group unfolds.

With the input of other members of the staff in the practitioner's agency, and interviews with potential members, a second practitioner designing a group format for older adults with similar characteristics decides to try out a different format focused on education about the effects of stress combined with demonstration and practice of specific stress-reduction techniques. The second practitioner decides to break the group into two components, a one-hour lecture and discussion about the effects of stress and how to cope with it, followed by practice using specific stress reduction techniques. This practitioner blends elements of therapy and education into the group.

It is not possible to evaluate which practitioner has chosen the most effective group format without understanding the needs, capacities, talents, and expectations of the members of each group, the purpose of each group, and the intent of each group's sponsor. Therefore, when reading the next five chapters, consider how the skills, methods, and practice principles that are described could best be combined and modified to meet the unique requirements of your particular practice situation.

5

Leading Support Groups

Support groups help members cope with stressful life events and enable them to grow and develop as they proceed through difficult life transitions such as retirement and widowhood. They also help to revitalize and enhance members' existing coping capacities so that they can more effectively adapt to problematic life events.

Some examples of support groups for older persons include

• A group of older persons who recently became widows and widowers who meet together at the local senior center.

• A group of recently discharged inpatients who meet once a week at a day treatment center to discuss their adjustment to life in a group home.

• A group of outpatients who meet together to help each other cope with and adapt to a medical diagnosis of cancer.

• A group of older employees who meet together at lunch hour on a biweekly basis to discuss plans for their impending retirement.

• A group of individuals in a rehabilitation hospital who meet together to discuss the effects of a cardiovascular accident on their ability to live independently.

Support groups help older adults cope with difficult life transitions and stressful life events, such as the death of a spouse or other close family member, the onset of an acute illness or the flare-up of a chronic one, retirement, or a move to a new living situation in the community or an institution. Such events create stress that can threaten older persons' capacities to cope effectively. When stressful life events occur in combination, the risk increases that older persons' coping capacities will become overwhelmed. Older persons often turn for help to family and friends or member of the clergy, but these sources of support are sometimes inadequate, or altogether lacking. In these situations, membership in a support group can be particularly beneficial.

SUPPORT GROUP CHARACTERISTICS

In support groups, members are bonded together by the knowledge that they share similar concerns that are often not well understood by others.

Also, they take pride in having information to offer to each other that is derived from life experiences and from their ongoing efforts to cope with stressful life events. Because members of support groups share much in common and have much to offer to each other, cohesion and psychological closeness often develops more quickly in these groups than in the other types of groups described in table 4.4 (Lieberman and Bliwise 1985; Toseland, Rossiter, Peak, and Hill in press).

Meetings of support groups are characterized by much back-and-forth interaction among members. While in the beginning members may be too self-focused to respect or even notice others, when support groups develop in a positive fashion, a healthy respect for each member's input evolves, so that neither a single member nor a few members dominate. Members can participate at their own pace, revitalizing, adjusting, and enhancing coping capacities that they have developed over a lifetime. Thus, support groups are a resource for social contact and social support, helping older persons to overcome isolation and to expand their informal support networks. They provide a sense of hope that can counterbalance situational depression arising from losses and other traumatic experiences. Also, they provide normative guidelines for later life development that are often lacking or unclear.

There is frequently a high level of emotional self-disclosure related directly to the central themes of the group. Support groups encourage members to share intense emotional reactions and to explore new ways of coping with problematic life events. During group meetings, members are encouraged to listen empathically to each other, to support each other, and to give and receive information and advice about effective strategies to enhance their own coping abilities and those of their fellow group members.

There is also a high level of social interaction that may be related only tangentially to the central concerns of the group. This latter dynamic is important, however, because it helps to establish a social support network among members that is often relied upon between group meetings and after the termination of the group.

Support groups give older members an opportunity to demonstrate their wisdom and experience and to play a useful and meaningful role in helping others with their problems and concerns. They provide peer models of effective coping that older persons can readily identify with. These motivate members, enabling them to take the necessary steps to sustain and enhance their own coping capacities.

Support groups are also characterized by their informal operating procedures. For example, interventions used by the leader are typically less complex and less structured than in therapy groups (Lieberman and Bliwise 1985). Also, there is rarely a predetermined agenda. Instead, members share pressing issues and concerns in a spontaneous fashion governed by the level of safety and security they feel in the group.

THE ROLE OF THE PROFESSIONAL

Professionals may be directly involved in facilitating a support group, or they may be involved indirectly, by sponsoring or by consulting with a group. Many support groups for older persons are facilitated by peer leaders rather than by professionals. Research has shown that peer leaders can be as effective as professional leaders (see, for example, reviews by Berman and Norton 1985; Durlack 1979, 1981; Emerick, Lasser, and Edwards 1977; Hattie, Sharpley, and Rogers 1984; Nietzel and Fisher 1981).

In most support groups led by peers, one or two members often take responsibility for organizing and facilitating group meetings. Peer leaders emerge in many different ways in support groups for older persons. In some groups, leadership responsibility is shared by all members, and in others it is rotated among those who have the capacity and are willing to take on the responsibility. Members who demonstrate exceptional energy or interest may emerge as leaders, leaders may be elected periodically by the membership, or an individual may be appointed to leadership roles by an administrator of the agency that sponsors the group. Appointment by an administrator is often the least desirable alternative because members of the group may feel that a leader is being imposed upon them.

SPONSORING A SUPPORT GROUP

As sponsors of peer-led support groups, professionals can play at least four roles (Toseland and Hacker 1982; 1985). A common role for professionals is to help peer leaders gain access to material support such as meeting rooms, secretarial support, office supplies, and similar resources. A small amount of material support is often all that is needed to sustain the ongoing functioning of a group. Professionals also commonly serve as consultants to peer-led support groups. They can serve as guest speakers or identify others who could serve in that capacity. They can be available to members when specialized expertise is needed to help them cope with and resolve particularly troublesome or unusual problems. Also, they can provide advice or supervision to a peer leader about how to improve group functioning or to overcome obstacles.

A third role that professionals can play in peer-led support groups is to serve as a broker by referring individuals to the group and by helping self-help group members connect with and utilize community resources and services. Professionals should not view themselves as competing with peer-led groups for clients. The available data suggests that those who attend peer-led self-help groups are at least as likely to use professional services as those who do not attend such groups (Lieberman, Borman, et al. 1979; Powell 1987).

Professionals can also help to plan the development of a new self-help group with interested older persons. This may involve a variety of tasks, including meeting with interested individuals to help formulate and clarify their ideas about the group, assessing potential interest among a larger constituency, considering possible obstacles and impediments to getting started, helping interested individuals enhance their organizational and leadership skills, publicizing the group, and being available as needed to help the group to get started.

Concern has been expressed in the self-help group literature about the potential for professionals to take over or dominate peer-led support groups. Although occurrences of this type are rare, professionals should be cautious about becoming directly involved in peer-led groups, especially at the beginning of their development. When sponsoring a self-help support group, do everything possible to assist interested older persons to begin a group except agree to lead the group. Instead, work with the potential peer leaders, teaching them group leadership skills, helping them to plan for and to organize the group and to gain confidence in their own skills. National, state, and local self-help group clearinghouses can provide much assistance to those who plan to develop self-help support groups for older persons.[1]

FACILITATING EFFECTIVE SUPPORT GROUPS

As facilitators of support groups, practitioners should focus on developing a climate of trust, empathy, warmth, and cohesion in which members will feel safe to disclose their thoughts and feelings, to revitalize their own coping capacities, and to be open to advice about coping strategies suggested by their fellow group members. This can be accomplished by pointing out and highlighting thoughts, feelings, and experiences that members share. Praise members for any assistance they provide to each other. Use terms such as "we" and "us" when speaking to the entire group about shared purposes, accomplishments, and experiences. Help to develop a group identity by starting or ending group meetings with a summary of the

1. To locate the one closest to you consult the *Self-Help Sourcebook* (Madera and Meese 1986) or appendix 2 of *Self-Help Organizations and Professional Practice* (Powell 1987).

work that has been accomplished in previous sessions and by pointing out the work that needs to be done. Reduce intragroup conflict by pointing out the commonalities among members, by discussing the factors that might account for different perspectives, and by helping members to consider how different perspectives can contribute to an understanding of their own situations.

Members of support groups are usually highly motivated to reduce the stress they are experiencing. Therefore, as the group develops, the practitioner should act primarily as a facilitator and a guide, preventing obstacles from interfering with members' own efforts to help each other cope more effectively. Scanning the group by making eye contact with each participant, inviting members' participation when they appear interested in speaking, and listening in a focused fashion are often all the assistance that is needed to begin, and to sustain, the interaction process.

Because members expect support rather than "therapy," practitioners are likely to encounter resistance to efforts to produce change in members by stripping away their defenses or by pushing them to confront deep-seated psychological issues and conflicts that may have their roots in early development (Toseland, Rossiter, and Labrecque 1989a, 1989b, 1989c). As one-82-year-old group member put it, "Older people prefer to tell their own story, in their own way." Therefore, confrontive and probing interventions designed to help members explore potential areas of intrapersonal or interpersonal conflict, and those designed to elicit here-and-now responses about the relationship of one member to another should be used sparingly, if at all, especially in early sessions of support groups.

As the group unfolds, help members to show their respect for each other. Reinforce members' rights to express controversial or emotionally laden thoughts and feelings. Helping the group to develop norms of acceptance will do much to deepen members' trust of each other as the group progresses. Lakin (1988) has found that older persons tend to reveal more in groups than do younger persons. In contrast to the tense pauses that were found in children's groups, he found that there was "a virtually continuous flow from self-disclosure to reassurance or advice; an almost tranquil sharing followed by seemingly automatic comforting responses" (51). However, he also found that older group members were more tranquil in their responses to each other. For example, as compared to younger persons, he found that older group members responded empathically, but less intensely, to emotion-laden revelations made by fellow group members. Therefore, one of the important tasks of the facilitator of support groups for older people is to amplify and highlight subdued responses, and to help members respond empathically to each other.

Another important role of the facilitator of a support group is to foster smooth member-to-member communication. Some members may try to dominate the interaction. Others may try to begin side conversations. The practitioner can help to avoid these situations by discussing expectations for group participation in pregroup interviews and at the first group meeting. Some leaders find that posting agreed-upon "rules for group interaction" in the meeting room or going over them at the beginning of each meeting also helps to avoid problems in group interaction.

There tends to be more leader-member and member-leader interaction in groups of older persons than in groups of younger persons (Lakin 1988). Practitioners can facilitate member-member interaction by (1) acknowledging and praising members who respond empathically to each other, (2) pointing out and highlighting shared thoughts, feelings, and themes, (3) making connections among members' statements, (4) asking members to respond to a particular question in a group go-round, (5) involving individual members or the whole group in an interaction between the leader and a member, (6) suggesting that members speak directly to each other rather than through the leader, (7) asking members to respond to each other, and (8) asking members to elaborate on disclosures that are likely to be of interest to other members of the group. For example, the practitioner can say, "What are you thinking about what Mrs S. just said, Mrs. T.?" or, "Tell us more about what you had in, mind Mrs B."

Practitioners will find that it is helpful to have experience with the traumatic event that members have experienced. The ideal situation is for the practitioner to have grappled with the same experience faced by group members and to have successfully coped with it. However, because professional leaders are often younger than the members, they often simply have not had the same types of experiences. When this is the case, begin by taking extra care to tune into members' needs. Become thoroughly familiar with members' concerns and problems, their current life situations, and those aspects of their past that have influenced the nature of their current concerns. Provide encouragement and support for members as they express their thoughts and feelings. Avoid making suggestions and giving advice until you are thoroughly familiar with the situation and members appear to be open to learning about alternative coping strategies.

Avoid becoming judgmental or patronizing. Draw upon any previous experiences you have had in working with clients who have experienced similar problems, and imagine what it would be like if you had experienced life events similar to the ones members of the group have encountered. If members' verbal or nonverbal messages indicate that they doubt your ability to be helpful, acknowledge their communication and your limited experience with the particular problem or concern, and ask for their assistance in helping you to understand what it is like for them. Also, take every opportunity to become familiar with normal and abnormal coping patterns in regard to the life events that members have experienced by reading scholarly literature on the topic, by attending meetings of existing support groups, and by discussing coping strategies with older individuals who have successfully negotiated similar experiences.

Burnside (1970) has pointed out that loss is a constant theme in group work with older persons. The theme of loss comes up frequently during the middle phase of support groups. Older people turn to support groups for help in coping with the loss of spouses, friends, relatives, and acquaintances as well as to cope with gradual declines in, and sudden losses of, their own physical stamina and functioning. To help members who have experienced losses, facilitators of support groups should become familiar with normal grieving processes. In the original conceptualization of the grief process, Kubler-Ross (1969) postulated a five step process: (1) denial and isolation, (2) anger, (3) bargaining, (4) depression, and (5) acceptance. While grief reactions do not always manifest themselves in a straightforward, linear manner, shock, denial, anxiety, anger, guilt, depression, resolution, and acceptance are associated, to some extent, with all losses that older people experience.

The duration of the normal grieving process and the intensity of the feeling states are directly affected by the centrality of the loss to the individual experiencing it. The loss of a spouse, for example, generally creates a more intense grieving process than the loss of an acquaintance. Also, the grieving process is affected by the individual's expectations. For example, the sudden and unexpected loss of a spouse will often precipitate feelings of shock and disbelief, but the death of a spouse after a long chronic illness usually will not.

When helping members with losses, support group facilitators should begin by making sure that members realize that grieving is a normal process that should be experienced rather than avoided. Because individuals' reactions to losses vary considerably, the facilitator should proceed by helping members move at their own pace through the feeling states associated with loss. Provide a safe and empathic environment where members feel free to express emotional reactions. This will encourage the unfolding and working through of emotions that are associated with the grieving process.

Gradually, as members who have sustained losses move through the grieving process, encourage them to begin the process of redefining and replacing lost roles with new ones. Although each member's method of coping is different, and members must find their own way, it is often helpful to have members who have experienced similar losses in the past reveal how they have coped with, and adapted to, the loss. These members help to normalize feelings, thoughts, and actions associated with the grieving process, and to instill hope in members who are feeling as if they can't go on. Also, they act as role models for those who may feel guilty about replacing lost roles with new ones.

Occasionally, grieving members become stuck in one feeling state and are unable to move beyond it. When this occurs, the practitioner should help the group to provide feedback to the member, to be available to the member for reality testing, and to support the member as he or she struggles to develop insight into the causes for the inability to move through the grieving process. Helping members who are stuck may require probing into emotionally charged aspects of their psychosocial development. Depending on the culture that has been established in the support group, this type of intervention may not be appropriate. Also, a member may be so needy that he or she inadvertently prevents other group members from getting what they need out of the group. In these situations, help the member to accept a referral and to recognize the benefits that more intensive psychotherapy might be able to provide.

During the middle phase, the practitioner should also encourage members to explore ways to revitalize and enhance their existing coping capacities. Reflective listening that enables members to sort out conflicting feelings and the sharing of alternative perspectives or suggestions about ways to cope with a particular problem can be helpful. Other effective intervention strategies are pointing out any obstacles to mutual sharing and reciprocal helping among members, gently helping members to confront taboo areas that they are uncomfortable discussing, exploring resistances rather than avoiding them, and sharing any specialized information about resources or services that members request or are likely to find helpful.

As support groups enter their ending phase, practitioners can help members prepare for termination by relying less on the group and more on other informal and formal helping resources. Members should be encouraged to share information about formal support services that they have found useful in the community. Members should also be encouraged to solidify informal support networks that were developed in the group. Ask members if they would like to exchange telephone numbers or meet informally after the group ends. Encourage members to socialize before or after meetings, during coffee breaks, and between meetings (Toseland and Coppola 1985).

Members who are nearing termination should also be given the opportunity to share their experiences of what it was like to be in the support group with those who are considering joining. Seasoned members benefit from this opportunity by reflecting on what the group experience has meant to them. New members benefit by learning directly from an experienced participant what it is like to be in the group. This has been referred to as the "helper-therapy principle"; that is, the process of helping another person benefits the helper as much as the person who receives the help.

CASE

The following case example presents excerpts of a dialogue from a support group for recent amputees that took place in a large skilled nursing facility that has a rehabilitation orientation. Ms. P., the Director of Social Services, contacted several individuals who had amputations and who had been discharged from the facility, asking for their help in planning and leading the support group. One person, Mr. M., agreed to participate in the planning process and to serve as cofacilitator.

Mr. M. and Ms. P. contacted residents who had recent amputations and invited them to participate in the group. Having Mr. M. interview potential group members was very helpful to Ms. P. He was able to identify with what the residents were going through because he himself had gone through it, and was able to point out how the planned group might be helpful in getting the members through the trauma and loss they were experiencing. Six of fourteen individuals who were contacted by Mr. M. and Ms. P. came to the first group meeting, and two others attended subsequent meetings after hearing positive things about the group from those who were attending.

Much of the first group meeting was taken up with an introductory exercise. Members were asked to move (three were in wheelchairs) next to someone whom they did not know, to introduce themselves, and to spend five minutes getting to know the person. Members then returned to the circle and introduced their partner.

In the first meeting, as well as in subsequent meetings, Ms. P. and Mr. M. highlighted common themes and made connections among what members were saying. At first, members spent much of the group's time ventilating angry feelings about the nursing home and its staff, about doctors, nurses, and aides, and about the health care system in general. The following dialogue, taken from a transcript of the second session, illustrates how the group leaders handled the members' need to ventilate their anger and their feelings of loss.

Ms. P.:   Ann, I can see you're really angry at how you have been treated in this place, and at St. Christopher's [Hospital]. *[to the group]* Many of you seem to feel that way, too. I wonder if you want to continue discussing your anger at the care you've received, or want to move on and begin to grapple with the effects of your recent surgery?

Ms. A.:   I would like to do both.

Mr. B.:   That's a good idea.

[Silence]

Ms. P.:   What about the rest of you?

Ms. Z.:   I don't see how the two can be separated. After all, we have to live here and deal with this place and this, too *[pointing to the missing part of her left leg]*.

Ms. L.:   What's there to talk about, . . . about my operation? I just want to forget it. Put it behind me. *[looking at Ms. P.]* I don't know how you can help!

Ms. P.:   Are you wondering how I can be helpful because I did not have to go through what you have gone through? *[Ms. L. looks directly at Ms. P. but does not say anything.]* You have a right to feel that way. I don't know what it's like, but I will try my best to understand what you are going through. I'll need your help. In fact, I hope we can all help each other.

Ms. Z.:   I think it will be good just to talk, to get some things off my chest and to hear how everyone else is coping.

Ms. P: What about the rest of you? *[scanning the group for responses]*

Mr. M: I think at this point it's important to leave time both for discussion of the quality of care around here as well the effects of the surgery.

Mr. B.:   I'm glad you're here Mr. M., not only because you're the only other man in the group, nothing against you ladies but . . . *[laughter from several group members]* but also because maybe you can tell us how it is for you now that the surgery is behind you. You seem to have managed so well.

Mr. M.:   Be glad to. It was hard for me at first, too. Don't kid yourself. Really hard. Like I expect it is for you. I can remember sitting in my room and crying like a baby. But it gets better. Much better. In fact, in some ways the experience was good for me. It helped me put my life in perspective. Helped me think about what was really important, what I wanted to accomplish with the rest of my life.

[Pause]

Ms. P.:   Does anyone else have anything to say about the direction of the group? *[scanning the group]* Okay then, hearing no objection, I guess we have a consensus that it is okay to talk both about the care we are receiving here as well as about the effects of the surgery.

In this portion of the dialogue, Ms. P. helped to deepen the group interaction by addressing Ms. L.'s covert message that the group might not be helpful. She also helped to guide the group interaction by helping to clarify what was appropriate to discuss in the group, and to enhance the group's cohesiveness by pointing out that there was consensus and by using the term "we" in reference to the decision about how to proceed. The dialogue also illustrates that Mr. M.'s successful coping with life after experiencing the amputation of a limb helps to make him a role model for the members of the group.

Ms. P. and Mr. M. realized that in many situations members' complaints about medical care have a basis in reality. However, in this situation they believed that members' expressions of hostility about the care they had been receiving helped them to avoid a discussion of their pain in trying to cope with their recent loss. Neither pressed to change the course of the group discussion because both realized that it was premature to help members confront their denial of what they were experiencing. They realized that a confrontation at this point might create defensiveness and resistance and might be counterproductive to the building of a trusting, supportive, and empathic group environment.

As the support group continued, members ventilated their feelings about the poor quality of the food served to them, the fact that they did not receive enough physical care and attention, and the financial costs associated with their care. Some complained that the poor-quality care they were receiving could be ameliorated. For example, members in wheelchairs complained that in the evening they often had to wait long periods for nurses and aides to help them to go to the toilet or to transfer themselves to their beds. After consulting with the group and asking if she could share this portion of their confidential meetings with staff of the facility, Ms. P. mentioned the problem to the head nursing supervisor, who looked into the matter. By the next group meeting, the members mentioned that there had been some improvement. The administrator of the facility also asked Ms. P. to announce during the group meeting that the facility was short-staffed in the evening but that an active effort was being made to hire additional staff.

Ms. P. and Mr. M. gradually helped members to confront how they were coping with the loss of a body part. Dialogue from the transcript of the fifth session illustrates how this was accomplished.

Ms. A.: It really bothers me to wait for someone to help me go to the bathroom.

Ms. J.: I remember when my husband was dying. He had to start using a bedpan when we had him home. He was really depressed by that.

Ms. L.: They [the staff] don't care how you feel.

Mr. M.: I remember being really angry. Then you know what I discovered? I was really angry at feeling helpless. Also, I kept thinking, Why me?

Ms. A.: Yeah, I feel like I'm trapped, a prisoner. I used to be able to do so much.

Mr. B.: Why, I remember the time that I was working two jobs and . . .

Ms. P.: Mr B., can I interrupt you? I wanted to ask the group something about what Mrs. A. just said.

Mr. B.: Yup.

Ms. P.: Well, I was wondering what everybody felt about what Ms. A. just said about feeling trapped and how she was able to do so much more before she got ill.

[Mr. M.'s self-disclosure and Ms. P.'s invitation to focus on Ms. A.'s statement led two members to comment on their situation.]

Ms. S.: I can't even walk to the nurses' station without getting exhausted.

Ms. Z.: *[looking at Ms. P.]* I get tired easily too. But I feel lucky to be alive—and I'm getting around better with this *[points to prosthesis]*.

Ms. P.: Mrs. Z. was looking at me, but I think she was speaking to us all. How about the rest of you?

Mr. B.: I've been feeling a little like you [Ms. Z.]. It's not easy, but I'm getting used to it.

Ms. P.: Let's go around the group and each person who cares to can say what's been the worst thing about having a body part amputated and one thing that you have done to help yourself recover.

As the group continued, members discussed a variety of topics related to coping with the effects of an amputation, ranging from how they were progressing in physical therapy to how family and friends reacted when they came to visit. Ms. J. announced that her great-granddaughter was coming to see her the following week. She was really looking forward to it. At the beginning of the sixth meeting, the following dialogue occurred:

Ms. A.: *[to Ms. J.]* Did you get to see your granddaughter's child?

Ms. J.: Yes *[with apparent discomfort]*.

Ms. S.: Oh! What is it? Didn't the visit go well?

Ms. J.: Yes, it did, well, . . . sort of. It was good to see Debbie and Becky [her granddaughter and great-granddaughter].

Mr. B.: So what's troubling you?

Ms. J.: Well, it's just that when she came in, she looked away, like she was horrified or something. She didn't warm up to me until nearly the end of the visit.

Mr. B.: Your granddaughter?

Ms. J.: No, no, *[pause]* my great-granddaughter.

MR. B.: Well, she's young, what do you expect?

Ms. J.: She's already eleven.

MR. M.: How did you feel?

Ms. J.: Bad. It brought back all the feelings I had about having the operation, fearing how ugly and helpless I'd be.

Mr. B.: Ah! You look fine.

Ms. P.: It's difficult adjusting to it, isn't it—and sometimes people who are close make it harder . . .

Ms. J.: They don't mean to. It's hard for them too.

Notice how both Mr. M. and Ms. P. intervened to soften the comments that were made by Mr. B. By softening unempathic responses and amplifying empathic ones, the leaders of the support group helped to create a supportive, warm, and caring atmosphere in which members felt free to share emotion-laden experiences.

The group spent the remainder of the session discussing how different people reacted to seeing them after the amputation and their responses to the reactions. Humor helped to lend a feeling of support and comradery to the group. For example, one group member said that he had never received so much attention for losing something before, and another member said that she never cared for how her legs looked anyway.

As the group progressed, Ms. P. noticed that the support network that developed in the group began to expand beyond the group meetings. Members could be seen talking in the corridors to each other and sitting next to each other at meals and other events. Ms. P. and Mr. M. encouraged this by suggesting that members continue to discuss issues that were brought up in the group. Also, before the close of each group meeting, Ms. P. summarized what had been discussed during the meeting and suggested how members could follow up on certain topics during the week. Mr. M. often came early to group meetings and stayed after they ended to talk with members.

Although the group's tone became more hopeful and less angry with time, setbacks were encountered. One group member, Ms. D., who had come to the first few meetings, was rehospitalized, and the group learned that she was going to have a part of her other foot removed because of complications resulting from diabetes.

Ms. Z.: Isn't it terrible about Mrs. D.?

Ms. L.: I remember her talking about wanting to go home and how her brothers and her only child couldn't . . .

MR. B.: Wouldn't is more like it! After all we've done for them, and they don't want to help when we need it! A disgrace!

Ms. S.: Sometimes I feel no one cares.

Ms. J.:   At least my kids care.

Ms. S.:   So do mine. My daughter comes just about every day! Seeing her really helps when I get to feeling blue.

Ms. A.:   We don't have any children, but my husband's been a big support, even through the latest.

Ms. L.:   What do you mean?

Ms. A.:   ˙The circulation in my other foot is real bad. The doctor told me if my circulation problems get any worse I may have to have some of my other foot amputated.

[The group grew silent.]

Mr. M.:   I think I understand how you feel. When I was here I made friends with a guy, name of Ed, almost from the start. He was a carpenter so we had a lot in common. He died two days before I left for home. I remember really feeling down, sorry for myself.

Ms. A.:   I guess we have to try and stay positive. Otherwise, you really get to feeling blue.

Ms. P.:   You know I really admire all of you for coping as well as you do. I'm not sure I'd do as well.

Mr. B.:   Oh! Sure you would honey. What else can you do? I'm with Mrs. A. and Mr. M. I try to keep thinking positive. I'm lucky. My wife will take care of me as soon as I'm done with physical therapy and can get back home. Soon, I'll be back to my old self! Driving my wife crazy.

[Laughter from the group]

As the group continued to meet, some members were discharged and others were added. As the following dialogue illustrates, discussions of discharge plans were helpful to other members who were soon to be discharged as well as to those who were in earlier phases of rehabilitation.

Mr. B.:   I'm going to be leaving next Thursday, so next week will be my last group session. I'm going to miss our little get-togethers.

Ms. Z.:   *[speaking directly to Mr. B.]* Ms. P. said she was going to see if she could find out about that stair lift for your daughter's house. My home also has an upstairs and a downstairs, and I'm going to have to do something too.

Mr. B.:   Well, remember, I told you, my daughter had a big corner house. I asked her about getting the back porch and mud room winterized. I could use it as an apartment. Since it's on the first floor, I don't need the stair lift. My son-in-law has a good friend who is a contractor. He says his friend can do the work as soon as he finishes the job he's working on now.

Ms. P.:   *[turning to Ms. Z.]* I did get that information for Mr. B., so I can pass it on to you. I'll give it to you after the meeting.

Ms. Z.:   Thanks. *[to Mr. B.]* I bet you're looking forward to going home.

Mr. B.:   Well—It's not really home—but I think having my own separate little apartment will help. I was really worried about getting in the way. Carol [his daughter] has four [children] to take care of.

Ms. L.:   I'm worried about how my son-in-law is going to take it. My daughter says that sometimes he complains about how much time she spends with me.

As the group continued to meet, members discussed efforts to cope with the effects of their illness and their plans for the future. Within the course of a year, two members were discharged to live with family, and two others were placed in lower levels of care. As members left the group, new ones were recruited, providing an opportunity for those who had been with the group for longer periods of time to share their perspectives on the group's development and to help new members coping with feelings and issues to which they had successfully adapted.

SUMMARY

This chapter has described techniques for working with older adults in support groups. It began with a discussion of the characteristics of support groups. Next, the roles of professionals as sponsors and facilitators of support groups were described. The middle portion of the chapter focused on the skills necessary to work effectively with support groups. Emphasis was placed on the importance of basic helping skills such as empathy, instillation of hope, mutual sharing, and mutual aid, as well as helping group members through grieving processes that result from the losses that so often accompany difficult life transitions. The chapter closed with a case example of a support group in action.

6

Leading Therapy Groups

Therapy groups help older persons to restore impaired abilities and to cope with irreversible chronic disabilities. Examples of therapy groups include

• A group of older persons, discharged after inpatient psychiatric care, who meet together once a week in a community mental health center for long-term psychotherapy designed to prevent relapse and to promote their continued growth and development.

• A group of older persons attending an adult day treatment center in a psychiatric hospital who meet together twice a week to resolve problems associated with their chronic mental health problems.

• A group of older patients in a rehabilitation center who meet together to learn independent living skills and to become involved in the development and implementation of their own discharge plans.

• A group of inpatients in a state psychiatric facility who meet together twice each week for remotivation therapy to help reduce the negative effects of their long-term institutionalization.

• A group of older persons with dementing illnesses in a nursing home who meet together for reality orientation sessions.

In this chapter, the term "therapy group" is used to refer to a broad continuum of groups designed to restore, maintain, and enhance older persons' abilities and to help them function as independently as possible. Some groups are designed to help members with severe impairments maintain their abilities and slow down progressive deterioration. Others are designed to help members develop more effective coping and problem-solving skills. Although less common, some are also designed to help members gain insight into their own development and to make changes in long-standing personality traits and behavior patterns.

THERAPY GROUP CHARACTERISTICS

More than any of the other types of groups listed in table 4.4, therapy groups are designed to help members change dysfunctional behavior patterns. In therapy groups, practitioners often play the role of expert and change agent. They use their knowledge of normal and abnormal development in later life to assess each member's abilities. They also use technical behavior change procedures and strategies, and their knowledge about helping resources and services, to enable members to solve problems and to develop more effective coping skills.

Even when members share similar psychiatric disabilities, different life circumstances make each member's problems unique. For this reason, therapy groups are often characterized by a focus on the concerns of individual members who take turns receiving assistance from the group. However, the extent of focus on individual members varies considerably depending on practitioners' theoretical orientations and members' abilities to interact with each other. For example, while some practitioners encourage as much member-to-member interaction as possible, others prefer to work intensively with one member of the group at a time, thereby limiting interaction among members. The latter approach can be effective, but only when the other members of the group remain involved and can benefit from the dyadic interaction that occurs between the practitioner and a single member. A focus on one member should not continue for an extended period of time without the involvement of other members.

There is an expectation of a high level of self-disclosure in therapy groups. Members are expected to share difficult, emotionally charged issues and to work on resolving them in the group. Like younger people, older group members are likely to be reluctant to self-disclose unless a supportive and trusting environment is first built up in the group. Even with such an environment in a group, some older people may have a difficult time self-disclosing. Having a long history, they are more likely to be aware that opening themselves up to others makes them vulnerable. Also, they may have had negative experiences in previous therapy. For example, they may have experienced the pain of opening themselves up to others only to find themselves being judged, rejected, put down, or in some other way harmed by the experience. Thus, some are more likely to proceed with caution, taking fewer risks and waiting to see what the group has to offer before sharing intimate, emotionally charged issues and concerns with the group.

A sense of futility about their condition sometimes makes it difficult for frail and devalued elderly to invest energy in the therapeutic process. The loss of loved ones, of meaningful roles, and of physical health is sometimes reacted to by depression and despair. It is not uncommon for older persons to see little purpose in therapy groups. They demonstrate their feelings by making statements such as, "I'd rather be left alone to die," or "What's the use?"

The very old tend to be less introspective (Lieberman and Tobin 1983). This may occur because, as they reach an advanced age, they choose to conserve energy to meet basic physical needs rather than to expend it on dealing with emotional problems and needs. Also, they may be reluctant to invest in other group members whom they do not know well, and who may die and abandon them.

Particular psychiatric problems may inhibit the sharing of emotionally charged issues. For example, dementing illnesses and other severe mental health problems limit members' ability to express themselves and to explore and grapple with their problems. When working with groups of severely impaired elderly in a state mental hospital, for example, Bienenfeld (1988) found that much time was spent on concrete issues such as daily events and food. He also observed that group discussions were not always conducted on a coherent, sophisticated level.

Other factors can also inhibit self-disclosure. For example, the current generation of older persons grew up at a time when therapy was less available and more negatively stereotyped. This cohort effect tends to decrease the current generation of older people's enthusiasm about participating in community groups focused on growth and prevention. Also, there is a normative expectation that older people possess wisdom accumulated from extensive life experience that can be used to problem-solve. To some extent, this normative expectation conflicts with the group therapy expectation that participants freely reveal problems with which they are having difficulty coping.

Therapy groups are also characterized by careful planning as practitioners attempt to ensure that each member receives appropriate help to solve specific problems and to develop and use more effective coping skills and resources. Individuals who may be in need of therapy should be asked to participate in an intake interview so that practitioners can determine the nature of their needs, their suitability for the group, their motivation for working on their concerns, and their expectations regarding the therapeutic processes to be used in the group. With the permission of the older adult who is being considered for inclusion, family members and others who are familiar with the applicant's behavior may also be contacted.

ROLE OF THE PROFESSIONAL

Leaders of therapy groups for older persons are often told to be "active" (Foster and Foster 1983; Pfeiffer and Busse 1973; Weinberg 1975; Yesavage and Karasu 1982). Unfortunately, this term is rarely defined (Bienenfeld 1988). Some professionals develop agendas without soliciting members' input or involving them in the goal-setting process. Imposing an agenda can lead to resistance because members have no stake in the group.

It can also lead to members becoming angry at being treated as if they do not have the skills and capacities to take charge of their own lives. The message conveyed to members is that they are so helpless, incompetent, and powerless that they must be told what to do.

When practitioners treat members as if they are incapable and incompetent, a self-fulfilling prophecy can be created, leading members to act out or to behave irresponsibly. It is almost as if members are saying to the leader, "If you do not value and respect me, and if you expect me to behave poorly, then I will act the part." Therefore, practitioners should encourage members to have as much input about the direction and goals of the group as their capacities allow. They should also make certain that all members are given the fullest opportunity possible to participate in the ongoing work of the group.

As the group meets, it is also a good practice to point out members' abilities and capacities. Instead of focusing on negative behaviors, ignore them, and praise members as much as possible for their positive contributions to the group and to their own goal-attainment efforts. Encourage members to use their abilities to the fullest extent possible, and acknowledge when they do so. Also, be sure to demonstrate hopefulness, that is, your belief in members' capacities to improve their situations. If you convey an attitude that members are too old to change, then you may do more harm than good. Therefore, strive to show realistic confidence in members' abilities to improve their situations.

The role of the practitioner in a therapy group varies with the type of psychiatric problems experienced by the members of the group. Older adults with mild psychiatric problems such as adjustment and dysthymic disorders have the ability to organize, direct, and take responsibility for their own behavior. Therefore, a facilitative and egalitarian leadership stance is most appropriate with these individuals. Members with mild psychiatric impairments should be encouraged to define their own goals and to engage in a mutual helping process with the other members of the group. They should rely on the practitioner primarily as someone who can help when they encounter obstacles and impediments during the process of figuring out how to cope with, adapt to, and make changes in the way they think, feel, and act. Thus, the practitioner helps less impaired members to feel safe and secure enough in their own abilities to move beyond mere ventilation of problems and concerns to greater self-understanding and to an active consideration and implementation of alternative coping strategies.

Group therapy sessions provide a time for members to evaluate their current functioning, to identify what they would like to change, to discuss alternative action plans, and to clear away obstacles and impediments to implementing them. However, do not try to help members define goals too quickly. Premature efforts to help members define goals often fail because feelings of safety and trust have not yet developed in the group. At the same time, do not allow the group discussion to become directionless. Help members clarify what they are trying to accomplish by summarizing the work being done in the group briefly and frequently. Clarify vague statements, and help members to make them more concrete. Point out and highlight work that has been accomplished, and make connections between the work two or more members are doing in the group. Ask each member to write down a goal and to report on efforts to accomplish it during the next meeting. Also, bring up for group discussion unfinished work from previous sessions.

A structured check-in period at the beginning of each group meeting can be helpful to build continuity with previous group meetings. During the check-in, encourage members to share any issues or concerns they would like to address during the current meeting, and briefly review what each member had agreed to work on during previous meetings. A check-in period helps to ease members back into the focus of the group. It also helps members to recall and to clarify purposes and goals articulated in previous meetings.

During the check-in, practitioners should help members to stay focused on the agenda rather than to drift into social conversation or lengthy reviews of their life experiences. Gently but firmly encourage members to save interactions of this type for the coffee break or for the social time at the beginning or end of the group meeting. Structure the check-in so that each member is given a relatively brief period of time to present. Do not rush members, but if they get off task, or go on for an extended period, remind them of the purposes of the check-in, and that additional time has been set aside later in the group meeting to focus, in detail, on particularly pressing concerns brought up during the check-in.

Self-disclosure and effective problem-solving work are enhanced when each member feels he or she can share problems and get an empathic, nonjudgmental response. In a warm, supportive, trusting atmosphere members feel less vulnerable and less defensive about their problems and flaws. As one member put it, "I can be myself here. I don't have to put on any airs, like I do for my daughters, or my son. You know they worry about me, and I hate to be a burden, so I try not to tell them when I'm feeling down, like life isn't worth living."

When a supportive atmosphere is present, group members are also more likely to engage in the emotionally draining process of figuring out what their own role in the problem is, and what changes they can make to better cope with the situation. For example, in an outpatient group, one older member stated, "Well, he [her son] turned out a lot like his father.

Selfish. I don't say anything to him about it, just like I never used to say anything to Tom [her deceased husband]. So I guess, I've allowed both of them to get away with it, treat me like that, I mean. You [the group] have helped me see that."

In general, the practitioner should avoid giving advice unless it is requested by a member. It is usually more helpful to tune into members' needs, wants, and expectations when they share something with the group. When members are helped to explore their own thoughts, feelings, and reactions, a process of self-discovery occurs. With input from other group members and the leader, members arrive at their own answers and their own solutions. Such an approach helps members to rely on their own coping abilities.

Similarly, avoid developing plans for members. Instead, encourage members to help each other develop action plans to accomplish self-defined goals. As members begin to identify and achieve goals they have set for themselves, they take pride in their accomplishments. They begin to feel that something meaningful can be accomplished in the group. Goal definition and accomplishment by some members encourages others to define and accomplish their own goals, to remain hopeful about their situations, and to continue their problem-solving efforts. Also, members are more likely to take responsibility for their own behavior and to implement whatever plan of action has been developed through their participation in the group.

Depending on practitioners' theoretical orientation and members' ability to form intimate relationships, some practitioners prefer to focus on the here-and-now of group interaction, while others prefer to focus on the there-and-then experiences of members. Although Yalom (1985) has indicated that a here-and-now focus is what separates therapy groups from other types of groups, older persons seem to prefer a there-and-then focus. As Lakin (1988) states, "In contrast to the procedures of many contemporary group therapies, here-and-now issues were ignored, and the idea of analyzing one's own interactions with other group members was regarded as irrelevant" (52). A preference for then-and-there interactions may be due to the importance of memories in older persons' lives and the enjoyment they get from reviewing previous positive life experiences. Early socialization processes and previous life experiences that denigrate the value of a direct approach to the expression of thoughts and feelings about another individual's behavior may also help to account for the preference for a there-and-then focus among the current generation of older persons.

There is some evidence suggesting that older persons may actually be more comfortable self-disclosing certain personal issues in groups than are younger persons (Lakin, Oppenheimer, and Bremer 1982). However, these tend to be concrete issues, such as financial difficulties or experiences of bereavement and isolation, that arise outside of the group rather than issues that pertain to here-and-now interactions among members. Thus, even in long-term intensive psychotherapy groups, confrontations designed to elicit intrapersonal or interpersonal tensions and conflicts should be avoided (Lakin, Oppenheimer, and Bremer 1982).

A modified here-and-now approach can be effectively used with older persons in long-term, insight-oriented psychotherapy groups by promoting the developing of a "safe, self-esteem supporting milieu" within the group (Leszcz 1987, 332). Members' concerns should never be trivialized or ignored. Trust should be developed gradually by empathically responding to each member's concerns and attending to them in a timely fashion. When an accepting, affirming, encouraging, and supportive group environment is present, clarification and mild amplification of feelings can be used to build interpersonal connections within the group (Lakin, Oppenheimer, and Bremer 1982; Leszcz 1987).

When summing up some of these ideas, Leszcz (1987) has suggested (1) tuning in empathically to the inner world of each group member, (2) understanding important relationships, functions, and talents from the subjective perspective of each member, (3) encouraging members to address each other directly using names rather than pronouns such as "he" and "she," (4) helping members to acknowledge the importance of other members' contributions, and (5) promoting and reinforcing members' efforts to recognize, describe, and discuss the personal impact of other members' self-disclosures.

Clinical experience suggests that older group members often find a developmental perspective on their own lives, and the lives of their fellow group members, particularly appealing. Many are ready to review their life histories and to put previous experiences into perspective. Later life is a time when individuals strive to come to terms with positive and negative life events and, as one elderly group member stated, "put them behind you, so that you can get on with life." Putting current events into a developmental perspective also helps members to rediscover past strengths and supportive resources that they have used successfully in the past to cope with problematic events. These may be overlooked when practitioners focus exclusively on specific deficits in members' here-and-now functioning and on how to remedy them.

Life review procedures can be particularly helpful in the early stages of therapy groups when members are reluctant to become too interpersonally intimate (Lesser, Lazarus, Frankel, and Havasy 1981). Leszcz (1987) suggests encouraging each member to think about and discuss his or her personal reactions to the parts of another member's reminiscences that are personally meaningful (Lesser, Lazarus, Frankel, and Havasy 1981; Leszcz, 1987). Asking members to respond with their own personal reactions also guards against a common group problem—one member dominating the group discussion by repeatedly sharing lengthy stories about previous life experiences.

It is also important to help members identify, explore, and assess the impact of current and previous behavior patterns on their future ability to cope with stressful life events. A developmental perspective can help members assess whether circumstances that led them to behave in certain ways in the past still apply. Sometimes, the resulting insights motivate members to make changes in coping patterns that are no longer functional. At other times, members become more self-aware and more self-accepting.

Encouraging members to use coping responses that are viewed as congruent with their previous adaptive efforts can also be helpful in over-coming resistance to self-disclosure and to change. Coping with stressful events in familiar ways is much preferred by older persons to using totally new and different coping mechanisms. New coping mechanisms are more likely to be viewed as externally imposed and completely alien to older members' well-established, albeit impaired, functional abilities. For this reason they may not be tried. For example, a group member who enjoyed writing, but had always been shy, resisted a suggestion to contact her estranged sister in person for the purpose of improving their relationship. She was open, however, to a suggestion about sharing her feelings about her relationship with her sister in a letter.

Practitioners should be especially careful to treat older people who participate in therapy groups with dignity and respect. Because they have been identified by others as having psychological problems and are accustomed to thinking of themselves as impaired, they often have poor self-concepts and inappropriately low expectations of their own competencies. There is a danger that, if practitioners adopt these same attitudes about older group members, they will only reinforce members' negative self-images and perceptions of themselves as disabled.

Because older adults with psychiatric problems sometimes have unappealing personal characteristics or engage in behaviors that make them unattractive or difficult to work with, there is a danger that the practitioner will assume that members are less competent and capable then they actually are. There is also a danger that if practitioners find members' behaviors or personal characteristics offensive, they will neglect them or unwittingly undermine their existing skills and capacities. To prevent negative attitudes from interfering with effective leadership of therapy groups, review each session soon after it occurs. In the review, focus on interactions that evoked particularly strong emotional reactions. These interactions often provide insight into the way members relate to each other and to you. Also, be aware of your own reactions to members and to their particular self-disclosures. If certain members, or certain disclosures, evoke strong feelings or painful memories, it may be helpful to review the group meeting, and your own feelings, with your clinical supervisor.

Often, more guidance, direction, and structure are needed by those who suffer from dementing and schizophrenic disorders and other psychoses. By definition, older people with these disorders have difficulty organizing and taking responsibility for their own behavior. As disabilities increase, members are more likely to have difficulty engaging in helpful member-to-member interaction and developing the level of intimacy that is a prerequisite for a high level of group cohesion, for establishing and adhering to therapeutic norms and role behaviors, and for contributing to a therapeutic environment within the group. Depending on the nature of their disabilities, members may also be less responsive to leaders' efforts to develop therapeutic group dynamics and to correct problems in group functioning as they occur.

With severely impaired group members, keep group meetings fairly brief. Follow a routinized agenda so that members can anticipate what to expect in the group. For example, each meeting might open with a check-in in which members mention one positive and one negative thing that happened to them during the week. This might be followed by a sentence completion exercise in which each member responds to the following statement: "When I felt good this week I . . ." Similarly, members might be asked to respond to the following statement: "When I had a problem this week I coped with it by . . ." After a period of open discussion in which any member can bring up something for discussion, a skills training exercise, or a program activity, the group meeting might be closed by summarizing what has occurred, by highlighting the contributions of particular members, and by asking if members have any feedback about the meeting or any requests for what could be covered during the next meeting. Following the same format each meeting helps members to feel secure and in control because they know what to anticipate and what is expected of them.

When working with older adults with severe psychiatric impairments, make sure that whatever is done in the group is commensurate with the members' abilities. Avoid demanding situations. Encourage members to participate, but do not attempt to force them into verbal interaction. During go-rounds and other group exercises, allow members to pass when it is their turn and they do not feel like participating. Also, avoid highly emotionally charged issues, confrontations, and work focused on development issues and in-depth personality change. Some research suggests that this approach can actually stimulate psychotic symptoms (see, for example, Simpson and May 1982). Instead, utilize a supportive approach that focuses on education, problem-solving, and skills training for coping with and adapting to current and anticipated living situations. For example, skills training might include having members practice how to make appropriate requests of each other, staff, and family members. It also might include education and practice of independent living skills such as personal hygiene, staying within a budget, balancing a checkbook, taking medication, using public transportation, avoiding exploitation, shopping wisely and, planning and cooking meals.

Older adults who do not really want to participate in group therapy can provide a particularly difficult challenge for practitioners. It is not uncommon for older adults to be urged, or forced, to seek treatment by relatives, professionals, and the larger society, who are worried that their mental health problems may make them a danger to themselves or to others. In other situations, it is merely a matter of convenience. Staff in nursing homes, for example, may wish to make older people "more manageable." These older people often feel demoralized and completely helpless. Sometimes they express their profound sense of powerlessness at being coerced into participation in a group by withdrawing into themselves and by resisting the practitioner's attempts to engage them in treatment.

With these individuals, the practitioner should consider attempting to find the common ground between their needs and desires and the needs and desires of those who want them to participate in treatment. For example, the son and daughter of an individual in a psychiatric day treatment program insisted that their mother continue to receive treatment because past experience indicated that when she did not attend, she decompensated. During group sessions, the practitioner reviewed with the member what happened when she did not participate in treatment. After the member indicated that she had had problems as a result of not taking her medication in the past, the practitioner was able to reframe the member's perception that her children had insisted on her participation because "they think I'm crazy." Instead, she helped the member to view her children's insistence as concern and caring for their mother.

There are situations, however, in which the practitioner should not participate in attempts to engage older people in group treatment. Practitioners who work with older adults with mental health problems should be aware that there are specific laws governing an individual's right to refuse treatment. Sometimes, older adults who do not need or want treatment are coerced into it against their will by well-meaning family members or well-intentioned professionals. In other situations, treatment may be a way for family members or professionals to attempt to control the older adult. If an older adult who does not want treatment has been found to be competent,[1] group work practitioners should be aware that they have a moral and legal responsibility to respect the individual's right to refuse treatment. However, if an older adult has been judged to be incompetent, then the practitioner has a moral and legal responsibility to see to it that the individual is receiving the least restrictive and most appropriate treatment for his or her particular mental health symptoms. Also, make sure that reassessments of individuals who have been declared incompetent occur periodically, to ensure that this designation is still warranted.

Whether members have mild or severe impairments, it is important that practitioners do not limit assessments to the intake interview. Assessment should be thought of as an ongoing process that occurs throughout a member's tenure in a group. During the intake process and the first few sessions, older adults reveal data about a variety of different aspects of themselves and their life situations. In later sessions, the practitioner proceeds by filling in gaps in information, attempting to gain as coherent and comprehensive an understanding of each member of the group as is feasible. As the group progresses, the assessment process becomes more and more focused on helping members to overcome obstacles and impediments to achieving the purposes and goals they have set out to accomplish through their participation in the group. As termination approaches, the focus of assessment changes to evaluating the extent to which the member has achieved the purposes and goals he or she has set out to accomplish and to identifying what remains to be done.

The diagnosis and ongoing assessment of older adults' mental health problems requires specialized knowledge and skills. There can be complex interactions between older persons' physical and emotional states. For example, determining whether an older person is depressed or whether he or she is suffering from dementia can be difficult (Toseland, Derico, and Owen 1984). Also, psychotropic medications work differently with older people than with younger people, and drug interaction may be more complex due to the number and type of drugs some older people take for chronic disabilities. Therefore, practitioners who lead therapy groups for older adults should be familiar with standard diagnostic criteria such as those included in the *Diagnostic and Statistical Manual of Mental Disorders*

---

1. Methods to determine competency vary from state to state. The determination is often made by physicians and includes an assessment of whether or not an individual is able to make an informed decision, and whether an individual poses a serious danger to himself or herself or others (see, for example, Lamb and Mills 1986). If it is likely that you will be working with older adults in groups who have been mandated to receive treatment, be sure to check the laws that apply in your state, and the policies and procedures of the agency sponsoring the group.

(American Psychiatric Association 1980), as well as specific information about the assessment and treatment of mental health problems in later life (see, for example, Birren and Sloane 1980; Birren and Schaie 1985; Butler and Lewis 1982; Zarit 1983).

After carefully considering each member's needs, the practitioner composes the group and considers specialized intervention strategies that may help members with specific problems. During the group, and between group sessions, the practitioner reviews each member's progress, helping members to refine and adjust treatment plans as needed.

The procedures and skills used to facilitate therapy groups during their middle phase vary according to the theoretical orientation of the practitioner. For example, behaviorally oriented practitioners are more likely to use role playing and contingency management procedures, cognitively oriented practitioners are more likely to use rational self-analysis and self-talk procedures, and psychodynamically oriented practitioners are more likely to use insight-oriented procedures.

Although most treatment outcome studies have not established the clear superiority of one theoretical orientation over another (Smith, Glass, and Miller 1980), certain procedures seem to be particularly effective for helping older persons with specific disorders. For example, cognitive group therapy has been shown to be effective in the treatment of depressed older persons (Gaylord and Zung 1987; Yost, Beutler, Corbishley, and Allender 1986), behavioral group therapy has been shown to be effective for pain management in older patients (Sturgis, Dolce, and Dickerson 1987), and psychodynamic group therapy has been shown to be effective for individuals suffering from adjustment disorders of later life (Tross and Blum 1988).

SPECIALIZED SKILLS AND PROCEDURES

Depending on the nature of their impairments, many different procedures can be used when working with older persons in therapy groups. Some of the most widely used ones are presented in the following section. Although many of the procedures are presented as if they stand alone, in actual practice multiple intervention procedures are often incorporated eclectically into short-term and long-term therapy groups.

Reality Orientation

Reality orientation is a widely used procedure for helping confused older persons who are not fully oriented to time, place, or person. The goal of the procedure is to reduce confusion and help older persons remain as oriented as possible by providing them with basic information about their environment. The developers of reality orientation began with a thirty-minute group program for severely confused residents, but soon realized that reality orientation should occur on a twenty-four-hour basis (Folsom 1968; Taulbee 1986). They found that it was important to teach reality orientation to staff, family members, and other individuals who interact with the confused older persons on a regular basis.

To implement a successful reality orientation group, begin by paying careful attention to the composition of the group. Be sure that all members have similar levels of impairment. This will avoid boring high-functioning individuals and overwhelming low-functioning members. Also, limit membership. Five or six older persons and a coleader are ideal because confused older persons need much individual attention.

Because of cognitive impairments and possible hearing deficits, speak slowly and clearly, repeating key phrases frequently. To increase knowledge acquisition, use a blackboard or other visual medium, as well as objects that can be seen and touched. Clocks, calendars, photographs, and other props can also be used to help orient older members to upcoming holidays and other special events. A reality orientation board listing basic facts such as the time of day, today's date, weather conditions, and the season of the year also can be used to help reduce members' disorientation and to help them participate as fully as possible in the group.

Leaders of reality orientation groups should not neglect the relationship between themselves and the group members. Show genuine concern and caring. Do not treat confused older persons as children or as incapable of any meaningful interaction. Be positive by praising group members' accomplishments in remembering information and by focusing on their abilities rather than their disabilities. Do not begin an interaction with the anticipation that the older person will not understand or will be confused by your statement. Treat even the most disoriented member with respect and dignity.

Reality orientation procedures may not be appropriate for all confused older persons. If a confused group member does not retain sufficient knowledge after being exposed to a reality orientation group program for some time, it may be better to discontinue treatment and to try again at a later point (Taulbee 1986). Less intrusive and less intensive twenty-four-hour milieu reality orientation should continue, however, until a second trial of group reality orientation can be arranged. Also, because an individual's condition may change over time, frequent reevaluation of each group member is highly recommended.

The effects of dementia frequently make it difficult to keep members involved in group processes and content. To help members stay engaged, it is often helpful to invite one or two co-leaders to participate in the group. Nurses' aides, mental health therapy aides, or volunteers can serve in this capacity. They should not sit next to each other but rather should be dispersed among members, helping to reorient members when they drift off. Also, the use of concrete prompts can be helpful. For example, a large beach ball or baton can be passed to members to cue them that it is their turn to respond to a question or to participate in a program activity. For example, when a member is through giving his or her name and place of residence, the member can pass the baton or toss the ball across the circle. The person who catches the ball or is handed the baton takes the next turn. Similarly, objects symbolic of a season can be used to spur members' memories. For example, a pumpkin can be displayed when members are asked about the Thanksgiving holiday, and colored eggs can be passed around during Easter.

Clinical experience from many years of working with disoriented nursing home residents suggested to Naomi Feil (1982, 1983) that mildly and moderately disoriented older persons responded well to reality orientation and remotivation procedures, but severely confused older persons did not. Responding to the need for better procedures for working with this latter group of residents, Feil (1982, 1983) developed the following procedures: (1) assess the severity of the disorientation to determine the appropriate treatment approach, (2) explore each member's past, take a history, and establish a trusting one-to-one relationship, (3) select five to ten residents who are severely confused, (4) develop a role for each member in the group, (5) conduct all activities in a small circle without a table in between members, (6) involve staff in goal setting for group members and the whole group, and (7) follow the same agenda each week. The agenda should include a warm welcome, followed by some music, discussion of thoughts and feelings, an activity or exercise requiring movement, followed by refreshments and the formal ending of the meeting.

Denial of reality and retreat inward into a fantasy world with the help of memory fragments are methods that individuals with severe dementia use to cope with the profound changes they experience in their functioning. By taking away these coping mechanisms, standard reality orientation procedures may not be therapeutic. Instead, the group worker should respond empathically, attempting to tune in to the disjointed fantasies and fragments of previous memories that members vocalize. According to Feil (1982), the calming effect that occurs when fantasies are validated occurs because early memories replace intellectual thinking for the severely disoriented, and they are the only aspects of the self that remain intact. She speculated that validation, support, and empathic understanding help severely confused older persons to draw on memory fragments for sustenance and dignity, to bring closure to unfinished or unresolved events, and to review their lives in preparation for death.

Feil (1982) has offered some evidence for the effectiveness of her method, which she calls "validation." Given the failure of conventional reality orientation methods with severely disoriented older persons, her method deserves greater attention by those who work with severely impaired older person.

Remotivation

The remotivation technique is designed to stimulate older people to relate to each other and to think about and discuss topics associated with the real world (Weiner, Brok, and Snadowsky 1987). For example, the residents of some institutions rarely, if ever, leave the building, and their daily routine does not vary. News of current events may be unavailable or difficult to access due to sensory impairments.

Remotivation is particularly appropriate for moderately withdrawn individuals who are able to follow a conversation and contribute to it, but who need the structured socialization that a remotivation group can provide. In general, six to ten individuals, able to attend weekly or biweekly one-hour sessions, are ideal for a remotivation group.

The leader of a remotivation group acts as a teacher, taking responsibility for the subject material and any materials that are necessary for the program activity. The leader also takes responsibility for the structure of each remotivation group meeting by (1) creating a climate of acceptance by greeting members warmly and encouraging their participation in the group, (2) creating a bridge to reality by reading a short poem or by using other appropriate audio and visual materials that focus on a particular topic, (3) reinforcing members' appropriate responses to the topic, and encouraging them to talk about and share in the world of reality by asking questions and by using additional audio and visual materials to develop a particular topic, (4) demonstrating an appreciation for the work of the world by stimulating reminiscences, sharing experiences and developing ideas and questions about the type of work that can be done in relation to the topic, and (5) creating a climate of appreciation by acknowledging members' contributions and by inviting them to bring poems, songs, and other program materials to the next regularly scheduled meeting.

Within the relatively rigid structure of each meeting, leaders are encouraged to be creative by using a variety of different materials to stimulate interest in the topic. For example, in a ten-week remotivation group, two students I was supervising included the following topics: (1) cats and dogs, (2) trains, (3) farming, (4) horses, (5) maple syrup, (6) St. Patrick's Day,

(7) coin collection, (8) spring flowers and foliage, (9) Easter, and (10) cooking. For the last session, cookbooks, cooking utensils, and a chef's hat were all used to stimulate members' interest. Also, questions were developed about members' cooking abilities, their favorite recipes, and what kinds of jobs involve cooking.

When leading remotivation groups, it is particularly important for practitioners to stimulate member-to-member interaction and high level of cohesion. Practice principles described in chapter 2 can be used for this purpose. Stimulating member-to-member interaction fosters the development of an informal support system among members that they can, in turn, rely on outside of group meetings as they prepare to leave the institution, and after they are discharged. For example, four members of a remotivation group in a state psychiatric hospital were placed in the same residential community facility upon their discharge from the hospital. When interviewed six months later, three of the four members indicated that they had become confidants through the group experience, had supported each other through the transition to community living, and had continued to provide support and friendship to each other as they dealt with the daily living problems they encountered in the residence and in the community.

Problem Solving

The problem-solving technique is a structured procedure designed to help members resolve problematic situations and cope better with situations that are chronically stressful. A ten-step model is recommended: (1) achieve a calm state of mind, (2) define the problem as specifically as possible, (3) gather assessment data, (4) list as many action plans as possible, (5) list positive and negative aspects of each plan, (6) identify the plan that has the best chance of succeeding, (7) identify any obstacles that might interfere with implementation of the plan, (8) implement the plan, (9) evaluate the outcome, (10) reevaluate periodically, adjusting the action plan as necessary.

Clinical research findings indicate that problem-solving techniques can be used effectively with older persons in many types of therapy groups (Toseland 1977; Toseland and Rose 1978; Toseland, Rossiter, and Labrecque 1989a, 1989b, 1989c; Tross and Blum 1988). Because problem-solving is difficult work that requires much energy while the social aspects of group interaction are also rewarding and therapeutic, there is a tendency for members to become sidetracked by social conversations that are interesting but have little or no relevance to solving a particular problem. Digressions can be reduced by setting aside time during each session for problem solving, by writing and displaying the steps of the problem-solving process on a blackboard or a poster board at each group session, by redirecting member's comments that are unrelated to the problem-solving process, and by helping members to participate as fully as possible in the problem-solving process.

Relaxation Techniques

Relaxation procedures such as deep breathing, progressive muscle relaxation, and cognitive imagery can be used effectively with older group members. Group meetings offer members an opportunity to practice relaxation procedures until they become comfortable using them outside the group. Because a variety of circumstances can interfere with members' use of relaxation procedures, it is important for the leader to inquire about what relaxation procedures have the most appeal for each member and about what obstacles, if any, each member is likely to encounter when implementing a specific relaxation procedure outside of the group.

Clinical experience suggests that older persons find deep breathing to be a particularly useful relaxation technique, perhaps due to the convenience and ease of implementing the procedure. To perform the procedure correctly, members should be instructed to (1) close their eyes, (2) get into comfortable positions (the ideal position is to be seated in a high-back arm chair with feet on the floor), (3) breath in and out deeply and slowly three times, and (4) focus on breathing rather than on other thoughts. After an individual becomes comfortable using the procedure, steps 1 and 2 can be modified to accommodate to the exigencies of a particular situation. Older persons report using the deep-breathing technique very successfully in many different kinds of stressful interpersonal situations.

Some older group members also find progressive muscle-relaxation procedures to be helpful. As described by Bernstein and Borkovec (1973), progressive muscle relaxation involves the tensing and relaxing of muscle groups while focusing awareness on the feelings of tension and relaxation that the procedure engenders. Clinical experience suggests that the procedure can be quite beneficial for certain group members. It is helpful to distribute audiotapes with progressive muscle-relaxation procedures so that members can use them outside the group. Two audiotapes that provide enough space for four sets of progressive muscle-relaxation instructions that become progressively briefer allow members to change instructions as they gain experience.[2] In addition to reducing stress and anxiety, some

2. These tapes were developed under the direction of Dr. Blanchard and Dr. Barlow, who are internationally known for their work in anxiety and stress disorders. Their generosity in sharing these tapes with me is gratefully acknowledged. More information about their work can be obtained by writing them directly at the Stress Disorders Clinic, Psychology Department, University at Albany, State University of New York, Albany, New York 12222.

older group members have also reported that using a progressive muscle relaxation tape just before bedtime helps reduce insomnia.

Cognitive imagery can deepen the feelings of calm and relaxation that some members experience after engaging in the progressive muscle-relaxation procedure. Therefore, it can be helpful to end relaxation tapes with a brief cognitive-imagery procedure. For example, the person who is listening may be asked to imagine himself or herself on a beach listening to the sound of the surf and breathing in the clear, salty air.

Cognitive Therapy

Group cognitive-therapy techniques for older persons have been described in detail by Yost, Beutler, Corbishley, and Allender (1986), who suggest a four-phase treatment model: (1) preparation, (2) collaboration and identification, (3) cognitive change, and (4) consolidation and termination. In the preparation phase, screening and evaluation occur to make sure the person is appropriate for a group. Before therapy begins, rapport should be established with each group member. The preparation phase is also a time to provide corrective information and reassurance about the nature of the group and what is expected of each participant.

In the collaboration and identification phase, it is important to establish a working partnership with each group member and an accepting atmosphere in the group-as-a-whole. Members can be introduced to basic cognitive therapy principles. To accomplish this, the leader is encouraged to play the role of educator, teaching group members to identify and describe (1) the situation, (2) rational and irrational thoughts and beliefs about the situation, and (3) feelings, moods, and behaviors that result from these thoughts and beliefs. Also, Yost et al. (1986) suggest teaching members about common cognitive errors and distortions such as (1) overgeneralizing, (2) "awfulizing," (3) exaggerating self-expectations, (4) making unrealistic demands of others, (5) exaggerating self-importance, (6) mind reading, and (7) being overly self-critical.

The following example illustrates how cognitive distortions can affect the mental health of older adults. In a therapy group I led in an outpatient mental health setting, one member who was usually quite talkative sat quietly, not interacting and wearing a sullen expression. I asked the member what was the matter, and she mentioned that her daughter did not love her. She said that her daughter had stopped calling her and had said that she did not want her mother to call her. I asked for the member's permission to speak with her daughter, which she granted.

The daughter was surprised at what her mother had said in the group. She told me that she had spoken to her mother about telephoning because in the past several months the frequency of her mother's calls had increased to the point where her mother was calling several times during each day while she was at work, and at least once every evening. She mentioned that this was causing her problems at work, and she told her mother to limit her calls to once per day, preferably in the evening, unless there was an emergency.

In the next meeting, I spoke to the group about overgeneralizing, "awfulizing," and making unreasonable demands. I asked the member if I could use her situation as an example. The group member agreed. She said she did not want to cause her daughter any trouble at work. I told her that her daughter had said she cared for her mother very much. The group member said that her daughter had spoken with her and that she guessed she had overreacted to her daughter's initial statements about not calling. She said, however, that it was hard for her to call in the evening because she could not call until her daughter had put her three children in bed, and by that time it was late. One member suggested that perhaps her daughter would be willing to call her mother during her lunch hour. The group member in question liked this suggestion and said she would talk with her daughter about it. At the beginning of the next meeting, during the check-in period, the group member mentioned that her daughter agreed to talk with her for fifteen minutes by telephone each lunch hour.

In the cognitive change phase, members are given simple homework assignments. At first, assignments are geared toward identifying problematic events and the thoughts and feelings associated with them. Then the leader helps each member to develop a series of assignments that are graded in regard to difficulty and tailored to specific needs and capacities. Members work on these assignments between group meetings and report their experiences in subsequent meetings. For example, the member in the previous example first agreed to speak with her daughter. In later group sessions, she agreed to talk with her daughter about her feelings that her daughter did not love her, to write down what she said to herself when she felt that her daughter was not paying attention to her, and to rationally dispute her self-statements with objective facts about how often she talked with and saw her daughter and about what her daughter said to her and did for her.

In the consolidation and termination phase, members are encouraged to complete tasks, to work toward eliminating any cognitive distortions that continue to interfere with their functioning, to anticipate obstacles that may occur in the future, and to build support networks outside the group.

Cognitive therapy requires alert group members who have some intellectual abilities. Clinical experience suggests that apprehensions about the procedure being too difficult for older persons are unfounded. Once group norms are established and older persons overcome their own stereotypes about not being able to learn new concepts, most have no difficulty learning cognitive therapy principles or using them in their daily lives. However, experience suggests that depressed older adults often have a difficult time following through on homework assignments. Therefore, it may be better to have members practice the techniques in the group and report on experiences in which they used the techniques between meetings, but not assign members formal "homework."

Role Playing, Psychodrama, and Sociodrama

Procedures to dramatize events can be used effectively with older persons in therapy groups (Altman 1983; Buchanan 1981; Schloss 1988). Role playing offers older persons the opportunity to practice interpersonal skills and to get feedback from peers about how they appear in social situations. It also gives them an opportunity to explore alternative ways of responding, to discover an effective approach, and to practice it in the supportive environment of the group before trying it in social situations outside of the group.

Sociodrama and psychodrama take role playing a step further by giving members an opportunity to dramatize problems using the procedures described in table 6.1 (Blatner 1973). By asking member's to act out a situation suggested by the leader or the group members, sociodrama gives older persons an opportunity to explore themes of common interest without focusing on the life experiences of a particular group member.

In contract, psychodrama allows members to dramatize events that have happened to them. It can heighten the emotional involvement of all group members beyond what is typically achieved through verbal description alone. Therefore, it is a particularly useful way to help members explore their feelings about particular events.

Older group members can be reluctant to engage in dramatic enactments. Concern about physical appearance, limitations in mobility, low energy levels, and lack of motivation can be impediments to role playing. To counteract this tendency, it is useful to ask if anyone in the group has ever had any acting experience. Members who have had acting experience are generally proud to share it. Also, they are often willing to volunteer to participate in a role play or other dramatic enactment, thereby serving as role models for other members. Clinical experience suggests that older persons respond well to retrospective enactments that incorporate life review processes, and those that focus on "unfinished business" (Schloss 1988).

TABLE 6.1: Role-Play Procedures

Procedure	*Description*	*Use*
Own Role	Member plays the protagonist and asks for a volunteer to play the antagonist	Enables a member to demonstrate how he/she acted in a situation and to practice new roles
Role Reversal	Member plays the antagonist and asks for a volunteer to play the protagonist	Enables a member to experience a situation from another's point of view
Chairing	When occupying one chair the member initiates a dialogue with one or more empty chairs, then occupies a second chair and responds to what he/she has just said.	Helps members to see the various roles they play and the conflicts in these different roles
Sculpting	The leader directs members in a drama that represents a symbolic or real situation in one member's life	Designed to immerse a number of group members in intense participatory involvement in a situation of concern to a member
On-the-Spot Interview	The leader stops the action and interviews a member who is role playing	Clarifies what the role-playing member is thinking or feeling
Soliloquy	The member stops the role play action and describes what he/she is thinking or feeling	Allows a member to express thoughts or feelings he/she is having while playing a role
Doubling	A member stands beside or behind the protagonist and plays a part of the person, that is, a feeling, thought, or action that is not directly expressed during the role play	Helps a role-playing member to get in touch with feelings or thoughts he/she is not fully conscious of having
Mirror	A member mimics what the protagonist does, sometimes in an exaggerated fashion	Demonstrates to a member how he/she appears to others
Sharing	Members discuss their reactions to a role-play procedure	Provides feedback, advice, and suggestions to those who acted in a role play

CASE

The following case example of a problem-solving group took place in a geriatric day treatment program in a community mental health center. Transportation to the center was provided by a van, and participants were provided with lunch. The day treatment program served thirty to forty individuals over the age of fifty-five with a wide range of mental health problems. Approximately half the program participants had Alzheimer's disease and other dementing illnesses. They participated in reality orientation groups, music groups, arts and crafts groups, and movement groups that were appropriate to their level of functioning. The remaining participants had other psychiatric problems. They participated in problem-solving groups, health-education groups, and social and recreational groups. All participants ate together, rode in the van together, and participated together in special events programming to celebrate birthdays, holidays, and similar festive occasions.

The problem-solving group for those with psychiatric problems other then dementia met for one hour and thirty minutes twice each week. It followed a structured format. The first half hour was spent "checking in." A group go-round gave each participant an opportunity to (1) discuss briefly any important events that had occurred since the last meeting, (2) report on the results of anything they agreed to do in a previous meeting, and (3) share their experience using the coping skills described in previous meetings. The second half hour was spent on a presentation by the group leader about a particular coping skill, followed by group discussion. The remaining half hour was spent helping two or three members to resolve particular concerns using the problem-solving model described previously in this chapter. Whenever possible, the coping skills described and discussed in previous group meetings were incorporated into the action plans developed as a part of the problem-solving process.

The following transcript illustrates how the "check in" helped to focus group interaction and to lend continuity to the group meetings.

Ms. A. *[group leader]:* How about you, Mrs S.? We missed you on Tuesday.

Ms. S.: *[hardly audible]* I wanted to come but I wasn't feeling well. [I] must have had that bug that's going around. *[Long pause]*

Mr. J.: I was wondering about the party for . . .

Ms. A.: Mr. J. would you mind holding onto that thought for a moment? I'd really like to hear about Mrs. S.'s week.

Mr. J.: Sure. I thought she was finished.

Ms. S.: Did you see that TV movie last night about that girl who was abused?

Mr. J.: People like that should be put in jail—or worse.

Ms. M.: Isn't it terrible what's happening nowadays!

Ms. A. *[to Ms. S.]:* Did you use the relaxation tapes I gave out last week?

Ms. S.: Well, I tried them, But, to tell you the truth, I only listened to them once. They're kind of long.

Ms. M.: That's what I said last time we met. Who has the time to sit quietly like that! Harry [her husband] always needs something, and then there's shopping, cooking, and cleaning. It never ends. I like the breathing exercise, though. Since I've been doing that I find I catch myself before I get too upset and nervous with Harry. Even he noticed a difference!

Ms. S.: The breathing [exercise] is good—I use that. It's really made a difference in my relationship with my daughter-in-law. When she gets upset with me, I just take a few deep breaths and say to myself not to get mad at her because my son wouldn't like it.

Ms. A.: Do you all feel that way? I won't use the tapes anymore if you *[to the group]* don't feel that they are helpful.

Ms. H.: Oh, I don't know. I like those tapes you gave out *[looking at Ms. A.]*. I listen to them at night just before bed. They put me to sleep. I don't even hear the tape recorder click off.

Ms. L.: I like them too—they're very relaxing.

Ms. A.: I guess that just shows you that different relaxation procedures appeal to different people. I'm just really pleased that you *[to the group]* are trying the coping skills we go over to see whether or not you find them beneficial.

Mr. J.: I keep a diary like you suggested a while back. It helps me to organize my thoughts—I write in it just about every day. *[Two other group members nod as if they find it helpful too.]*

Ms. S.: Maybe I'll try the tapes again. I had a hard time this past week. Besides being sick, I've been kind of blue.

Ms. A.: Have you been taking your medication?

Ms. S.: Oh yes. I take it twice a day like I'm supposed to. My daughter is always checking up on me. I don't like taking medication, but it seems to help. I don't get as low as I used to, but sometimes I get to thinking about Tom [her late husband] and feeling sorry for myself. I get to feeling, What's the use?

Ms. A.: I wonder if we would talk some more about your mood after everyone has had their turn to check in. What do you say?

Ms. S.: *[in a quiet tone]* Okay.

In many therapy groups for older persons, especially those with severly impaired members, leaders spend much time helping members to share their thoughts and feelings. The first part of this transcript illustrates that the leader was active in soliciting Ms. S.'s input during the "check in." Previous experience suggested to Ms. A. that Mr. J. was uncomfortable with silence. If allowed the opportunity, he would dominate the group conversation, and Ms. S. would be left to lapse into silence.

The effective leader also has to be assertive in keeping the group focused. Members easily slip into social conversations about television programs and other present and past experiences that frequently are irrelevant to the group's work. Experience suggests that these "social topics" may interest some members while boring others. To accommodate members' social needs, time was set aside at the end of each meeting for coffee, donuts, and social conversation. This time was helpful in solidifying social support networks developed during group meetings.

The transcript reveals that members felt free to disagree with each other about the usefulness of the different coping skills that had been presented by the leader in earlier group meetings. Earlier in the life of the group, most disagreements were avoided, and the few that did occur resulted in diminished interaction. An ability to disagree without getting into a protracted conflict is characteristic of a well-functioning group during the middle phase of its development.

The transcript also reveals that the comment by Mr. J. about his use of the relaxation tapes helped motivate Ms. S. to state that she would give them another try. This is reinforced by Ms. A.'s comments about being pleased by the members' attempts to us the coping skills she presented in previous meetings. Both comments illustrate the power that group dynamics have over individual members' behaviors.

A portion of the transcript from later in the same group meeting illustrates problem-solving work in a mature therapy group.

Ms. A.: Has everyone checked in *[scanning the group]?* Good. Well then, let's move on and see if we [the group] can assist Mrs. S. If we have time after the break, we can help Mrs. M. with her problem about feeling manipulated by her husband, If not, we will discuss Mrs. M.'s problem during our next meeting. Okay? *[looking at Ms. M. and Ms. S. who both nod their heads in approval]*

Ms. M.: It's been going on for so long. [I] guess I can wait another week.

Ms. A.: Good, well, here's our problem-solving model again *[putting a sheet of newsprint with the outline of the previously described ten problem-solving steps on an easel]*. Okay, Mrs. S., take a few deep breaths. Are you relaxed and calm? *[referring to the first step of the model]*

Ms. S.: Uh hum.

Ms. A.: You said you have been feeling blue, especially when you think of Tom. Can you be any more specific?

Ms. S.: I guess I just get sad thinking of him and the way it used to be.

Ms. A.: Oh, Mrs. S., I feel for you, it's really hard after so many good years. *[pause]* Let's see if there's anything we can do to help. Anybody want to ask Mrs. A. any questions? *[silence]* Well, I have one. What happens when you get blue?

Ms. S.: Not much. I just sit, sit and think about him and how it used to be.

Mr. J.: I bet you're feeling low because you've been sick. Why don't you try . . .

Ms. A.: Excuse me, Mr. J., but remember we are on this step *[pointing to step 2 of the problem-solving model]*. Let's gather information before making suggestions about possible courses of action.

Ms. M.: I have a question. What do you do to keep your spirits up?

Ms. S.: Well, I used to go to a movie matinee once a week with a neighbor. But, I haven't been doing that lately.

Mr. J.: Do you exercise?

Ms. S.: I used to go for walks. But it's awfully cold out these days.

Ms. L.: Do you have any friends or family that come and visit you?

[Further exploration and questioning continued for the next ten minutes.]

Ms. A.: Well, if no one has any other questions, let's get some suggestions about what Mrs. S. can do to help herself. After we get everybody's ideas, Mrs. S. and everyone else can discuss the positive and the negative aspects of each suggestion. Okay?

Mr. J.: You said you like to walk, but it's too cold out, right? *[Ms. S. nods.]* What about going to the mall and walking around there? It's heated, and there's plenty of room to walk around.

Ms. M.: That's a really good idea. I never though of that. I'll have to try it with some of my friends.

Ms. L.: I have another suggestion, about your neighbor, the one who used to go with you to the movies. Why don't you ask her if she'd like to start going again?

Ms. H.: You know, when I lost my husband I went to a widow's support group for about a year that met at the Carver Community Center. I found it very helpful.

Ms. S.: How often does it meet?

Ms. A.: I think it meets once every two weeks. Notices are posted on the bulletin board by the entrance. You know which one I mean? *[members nod]* *[To the group]* I'm writing down all the ideas you have come up with. Let's hold off on a discussion of each one until after we get everybody's ideas. Okay?

Ms. A.: Anybody else? *[pause]* Okay—then let's move to the next step. Mrs. S., what do you think about these ideas? *[Pointing to the ideas listed on a separate sheet of newsprint]*

This section of the transcript illustrates that the leader takes an active role in focusing the group's problem-solving work. She posts the problem-solving model on an easel and directs members' attention to each step as they work through the problem-solving model, focusing on Ms. S.'s concerns.

The group meeting continued with Ms. S., and the other members of the group, evaluating the positive and negative aspects of each of the ideas suggested by group members. An action plan was developed that she agreed to implement. Before this portion of the group meeting ended, the following dialogue occurred concerning the obstacles that Ms. S. might encounter in implementing the plan.

Ms. A.: Mrs. S., I wonder if you are going to feel shy about going to the first meeting [of the widow-to-widow group] all by yourself? Do you think you'll be able to do that?

Ms. S.: Ah. I don't know. I'll try.

Ms. A.: Would having company help? Maybe someone from this group would be willing to go with you?

Ms. S.: Yes, I think I'd like that.

Ms. H.: I'd be glad to go with you the first time. I haven't been there for quite a while, but I bet I still know some people I could introduce you to.

Ms. S.: That would be nice.

This dialogue as well as the proceeding portions of the transcript illustrate that with some active assistance from the group leader, members can help each other to cope with problematic situations. In doing so, members feel useful and appreciated. Thus, benefits accrue to members who are the focus of the problem-solving efforts, and also to the other members who participate in the problem-solving work of the group.

SUMMARY

This chapter has focused on the skills practitioners need to facilitate therapy groups composed of older adults. It began with a discussion of the characteristics that differentiate therapy groups from other types of groups. Next, some important aspects of the role of the practitioner in therapy groups were enumerated. Then, a number of procedures that are especially useful for working with older adults in therapy groups, such as reality orientation, remotivation, problem solving, relaxation techniques, cognitive therapy, and role playing were described. The chapter concluded with a case example of a therapy group in action.

7

Leading Social, Recreational, and Educational Groups

Social, recreational, and educational groups provide members with an opportunity to become actively engaged with peers in activities that enhance enjoyment, stimulate learning, and promote healthy growth and development. Examples of social, recreational, and educational groups include

- A current events discussion group for frail older persons that meets once a week in an adult day care center.
- An arts and crafts group that meets in a day room attached to a geriatric unit in a state psychiatric facility.
- A reading club that meets to discuss one novel each month at a local library.
- A folk dance group that meets regularly to practice dances and to perform them at local community centers.
- A life review group that meets once a week at a senior center.

There is a considerable body of evidence indicating that healthy later life development for both the well elderly and the frail elderly is promoted by participation in social, recreational, and educational groups (see, for example, McCormack and Whitehead 1981; Ragheb and Griffith 1982). They bring pleasure and enjoyment into older people's lives; they provide opportunities for continous learning, growth, and development; they provide a sense of purpose, of responsibility, and of fulfillment; they fill empty time and reduce loneliness; they increase morale and self-esteem (see, for example, Hastings 1981); and they help to keep older persons functioning well by exercising their physical, social, and intelectual abilities. Also, the group context fosters feelings of belonging, of community, and of family-like ties (Macheath 1984), a benefit of participating in social, recreational and educational groups that is particularly important for those who are socially isolated.

CHARACTERISTICS OF SOCIAL, RECREATIONAL, AND EDUCATIONAL GROUPS

Although separate chapters could have been written about social, recreational, and educational groups, a decision was made to include them in a single chapter because they share several overlapping features that distinguish them from the other types of groups listed in table 4.4. The first feature is their emphasis on primary prevention. Social, recreational, and educational groups emphasize the maintenance and enhancement of members' abilities. The gradual deterioration of physical, social, and cognitive skills that can accompany the aging process can be prevented, slowed, or reversed by active participation in social, recreational, and educational activities. Members are enabled to use skills, talents, and abilities that might otherwise lay dormant. As members engage in activities and learn new things, they acknowledge, affirm, and validate each other's abilities. This, in turn, helps them to feel useful and competent, building their senses of self-esteem, self-worth, and self-confidence (Kubie and Landau 1953).

A second distinguishing feature of these groups is their emphasis on building social support, comradery, and a spirit of community. They provide an opportunity for members to stay actively engaged with their peers. They promote the development of informal support networks that are essential for assisting older persons to live independently in the community for as long as possible. They provide a reference group, a sense of security and acceptance, and a forum to maintain and enhance members' own identity and personality and to experience it in relation to others. As a result of these experiences, isolation and social withdrawal can be prevented.

A third distinguishing feature of these groups is their reliance on program activities. Social, recreational, and educational groups use program activities as the medium for engagement, for social interaction, and for sustained interest in the group. Members' common interest in a particular social, recreational, or educational activity, and the experiences they share in common from engaging in it, form the bond among them.

Social, recreational, and educational groups are often led by paraprofessionals. Perhaps this is because program administrators believe that it is easier to lead groups when the focus is on later life development and growth than when the focus is on pathology or on difficult life transitions. Certainly, in social, recreational, and educational groups, the content is less emotionally charged and more inherently enjoyable than it is in therapy and support groups. Also, members are less likely to exhibit social and behavioral problems. Thus, a sensitive, caring paraprofessional can be effective in leading these groups. Still, leading social, recreational, and educational groups effectively is not as easy as it may first appear. Therefore, the remainder of this chapter presents guidelines for conducting these groups that both professionals and paraprofessionals can use to help elderly group members get the most out of their participation.

GETTING STARTED

The first step in developing social, recreational, or educational groups for the elderly is to become thoroughly familiar with the mission and goals of the sponsoring organization. There is a close relationship between social, recreational, and educational groups and the total program of the sponsoring organization. In senior centers, day treatment programs, and a variety of other community-based civic and religious associations, social, recreational, and educational groups account for a significant portion of an organization's programming, determining, to a large extent, who is served. In some settings, all group programming is designed for the same group of individuals, whereas in other agencies, different social, recreational, and educational groups are offered as a way of reaching out to diverse subgroups of the elderly. Whom they serve reflects, to a large extent, the policies, missions, and goals of the agencies that sponsor them.

Discuss the mission of the sponsoring organization with your supervisor or administrator. Does the agency mission statement and long-range plan indicate any preference for serving certain subgroups of the elderly population? To what extent are these individuals currently being served? What are the barriers to their participation? Consider carefully how to address these issues early in the planning process.

A second step in getting stated is to build a relationship with prospective group members. Describe the planned group, soliciting potential members' feedback and input. Spend as much time as possible with each potential member, developing rapport and trust. Describe previous groups, if any, and the benefits that members have derived from participating in them. Whenever possible, ask former members to share their perceptions of the benefits of participation with those who are considering joining the group.

The third step in getting started is knowing potential members' interests and motivations. Continuity theory has been shown to be the most useful framework to explain preference for particular leisure time activities in later life (see, for example, McGuire and Dottavio 1986, 1987). Continuity theory suggests that older people are more likely to be enthusiastic about activities that they have engaged in, or been exposed to, in the past. Conversely, it also suggests that they are less likely to be enthusiastic about activities that they are unfamiliar with. Therefore, inquire about how leisure time has been used in the past and about whether these activities still hold interest for the individual. It can be useful to have potential members fill out a personal interest inventory that asks individuals to describe the types of activities they currently engage in, have pursued in the past, and are interested in pursuing in an organized group (Ginsberg 1988). Responses can then be collated to determine what types of programming should be offered. Generally, expect anywhere between one half and one fifth of those who express interest in a social, recreational, or educational activity to participate when a group is developed. Do not decide to offer a particular type of group merely because it was mentioned by the largest number of individuals. It is generally more effective to invite a select group of participants with high interest than to offer a group for a larger number of individuals who are only moderately interested.

A fourth step in getting started is becoming attuned to the abilities, capacities, skills, and talents of the individuals who will be served. To plan appropriate program activities, it is important to find out about members' cognitive and intellectual abilities. At a minimum, gather data regarding the following questions: Do members suffer from cognitive impairments? What are their educational backgrounds? How long are their attention spans?

It is also essential to assess members' physical abilities. Program activities require different levels of gross and fine motor coordination, so it is important to assess this aspect of members' physical functioning. Chronic disabilities such as arthritis and impaired hearing and vision may also make it difficult or impossible for older people to participate in certain program activities. A working knowledge of members' physical limitations can help the practitioner to make appropriate modifications in program activities to accommodate members with disabilities and to help the group-as-a-whole avoid selecting activities that will exclude certain members.

When becoming attuned to prospective members' abilities and needs, do not neglect to inquire about what special skills and talents they possess. Older people are a rich resource, and they are proud to describe their accomplishments and any special skills and talents they possess. When an older person has special skills and talents in a program activity that is going to be used in a group, enlist that member's help in guiding the other members through the activity.

A fifth step is to consider the requirements of program activities and to match these to what is known about potential members' abilities. Toseland and Rivas (1984) suggest considering (1) the physical requirements of the activity, including the level of fine motor coordination, strength, and endurance, (2) the social requirements of the activity, including the level of verbal and social skills that are needed, (3) the psychological requirements of the activity, including the ability to be introspective or insightful, and (4) the cognitive requirements of the activity, including members' intelligence and their ability to deal with the abstract concepts that are needed to engage in the program activity. In addition, Knox (1986), suggests that practitioners should encourage members to diagnose their own learning needs. Also, consider assessing what type of activities would be most appropriate by observing members and analyzing their capacities and skills in a variety of settings.

When composing the group, invite members to join who have similar ability levels. Large discrepancies in members' abilities can create disharmony and tension by impeding some members and by placing too many demands on others. This is particularly true when high levels of cooperation and interaction are needed to engage in a particular program activity.

A sixth step in getting started is to consider the resources that will be needed to conduct the group. Is the physical space suitable for the program activities that are planned? It is helpful to have at least one large and one small meeting room so that different sized groups can be accommodated. A portion of the space should be set aside as a lounge where participants can gather and socialize informally in comfortable chairs before group meetings. However, avoid chairs and sofas that are low to the ground because older people have difficulty getting in and out of them.

In some settings, a particular space may be used for a number of purposes. It is very distracting when participants are disturbed by intruders, and the development of group cohesion can be adversely effected. Thus, careful planning is needed to ensure that the space will be available when needed and, more importantly, that participants will not be disturbed when they are meeting. Also, for program activities that will not be finished at the end of each session, secure a place to store unfinished projects.

Pay particular attention to lighting, acoustics, access, and decor. If possible, select a space with plenty of natural lighting. Avoid glare and shadows by using soft fluorescent and incandescent lighting that is well-dispersed throughout the room. Nonskid carpeting, as well as drapes, can be very effective for absorbing background noise that is very distracting for individuals with hearing impairments. Even when participants using walkers and wheelchairs are not expected to attend, handicap access is essential because it assures that those who have arthritis and other problems affecting their mobility will be able to attend group meetings, and because members' situations may change over time. Also, pay particular attention to the decor of the meeting room, because pleasant surroundings can add greatly to the enjoyment of participants.

Program activities frequently require supplies. The group leader should ensure that an adequate budget is available to purchase these and to keep them in stock. When expensive equipment is going to be purchased, careful consideration should be given to how it will be used. Preference should be given to equipment that is likely to be used frequently and for a number of purposes. Some basic equipment that should be available includes a speaker's lectern, a public address system, folding tables and chairs that can be easily moved to accommodate different program activities, display cases, bulletin boards that can be used for posting announcements and schedules of activities, a portable blackboard and/or an easel for newsprint, audio tape and videotape recording and playback equipment, film and slide projectors, and a record player.

A seventh step in getting started is to consider the composition of the group. Social, recreational, and educational groups can be composed of a more diverse membership than the other types of groups for older people described in table 4.4 Because they do not require a high level of self-disclosure, members tend to feel less threatened by each other. Members are often freer than in other types of groups to select their own partners, teammates, or companions, and to interact primarily with members of their own choosing. Also, as members become absorbed in the content of whatever program activity is the focus of the group, they are generally less preoccupied with each other and are more tolerant of diversity.

Through program activities, social, recreational, and educational groups provide opportunities for spontaneous and structured interaction. Therefore, they are an excellent way for older people to make new friends and to overcome preconceived notions, prejudices, and other biases that might otherwise interfere with their reaching out to someone new or "different." Too frequently, however, social, recreational, and educational groups serve only one segment of all the eligible participants. As they participate in programming on a regular basis, members sometimes form rather exclusive cliques that do little to make new members feel welcome. Practitioners can be as guilty as members in this regard by tolerating or even fostering group norms of selectivity and exclusivity.

To avoid this problem, remind current members about the policy of welcoming new members. Pay special attention to newcomers. Encourage current members to make newcomers feel welcome, praising those who do. Reach out to specific subgroups who are not currently being served by advertising special welcoming programs, by sponsoring specialized groups designed to interest them, and by encouraging new members to bring along their friends. Consider planning group programs around congregate meals. Individuals who come for a meal will often participate in a group program that immediately precedes or follows it. Health screening programs, bingo, and special events targeted to specific subgroups of the elderly population also are good ways to bring in new members who might not otherwise be exposed to the offerings of a particular agency.

Whenever possible, develop a variety of different social, recreational, and educational group programs that can be offered throughout the week. Salamon (1986) has pointed out that very few individuals attend all the activities that are offered at one site. However, given the proper programming, a large number of individuals will participate in at least some of the programming that is offered. Do not try to tailor each group that is offered to the entire consistency, but rather develop groups that have appeal to specific segments of the targeted population. Also, vary the format for engaging in program activities. For example, Knox (1986) has pointed out that in large educational groups lectures, panels, debates, subgroup discussions, and forums can all be used to enliven meetings. Similarly, in small educational groups, discussions, case analyses, simulations, and demonstrations can be used to help hold members' interest.

CONDUCTING THE GROUPS

Social, recreational, and educational groups are characterized by a facilitative approach to leadership. For example, when making suggestions about how to lead educational groups Brookfield (1986) pointed out that as people mature they are more likely to want to participate in self-directed learning activities. Therefore, the leader should help members to formulate their own goals and objectives for group participation (Knox 1986).

Once members have been recruited, the group composed, and goals and objectives agreed upon, major tasks of the facilitator include helping members to (1) select and prepare program activities or lecture and discussion materials that are interesting and commensurate with the members' abilities and interests, (2) make the necessary arrangements and acquire the necessary resources for conducting the activity, (3) facilitate members' participation in the activity, and (4) prevent obstacles from interfering with their enjoyment of it. Practitioners may also serve as guides during program activities by demonstrating an activity, by suggesting roles, by providing structure, and by helping members through activities.

Unless the leader is a recognized expert on the subject matter, and the members' purpose for joining the group is to learn from the leader, it is generally good practice to avoid making unilateral decisions about program activities. Leaders who make decisions for members run the risk of fostering dependence and preventing members from utilizing their own decision-making skills. Instead, help members decide on what they would like to do in the group by facilitating communication among members. Clarify, summarize, and organize members' ideas and suggestions. Feel free to make suggestions about different program activity options that may have been overlooked, but be sure to help members consider all options and to express their opinions about the ones they would most like to see implemented in the group.

When working with frail older persons, the leader generally has to take on more responsibility for the planning and organization of social, recreational, and educational groups than when working with the well elderly (Weisman and Schwartz 1989). Frail older members do not respond well to open-ended questions about what program activities they would like to see implemented in the group. They often prefer the leader to suggest activities and to structure their roles in them. Still, as Judith Lee (1983) has pointed out, even with frail older people, "One does not work on self-concept by simply doing things with people or talking about who they were. The skill of the worker is to develop a fine sense of who the individual is and to draw this out. It takes much time to learn who elderly people are, particularly when they can only reveal themselves very indirectly, subtly and slowly" (45). Thus, as the group develops, the practitioner strives to get to know each member as a unique individual who has something special to contribute to the group as a whole.

For example, Hiemestra (1972) found that the single most important barrier to participation in educational groups for seniors was a lack of transportation. In other situations, the cost of a program activity may be prohibitive for certain members. Senior discounts, fund raisers, and donations can be used to help members who can't afford certain activities. Other barriers include fear of going out in the evening, and lack of interest in the planned activity (Hiemestra 1972).

Despite the importance of helping members to identify and eliminate impediments that may inhibit their participation, do not push members to take on roles that they are uncomfortable assuming, and never force anyone to participate. Much harm has been done by following the misguided notion that active participation in social, recreational, and educational groups is a panacea for all older persons. Participation in social, recreational, and educational groups often includes some who attend most meetings and are actively involved, and others who attend fewer meetings and participate in a less active manner. As Salamon (1986) has pointed out, both forms of participation are beneficial and valid.

As members engage in a program activity, help them to feel good about their participation. Acknowledge individual members' contributions to the program activity, taking special note of what they are doing well during the activity and pointing out their accomplishments when an activity has been completed. Also, with members' permission, publicly recognize accomplishments by displaying completed projects or by posting accomplishments on a bulletin board.

Establish a positive, upbeat atmosphere in the group. Participate enthusiastically along with members. Help members to have fun and to enjoy themselves while they are engaged in the activity by encouraging laughter, playfulness, creativity, and experimentation as well as expressions of pleasure and satisfaction regarding their own and other members' accomplishments.

Although the level of self-disclosure is frequently low in social, recreational, and educational groups, strong bonds often develop among members. These result from the interdependence, cooperation, and team spirit that are required by some activities. Even when activities require little cooperation among members, strong bonds can also result from the shared experiences and memories that result from collectively engaging in an activity.

Help group members develop norms of interdependent and cooperative functioning. Encourage member-to-member interaction and mutual aid. Reduce competition by helping members to set goals for themselves rather than comparing their performance to others in the group. Also, promote responsible role-taking within the group. Do not let one member dominate the activity. If necessary, rotate roles. Also, do not allow one member to try to control the action of other members by making unwanted, intrusive suggestions about how to engage in a program activity. Instead, help members who engage in such behavior to focus on their own roles in the activity.

PROGRAM ACTIVITIES

The following seven categories of program activities are presented to illustrate the wide range of options that are available to practitioners as they plan social, recreational, and educational groups for older people. Also, additional sources of information are presented for those who are interested in exploring any of the program activities in more depth.

Discussion-Oriented Activities

Discussion-oriented activities are especially suitable for older people who are not severely cognitively impaired, and for those whose physical limitations prevent them from participating in groups that require more physical stamina. Two of the most popular types of groups using discussion-oriented program activities are current events groups and reading discussion groups.

In regard to current events groups, many older people who reside in the community are keenly aware of local, state, national, and international affairs. They follow news events carefully and have strong opinions about newsworthy events. They welcome the opportunity that current events groups give them to express their opinions, to be listened to, and to discuss events with each other. Current events groups are also beneficial to older people who reside in institutional settings because they help them to stay oriented to what is going on in the outside world.

Reading discussion groups are also very popular. Many older people are avid, lifelong readers. Reading discussion groups give them an opportunity to share their interest with each other and to discuss what they have read. In poetry discussion groups, one member of the group reads a poem and then members discuss their reactions to it. In literature discussion groups, members agree to read a book at their own pace between meetings, and then get together to discuss it in the group. A variation of this format is for the practitioner, or a designated member, to read a short excerpt from a book that stimulates group members' memories of historical events of interest, or that pertains to material that is controversial. Members are then encouraged to discuss their opinions about what has been read. For a discussion of the types of reading materials most enjoyed by older persons, see Kamin (1984) or Wilson (1977).

Facilitating discussion groups requires the practitioner, or a designated member, to come prepared with materials that will stimulate discussion. In current events groups, this means bringing in newspaper clippings and/or videotape or audiotape recordings of newsworthy events. In reading discussion groups, it means bringing in a poem, a play, or titles of books that members might be interested in reading. Also, it is helpful to develop a series of discussion questions prior to the meeting to promote discussion.

To ensure an orderly discussion, it is a good idea for the leader to remind group members of a few simple rules at the beginning of each group meeting. These include (1) one person speaks at a time, (2) side conversations should be avoided, (3) members should take turns sharing their thoughts, opinions, and ideas, with preference given to members who have not spoken, and (4) members should keep each comment fairly brief to avoid dominating the discussion. For additional ideas about discussion programs for older people, see Schlenger (1988).

Reminiscence and Life-Review Activities

Since the publication of Robert Butler's (1963) seminal article on the importance of life review and reminiscence in the lives of older people, there has been much interest in this topic in the gerontological literature. Practitioners should keep in mind that reminiscence is a naturally occurring phenomenon in the elderly that arises spontaneously in social interaction. Still, to promote life review and reminiscence, a number of different group programs have been developed (see, for example, Fry 1983; Ingersoll and Goodman 1983; Ingersoll and Silverman 1978; King 1982; Lesser, Lazarus, Frankel, and Havasy 1981; Lewis and Butler 1974; McMorde and Blom 1979; Sherman 1987).

Some life-review groups meet for extended periods of time, using writing and other media to stimulate a continually evolving exploration of the past and its implications for the present. Typically, however, life-review and reminiscence groups are short-term, with one or more group sessions focused on a particular developmental period, and with succeeding group sessions progressing from one developmental period to the next. For example, the first session or two may focus on earliest childhood memories, followed by sessions on later childhood, adolescence, young adulthood (ages twenty to twenty-nine), middle adulthood (ages thirty to forty-five), senior adulthood (ages forty-five to sixty), and the recent past. During the first session, and all subsequent sessions, the leader informs members of the focus for the following session. Members are encouraged to bring in photographs, memorabilia, newspaper clippings, and any other props that will help the group focus on a particular developmental period. In addition to bringing in props, it is helpful for the leader to develop a series of questions to stimulate members' memories of events. For example, for earliest childhood memories, members can be asked to recall what they can remember of the first place they lived, their first friends, and their favorite toys and games. Similarly, for later childhood, members can be asked to recall where they went to school, a favorite teacher, and what athletic activities they engaged in.[1]

Reminiscence and life-review techniques are presented in this chapter because they can provide older persons with opportunities for socialization and social reintegration and for maintaining a sense of self in the face of losses. However, practitioners should also be aware that with modifications that focus on working through unresolved issues and conflicts from the past, reminiscence and life-review techniques can be used in therapy groups as a way to resolve developmental conflicts, to combat depression, and to build feelings of self-esteem and self-worth (see, for example, Fry 1983; Ingersoll and Silverman 1978; Lewis and Butler 1974; Sherman, in press).

Educational Activities

There are three broad types of educational programs commonly offered to groups of older people. The first type consists of programs that present necessary information to help older people maintain their independence.

1. Other ideas for stimulating older members' life review and reminiscing can be obtained by writing Potentials Development For Health and Aging Services, Inc., 775 Main Street, Buffalo, New York 14203.

These include presentations on health and nutrition, social services, and legal and financial topics. The second type consists of programs related to the existing interests and backgrounds of older people. These include presentations on cultural, ethnic, and religious topics, as well as presentations on gardening, cooking, sewing, ceramics, dancing, languages, and similar topics. A third type consists of continuing education courses on topics that older people have not had the opportunity to pursue in the past.

When planning for educational groups, a primary task of the practitioner is either to find a person who can present on the topic or to locate and prepare information on the topic to present without the help of an outside speaker. Area Agencies on Aging, community planning agencies, and information and referral agencies are often helpful in locating guest speakers and information for preparing presentations. Other practitioner tasks include publicizing the program, making all necessary arrangements for it, introducing the speaker, facilitating a question-and-answer period or a discussion about the presentation, and learning how members can get additional information on the topic should they wish to pursue it further.

Physical Activities

When program activities require any degree of extensive physical exertion, it is very important to make sure that members' physical condition permits them to engage in the activity. It is a good practice to ask potential participants to discuss their participation with their personal physician prior to attending. Those who decide to attend should be asked to sign a form certifying that they have done so and releasing the sponsoring agency from responsibility.

When beginning an exercise program, it is generally wise to limit physical activity to less than one hour. Also, to avoid injuries, use warm-up and cool-down exercises and proceed cautiously, checking to ensure that individual members are not overexerting themselves.

In recent years, a wide variety of physical exercise programs have been developed for older persons. A presentation of the specific exercises that have been developed is well beyond the scope of this book. For information about exercises designed specifically for the well elderly, see Fisher (1989), Flatten, Wilhite, and Reyes-Watson (1987a, 1987b), or Foster (1983). For information about exercises designed specifically for the frail elderly, see Beisgon (1989), Helgeson and Willis (1987), Hurley (1987), or Killeffer, Bennett, and Gruen (1985). Also, the journal *Activities, Adaptation & Aging* is an excellent resource for current information about exercise programs and other activities for both the frail and the well elderly.

Expressive Program Activities

There are a variety of program activities that can provide a creative, expressive outlet for older people. These include music, dance, drama, and arts and crafts. It is well documented that music has a powerful effect on physical and emotional states (see, for example, Critchley and Henson 1977). One use of music is simply to have older people listen to it. Select the type of music to be played on the basis of the mood you would like to create or enhance in the group. For example, some music can have an immediate calming and soothing effect, whereas other music can be uplifting, energizing, and inspiring.

Music can also be used in a more active fashion by having members sing along while someone is playing a piano or other musical instrument or by having older people make music. Those with musical talents can be encouraged to form choral groups or music ensembles. For some excellent suggestions about using music as a program activity, see Hennessey (1986).

Dance and dramatic activities provide a stimulating combination of cognitive and physical activity. They give older people an opportunity to express themselves through their bodies, to touch, and to be touched. As members become absorbed in a particular dance or dramatic activity, they tend to become less cautious, less self-absorbed, less obsessed with their own problems and concerns, and more likely to abandon themselves to the here-and-now of the activity. For information about the use of dance and creative movement with older people, see Booth (1986) and Fisher (1989), and for dramatic activities, see Clark and Osgood (1985) and Thurman and Piggins (1982).

There are also many arts and crafts activities that can be done in groups. Wolcott (1986), for example, describes the use of collage, scribble drawing, and painting in an art therapy group in a nursing home. Arts and crafts activities are particularly good for exercising older people's fine motor skills and their eye-hand coordination. One danger with arts and crafts program activities, particularly in institutional settings, is that they can be misused by serving merely as filler activities that have little or no appeal to those participating. This only adds to members' feelings of powerlessness, abandonment, uselessness, and anomie. To avoid this, make sure that arts and crafts activities have some intrinsic appeal to those who are participating. Also, pick activities that will result in meaningful products. For example, in one nursing home, residents made dolls for preschoolers who were located in a facility adjacent to the nursing home. Residents enjoyed making the dolls. They also got a lot out of knowing that they were still able to do something useful for someone else, and out of seeing the joy on the preschoolers' faces when they gave the handmade dolls to them.

Special Events

A variety of special events programming are conducted in groups. Some involve planning parties, luncheons, or dinners to celebrate birthdays and anniversaries. Others involve planning for religious and civic holidays. Special events provide an opportunity for older people to use their organizational skills as well as their talents in cooking, baking, decorating, and similar activities.

Groups can also be formed to go on regularly scheduled field trips to the theater, to parks and other recreational sites, and on sightseeing/vacation trips. Because these are often lengthy activities that give participants many different opportunities to deepen their friendships, they are especially useful activities for developing comradery and lasting friendships.

Table Games and Other Program Activities

A variety of other program activities are conducted in groups. Some of the most popular of these include card games, bingo, and movie clubs. Although they are rarely thought of as group activities *per se,* group dynamics are present during these activities, and should not be ignored.

CASE

The following case example is taken from a group that met at a community center that was located on the first floor of a highrise housing program for seniors. The group was called Lifetime, and it was advertised as a way for residents of the highrise to get to know their neighbors, to share life experiences, and to reflect upon their present and past lives.

Members were recruited by the group leader, Ms. A., who placed a notice describing the group in the mailbox of each individual who lived in the building, asking all those who were interested to contact Ms. A. by telephone, in person at the community center, or by coming to either of two informational meetings that were held after the congregate noontime meal at the community center. Ms. A. also spoke directly with a number of individuals who attended the center regularly whom she thought might be interested in the group.

Eighteen people who expressed interest in the group were invited to meet with Ms. A. individually for a screening interview. Ms. A. answered questions that the potential members had about the group. She mentioned that the group would meet for twelve weekly one-and-half-hour sessions and would focus on recalling memories and discussing their significance and meaning for members' current lives. She also mentioned that the group was designed to help members get to know each other and to make the most out of their lives. During the interview, she screened potential participants for their appropriateness for the group, excluding two individuals who had mental health problems, one individual who had a severe hearing impairment, and one individual who could not meet during the day. Of the fourteen people who remained, nine persons came to the first group meeting and attended regularly thereafter.

The first portion of the following transcript was taken from the third group meeting, when members were asked to describe and discuss their childhood memories.

Ms. A.: Last week, if you recall, we focused on our earliest memories, and I mentioned that we would focus on childhood memories today. We really had some fun last week. There sure was a lot of laughter! *[group members nodding]* Even those of you who had difficult times when you were young really seemed to enjoy hearing about what others remembered. This week, let's move on to your memories of later childhood. Take a few minutes now and recall what it was like as a child growing up in your family. *[pause]* Some of you, I see, have brought some photographs, and some other memorabilia. That's great! Are all of you ready with a memory? If you are, remember to think for a moment about how that time in your life affects you now. *[pause]* Let's go-round and see what everyone remembers.

[Silence]

Ms. J.: I guess I can start.

Ms. A.: Feel free.

Ms. J.: I have fond memories of my childhood. I guess that's because we lived in the country near Lake Luzerne. *[Members nod, recognizing the name of the lake.]* I can remember swimming and playing by the lakeside all day long during the summer. But what I can remember best is the winter. There was so much snow. We used to go sleigh riding and ice skating and we used to build great big snowmen. Our neighbor next door had a horse-drawn sleigh. I can remember going out in it and then coming home to a warm fire and some hot chocolate that my mother made. You know at that time they didn't burn wood. They burned coal. Did you know that? *[looking at Ms. A.]*

Ms. A.: No, I didn't realize that. We had a coal-burning stove in our basement when I was really young and then we switched to oil. But I don't remember coal in fireplaces. I guess I'm too young. *[pause]* One experience I missed.

Mr. H.: Oh, sure. Everybody had coal stoves. It lasts a lot longer than wood. Seems to me that there's a lot less snow nowadays. I can remember great big piles of snow. We used to play king of the mountain and try to push each other off. But it didn't hurt because you landed in the snow.

Ms. L.: You know, Anna [Ms. J.], I've known you for a long time, but I never knew you grew up on a farm. So did I. I miss those days. Winters were really something then. Now, I don't look forward to the snow and the ice. But I still enjoy the sight of snow falling, and I remember how nice it used to be to go out and play in it when I was young.

The leader began by reminding members of what they had done in the last meeting, and how much they had enjoyed it. This provided a sense of continuity and cohesion and helped to develop and reinforce a norm that the group is meant to be enjoyed. The leader also reminded members of how they had agreed to proceed, providing a structure for the meeting. The last portion of the transcript illustrates how much members enjoy taking turns sharing how things "used to be." It also illustrates the usefulness of the group in helping members get to know each other better.

Ms. H.: I have a memory that I'd like to share *[looking at Ms. A.]*
Ms. A.: Jump right in!
Ms. H.: Well, when I was a very little girl, I don't remember when exactly, I can remember going to the home of a relative, an aunt, to visit. She always used to say to my mother, "Helen doesn't belong in the family, she has such a dark complexion compared to the others." I can remember that very vividly. She always used to say it, and I believed it. It took me a long time to get over. When I was scolded for any little thing, I believed I was adopted. This went on for a long time, a number of years, till finally something happened, I can't remember what, but it came out in the open. I said to my mother, "Well, of course, that's why I'm treated this way. I'm adopted." *[members of the group listening intently]* Well, you know, my mother was terribly shocked of course, and my father as well. They finally got out my birth certificate and showed me that I was their child. *[pause]* That went on for quite a while, and I can remember how upset I was. Isn't that something.

Mr. B.: Well, I can tell you there was nothing good about my childhood. I don't remember having time to play. I feel like I missed out on a lot. My parents were poor. I quit school at eleven when my father died, and went out and got a job to help my mother take care of the seven children. My mother and my brothers and sisters were wonderful, but it was hard.

Ms. L.: I didn't have much of a childhood either. The rules were quite strict in my family. We got up early, did chores, and went to school.

When I came home my mother wanted me to be a pianist, so I was expected to play the piano, every day! And then there were more chores, endless chores, because we lived on a farm. And I had to watch the younger two. My mother had seven of us.

Ms. A.: You *[looking across the group at Ms. L. and Mr. B.]* had it pretty hard as children. What about the rest of you? What do you remember?

Ms. C.: My life was terrible as a child. We came over from Ireland. I remember being hungry. My father used to drink. He'd get drunk, beat us, and worse.

Ms. A.: And despite all that, things have turned out well for you.

Ms. C.: *[nodding]* Yes, they have. I've had a good life, all in all.

Mr. S.: We all lived through the Great Depression, you know.

Ms. A.: I've heard about how hard that was. What was it like growing up then? How was it different from now?

Mr. S.: Oh! Everything was so different then. You respected your parents. I think parents are too permissive today. Kids have everything, and they're still not happy.

Ms. L.: I can remember when I would get a penny to go down to the store and buy candy, I'd be so happy. You could get a lot of candy for a penny in those days!

Mr. S.: I think about the bad times, but I don't dwell on them, the poverty, all the things I missed. I regret all the things I wanted to do but couldn't, *[pause]* but we didn't have the wherewithal to do them. Still, there were a lot of good times. I can remember the meals my grandma prepared, especially at holidays. I have a picture of her here, somewhere. *[pulling it out of his pocketbook, showing it to members, and passing it around the group]* She was my star. She had her hands full with all those children and grandchildren. There were lots of us.

Ms. J.: *[looking at the picture]* Look at the clothes. I can remember wearing a dress like that. And there's a hand-crank phonograph!

Mr. S.: I can remember my dad playing records of Caruso. He used to love his voice. I can remember vividly that dog on the phonograph. The dog had a name, but I can't remember what it was.

Ms. J.: Nipper, I think the dog's name was Nipper.

Ms. J.: Yes, you're right. *[pause]* Families sure were a lot bigger then, and there weren't all of these labor-saving devices we have today.

Mr. S.: This is not exactly a childhood memory, but I think it shows what a dollar meant in those day. I went out and worked at a baseball factory to earn some money after school when I was thirteen or fourteen. I came all the way from south Albany to Menands.

Ms. J.: You walked all that way!

Mr. S.: Sure, how else would I get there?

Ms. W.: Yeah, we were poor, too. I can remember my first job. That was before I got married. I got forty something dollars a week . . .

Ms. A.: Perhaps we should stick to childhood memories. We'll be discussing teen years and adult working years in a few sessions according to the schedule we agreed to in the first session. *[pointing to the board where the schedule of group meetings was posted]* Is that okay? *[nods from members]* We can change our schedule if need be, but let's wait to discuss that until just before we end today. Sound reasonable?

[Members nod]

The dialogue indicates that when members share their memories in early group meetings, they often do so in a parallel fashion, with the common themes among members' memories not always very clear. Ms. A.'s statement reflecting on what two members had in common helped to focus the discussion. Also, her statement asking about what it was like during the Great Depression helped to draw out a member who was waiting for an invitation to speak. Notice that the leader chose to refocus the group away from negative comments about early childhood memories by asking members to describe what it was like in the old days. Throughout the group session, cohesion among members was enhanced by their reflections on what the times were like when they were growing up. In contrast, had the life-review process been used in a therapy group context, the leader might have asked members to reflect on the relationship between their current coping styles and how they were treated as children. At the end of the transcript, Ms. A. obtained the group's agreement to continue with childhood memories, helping them to own the agenda, and giving them a clear signal that their input was welcome. This illustrates that an important leader role in a life-review group is guiding the group discussion and keeping it from drifting from one topic to another with little continuity.

The next portion of the transcript is taken from the eleventh session of the group. Members were asked to think about each developmental period of their lives and to pick the one they enjoyed the most.

Ms. W.: I wanted to say before we start that I've really been enjoying these meetings. I'm not a joiner. But since my husband died, I've been lonely, and needed to do something besides sit at home and think about him. I wasn't so sure I'd like this when I started. But I really look forward to coming, and I've made a number of friends here. In fact I had lunch with Sadie [a group member] on Monday. I really enjoyed it. It's the first time I've been out to lunch in quite a while.

Ms. L. [Sadie]: I really enjoyed it, too!

Ms. A.: Well! I'm so glad to hear that. I think the group is turning out really well, and each of you are responsible for that. *[pause]* Okay, who's going to start sharing about what was the best time of their life?

Ms. C.: The best time of my life was when the children were young. I had my daughter, Becky, and then we had a son. I can remember feeling like I had the world by the tail when he was born because we had one of each. Just what we wanted. There were hard times of course, like the time he got pneumonia. I can remember him getting a shot of penicillin for it. It was brand new then, during World War II. I can remember being so scared he was going to die. But he got better.

MR. B.: When the children were young we did all sorts of activities with them, like taking them to Coney Island. I've got a funny story to tell. Not too long ago my son came home and gave his mother a bottle of aspirins. She asked him what they were for, and he said, "For all those headaches I gave you when I was young." *[laughter from the group]* And he sure did give us a lot of headaches! *[more laughter]*

Ms. C.: Oh! Isn't that something!

Ms. A.: So, despite the hard times you *[referring to both Ms. C. and Mr. B.]* had growing up, things got better.

Ms. C.: Yes, they certainly did. *[Mr. B. nodding]*

MR. B.: I can't complain. I've had a good life.

Ms. J.: I think the best time of my life was before I got married. It was during the Depression. I had to go out and work. You know, that was unusual then, not too many women worked, not like today. I resented it at first, because we had a lot of money when I was growing up. But then my father died. *[pause]* He was a lawyer, so I had to go to work. But you know, it was really okay. I learned how to be independent, that I could make it on my own. I met my husband when I was working. He was staying in the hotel that I was working in at the time. We had great times together. When we were keeping company we'd go exploring all over the state. Once we went to Long Island, near Montauk Point. We liked it so much we bought a small piece of land. Built a cabin on it. We kept that for a while, but then a hurricane came along and blew it down. Here, I brought a picture of it. All the houses around there were so nice. I bet the neighbors were glad when it blew down and they didn't have to look at it anymore!

[laughter from the group]

Ms. A.: Sounds like a nice time in your life.

Ms. J.: Yes, and you know what? Going to work was really good for me. I stopped working after I got married to raise the children. But, when my husband died, I thought a lot about when I used to work. I think it helped me to feel that I could get along on my own, even though I missed him terribly. And recently, I've gone back to bookkeeping, two days a week. I really enjoy it, and the people I work for are really nice to me.

Ms. W.: Well, the best time for me was when I married Jack. I had been married before, and it was horrible. I . . .

Ms. J.: I didn't know that. You were married before Jack! I've known you for so long, and never knew you were married twice.

Ms. W.: Yes, well, eh, I don't talk about it much. You know how it was in the old days. People didn't get divorced. I'm not proud of it. It was a terrible mistake. My parents warned me that he was no good. But, I didn't listen to them. I was so head over heels in love with him. We got married two months after I met him. A really big mistake. Soon, I was miserable. He started running around, never brought home his pay-check. I put up with it for a while, but then one day he came home, we got into an argument, and he hit me. That was it. I moved back with my parents.

Ms. J.: You were smart for leaving when you did. I wouldn't put up with anyone hitting me.

Ms. W.: Yes, I was. And I met Jack. I was lucky. It feels good to talk about it.

Ms. A.: We've all done things we're not proud of. I'm glad you felt good enough about us to trust us with your secret.

The comment by Ms. W. early in this portion of the transcript illustrates that social, recreational, and educational groups can have a significant impact on the lives of older persons, particularly those who have experienced losses and are having difficulty finding replacements for the way they used to spend their time. The middle portion of the transcript illustrates that a life-review/reminiscence group can help members place events in perspective and get in touch with personally meaningful, and especially significant, events in their own lives. For several group members, difficult childhood events were mitigated, somewhat, by the joys of having children and raising them successfully. Also, notice the importance of the death of Ms. J.'s father, how it forced her to go to work, and the profound influence this had on her later development.

The closing comments by Ms. W., Ms. J., and Ms. A. also illustrate the benefits that a social group can have for members. Reminiscing is a spontaneous process in old age, but certain memories are rarely shared with others. The group provides a safe environment for members to share painful memories and to talk about them with others whom they trust. When members are able to share painful memories, they no longer feel so isolated and alone. Also, they become better able to accept, and integrate, parts of themselves that they could not come to terms with earlier in their lives. Thus, social, recreational, and educational groups can provide useful forums for helping older members to successfully negotiate important tasks associated with later life development.

SUMMARY

This chapter has focused on leading social, recreational, and educational groups. It began with a brief description of the characteristics shared in common by social, recreational, and educational groups. Next, methods to engage participants and to maximize the beneficial effects of the groups on participants were discussed. The middle portion of the chapter described a variety of different program activities that are particularly popular with older adults. The chapter concluded with a case example illustrating the use of life-review techniques in a social group with residents of a highrise apartment complex.

8

Working with Service and Advocacy Groups

Service and advocacy groups help members join together to accomplish tasks that benefit themselves, their peers, and the larger society. Examples of service and advocacy groups include

- A residents' council in a nursing home that meets once a month to discuss patients' rights and problems in service delivery within the nursing home.
- A meeting of the Grey Panthers focused on preparing testimony about low-income housing for an upcoming community forum sponsored by a local state senator.
- A tenants' association in a senior citizens' housing project that meets to discuss policies governing residents' behavior and the maintenance of the building.
- A chapter of the Retired Senior Volunteer Program (RSVP) that is actively involved in raising funds and volunteering time to benefit patients in a children's hospital.
- Members of a senior citizens' center who form a service club to visit homebound elderly.

While the other types of groups listed in table 4.4 are designed to provide therapeutic benefits exclusively to their own membership, service and advocacy groups are distinguished by their focus on helping individuals who are not part of the group. For example, members of service groups may visit homebound elderly, they may work as volunteers in a hospital, they may make toys and spend time with toddlers in a day-care center, or they may raise funds for a charitable organization. Although the activities of service groups are therapeutically beneficial to members, the activities of the group generally provide little or no direct benefit to members. In contrast, the operation of advocacy groups may benefit a larger constituency as well as members of the group. For example, changes in policies and practices resulting from the work of a residents' council in a nursing home benefit members of the group as well as all the other residents of the facility.

166

Despite the fact that service and advocacy groups are focused on the needs of a larger community outside the group, many rewards accrue to members who participate in them. Through their involvement in service and advocacy groups, members are able to engage in meaningful social roles. They are given the opportunity to share experience accumulated over a lifetime, to feel good about their ability to contribute to others, and to feel proud of the wisdom and experience they possess.

Service and advocacy groups provide opportunities for members to express their sincere concern for others and to continue to be productive and vital citizens. This, in turn, enables members to successfully negotiate the important later life developmental task of "grand-generativity," that is, caring for, and making meaningful contributions to the larger society as well as to immediate family members (Erikson, Erikson, and Kirmick 1986).

A great deal of satisfaction and pride in one's accomplishments can be derived by performing altruistic deeds in the service of others. Members gain the approval, admiration, and respect of those who benefit from their activities. They feel needed and useful and consider that they are using their time in a worthwhile, meaningful manner.

In service groups, members have an opportunity to socialize with their peers while pursuing their interests and displaying and using their skills and talents in a beneficial manner. Also, for isolated and impaired elderly who sometimes are encouraged to participate in service and advocacy groups, scheduled obligations impart needed structure, offer welcome distractions, and provide an opportunity to escape preoccupation with personal problems (Morris and Bass 1988). Thus, by being a part of a service group, members gain meaningful social roles that can help them avoid anomie and despair even as they are faced with losses of loved ones and reductions in their own capacities and abilities.

In advocacy groups, members can regain a sense of control and self-efficacy in their own lives. They can improve their own living situations as well as the situations of those whom the group represents (see, for example, Atlas and Morris 1971; Cox 1988; Devitt and Checkoway 1982; Horn and Griesel 1977; Newmark 1963). Also, by virtue of those whom they represent, and as a result of the actual or potential impact of their work, members of advocacy groups can gain power and status, two attributes that are often missing in older people's lives.

CHARACTERISTICS OF SERVICE AND ADVOCACY GROUPS

Older persons who consider joining service and advocacy groups often have an idea of what they would like to accomplish as members of the group.

Also, they generally have the potential, if not the actual experience to organize and lead their own self-directed group activities. Therefore, frequently, the primary role of the practitioner in these groups is to help organize, coordinate, and facilitate members' self-directed activities.

In groups with high-functioning members who have the confidence and the experience to operate autonomously, the practitioner is often called upon to serve primarily as a staffer. In this position, the practitioner provides technical assistance and any other aid that the members of the group deem necessary to accomplish their chosen purposes. In some retirement communities, senior housing complexes, and community agencies, older adults essentially direct the practitioner's activities by asking for assistance as they proceed with their own agenda.

Frail members need more assistance to get started. They may not know how to proceed, or they may lack confidence in their own abilities and skills. When working with frail members, practitioners are more likely to play the role of facilitator rather than staffer, working closely with those who demonstrate interest, desire, and leadership potential, helping them in whatever ways are necessary to plan and organize the group. Practitioners support and encourage members' fledgling efforts. They provide energy, enthusiasm, and hope when members encounter obstacles and become pessimistic about their chances of successfully achieving a group goal. This has been referred to as "lending a vision" (Schwartz 1961; Gitterman and Shulman 1986). Also, practitioners help indigenous leaders to identify needed resources, to anticipate obstacles, and to plan strategies for overcoming them.

In situations where members are very frail, practitioners may have to take a very active role in planning and leadership to form and sustain advocacy and service groups. For example, in skilled nursing homes, helping residents to participate in self-governance and to advocate on their own behalf is frequently not an easy task. Without considerable assistance from a practitioner, residents can have great difficulty forming, or sustaining, viable residents' councils (see, for example, Cox 1988; Devitt and Checkoway 1982). Advanced age, chronic physical and mental disabilities, and overmedication limit the amount of physical and psychic energy that members can utilize to participate actively. Also, long-standing policies and practices of nursing facilities frequently contribute to the problem by limiting residents' autonomy and by discouraging them from advocating for changes in routinized procedures.

The composition of service and advocacy groups is not determined by the problems of members, but rather by their personal interests, their desire to share their expertise, and the requirements of the task they wish to accomplish. Frequently, a large membership is desirable because it helps to ensure representation of all viewpoints as well as the person power, knowledge, and skills for a division of labor to accomplish the group's goals.

Service and advocacy groups frequently do not meet as often as the other types of groups described in table 4.4. Monthly or quarterly meetings may be reserved for announcements of new information, reports by the group's officers and subcommittees, and discussion of agenda items that affect the group-as-a-whole. Frequently, much of the day-to-day business of service and advocacy groups is conducted by individual members or by subcommittees that meet between regularly scheduled meetings of the entire group.

High levels of self-disclosure are generally not expected in service and advocacy groups, although as members get to know one another some, or all, may form close friendships that lead to such disclosures. Generally, however, communications are characterized by sharing information, clarifying ideas, and accomplishing specific tasks related to the goals the group has decided to accomplish.

The operating procedures of service and advocacy groups are often more formal than those found in the other types of groups for older persons described in table 4.4. The conduct of meetings may be governed by specific bylaws developed by a governance committee and approved by the membership. A written agenda may be prepared before each meeting. Parliamentary procedures are often used, particularly in large service and advocacy groups, to ensure democratic action, equality of participation, and well-organized, efficiently run meetings. Also, minutes of each meeting are often kept as a record of the business that has been conducted and as a way to inform members who may not be able to attend each meeting and nonmembers who may be interested in, or affected by, the work of the group.

WORKING WITH SERVICE GROUPS

Service group members are generally the well elderly. They are competent and capable individuals who feel fortunate about the kinds of life experiences they have had. Often, they are motivated to participate by their desire to give something back to society and to do something meaningful with their lives.

Sometimes, the impetus for the group comes from the practitioner. He or she identifies and works with individuals who express interest in being part of a service group. In other situations, motivated individuals take the initiative, contacting the worker, sharing their ideas for engaging in a service project, and asking for assistance in planning and developing the group. In either case, the practitioner's primary tasks are to work closely with interested individuals, building their leadership potential, helping them to formulate and clarify what they would like to accomplish in the proposed group, and assisting them to select and pursue meaningful and gratifying service activities.

When some preliminary ideas about the shape of the group have been established, it can be helpful to call a planning meeting, inviting all interested persons to attend. The planning meeting serves several functions: (1) it gives organizers a chance to assess how widespread interest is in the group, (2) it allows for a more extensive discussion of the purposes and goals of the group, and (3) it establishes the role of the worker as someone who stands ready to support and facilitate interested individuals' efforts to organize themselves. Frequently, holding a planning meeting also sparks additional interest in the group.

During the planning stage, the practitioner's primary function is to help members organize themselves. This frequently includes helping members to consider what resources the group will need and what remaining steps need to be taken in order to promote the group's development. It also frequently includes giving potential leaders some tips on how to conduct meetings, how to publicize the group, and how to work with the group's sponsor.

Morris and Bass (1988) point out that there are costs involved in volunteering that may impede members from engaging in service activities. For example, members may be reluctant to spend their own money for the materials needed for service projects or for the use of their own automobiles to go to and from service project sites on a regular basis. Practitioners can be helpful by assisting members to raise the funds that are necessary to cover these expanses.

Practitioners may also be asked to identify worthy service activities. Help members decide what types of activities they would like to engage in and what types of individuals they would like to serve. Also, identify high-quality agencies serving the types of individuals members are interested in serving, and inquire about whether these agencies would be interested in the types of activities the group members have identified. Inquiries should be directed to the volunteer coordinator, if one is available.

When service projects are time-limited, and there is a turnover of volunteers, practitioners often serve in coordinating and linking roles by evaluating the interests and skills of new volunteers, identifying appropriate service projects, matching volunteers' talents and interests to available service opportunities, making initial introductions, and ensuring that both the group members and the recipients of the service remain satisfied with the arrangements that have been made.

As the group develops, practitioners may be called upon for guidance in the development of bylaws and for the resolution of interpersonal conflicts or other problems in group functioning. Also, members may ask practitioners to provide technical assistance regarding the handling of problems that are encountered when performing service activities. For example, with the help of a county grant prepared by the practitioner, one service group was able to reimburse members for mileage for a friendly visiting program targeted at frail, homebound elderly persons. When making these visits, members occasionally encountered persons who had needs that they did not know how to service. On these occasions, the worker provided advice, consultation, and crisis intervention. In another situation, volunteers were placed in many different public and voluntary health and social service agencies in a large urban area. Occasionally, volunteers became dissatisfied with their placement, or the agency became dissatisfied with the volunteer's performance. In these situations, the practitioner investigated the situation, helped to determine how it could be improved, and acted as a mediator between the host agency and the volunteer to resolve conflicts and concerns.

WORKING WITH ADVOCACY GROUPS

When the concept of an advocacy group is introduced, practitioners should be prepared to encounter strong emotional reactions among potential members, and among those who may have to deal with the consequences of the group's actions (Getzel 1983). Some may feel that meeting as a group will be futile. Others may view the work of the group with suspicion because it threatens the status quo. One of the first tasks of the worker, therefore, is to be able to articulate the purpose of the group, indicating why its formation will be beneficial rather than harmful. McDermott (1989), for example, points out that when describing the purpose of a resident's rights campaign to the agency's administration and staff, instead of emphasizing such negative issues as patient abuse, the practitioner emphasized elders' capacity for reasoned decision making, and the good publicity and improved public image that would accrue to the facility as a result of sponsoring the campaign.

In situations where the group is likely to be a threat to the status quo, the worker should assess how likely it is for vested interests to attempt to sabotage the group's development, planning strategies in advance to overcome the potential threat. For example, when establishing a resident's council in a nursing home, it is helpful to begin by developing good relationships with administrators, department heads, and other key personnel in the facility, asking for and considering their input, discussing and addressing their concerns, and enlisting their support.

It is also important to interpret the needs and the perceptions of residents in a way that points out how particular policies and practices needlessly limit residents' autonomy. Indicate, for example, how an advocacy group would permit residents to have greater input into the day-to-day operation of the nursing home without causing undue disruption. Also, in some situations, it can be helpful to refer to standards and policies to which the administrators of the facility have committed themselves. This should not be done in a threatening manner, but rather with the attitude that the individuals involved wish to adhere to these standards and policies and that their intentions have been inadvertently undermined by the practices that have developed and evolved in the facility.

The frail elderly are often not very responsive to initial efforts to get them involved in advocacy groups (Cox 1988; Devitt and Checkoway 1982). In addition to their lack of physical energy, some fear sanctions and reprisals if they participate. When reluctance is encountered, it is often helpful to begin by establishing a personal relationship with potential members, gaining their trust, allowing them to disclose their fears and their reluctance about participating, and pointing out why their participation is important.

It is important to address any fears of reprisals that are expressed, discussing with potential members the nature of these, how likely they are to occur, and what can be done about them should they be encountered. When a relationship has been established and elderly individuals' fears about reprisals are considered and dealt with, they are much more likely to follow through on the practitioner's invitation to become a member of an advocacy group.

It is also important to make it convenient for members to get to meetings so that they do not have to expend too much energy to participate. For example, meetings of residents' councils may be held on each floor of a skilled nursing facility. Groups that meet on each floor could then send one or more representatives to a meeting of an executive council that would, in turn, deliberate about issues to be presented to the home's administrators. Similarly, access to a van may be needed to transport some older adults who do not drive or have access to public transportation, so that they can attend meetings held in a senior center.

There are several organizational issues that often need to be addressed when planning advocacy groups for the elderly. Although the ideal situation is for members to decide on their own structure for the group, experience suggests that in some situations members are not able to do so (see, for example, Devitt and Checkoway 1982). Thus, the worker is sometimes put in the position of taking a significant role in organizing the group. In nursing homes, senior housing programs, and other settings where there is a defined constituency, the practitioner should consider organizing an election so that members can choose the officers of their group. This approach has many benefits: it introduces members to the use of democratic processes that can be used later within the newly formed group; it often raises interest in the group and adds to the power and prestige of the elected officers; and it helps members to articulate their positions and their ideas for the group.

Unfortunately, elections are sometimes responded to with apathy (see, for example, Devitt and Checkoway 1982). In these situations, the practitioner should encourage those interested in leadership positions to assume the role for a specified time period, serving as the first officers of the newly formed group until greater interest can be generated and a second election can be held.

Another organizational issue has to do with the development of a structure for group meetings. The ideal situation is for members of a newly formed group to decide on bylaws and a structure for meetings. Again, however, experience suggests that in some contexts members find this difficult. One alternative is for the worker to suggest an organizational structure for the group that members can then modify as the group develops. Another is for the leader to actively assist members to consider different organizational frameworks in the first few group meetings. Although the first alternative creates less confusion and greater role definition and is usually readily accepted by members, the second alternative can result in greater investment in the group by its members.

As advocacy groups move from beginning, formative phases to middle, work phases, practitioners have four primary tasks: (1) to facilitate linkages and communication between the group and those who are in a position to implement the changes, (2) to encourage the fullest possible participation by those whose interests are being represented, (3) to enhance systematic problem-solving efforts, and (4) to ensure the group's continued development and effective functioning.

A number of steps can be taken to facilitate linkages between advocacy groups and those who are in a position to make the changes in policies, procedures, and practices that are the targets of the group's actions. One step is to invite key decision-makers to group meetings to learn about their perceptions of a problematic situation, to inform them about members' perceptions, and to discuss ways to improve it. For example, the head of the dietary department is invited regularly to meetings of a resident's council formed in an intermediate care facility to learn about members' concerns about the menu plan and the way food is served.

When inviting influential individuals to the group, it is important to welcome them as collaborators and advisors in the change process, rather than as adversaries. The latter approach often is counterproductive because it heightens tension, hardens positions, increases resistance to change, and may even heighten feelings of animosity. Before the individual arrives, suggest to members that they consider toning down quarrelsome comments, pointing out how these have the potential to damage their cause. Instead, encourage members to begin by pointing out what is being done well by the individual who has been invited and what positive changes, if any, have occurred since the last time the person was invited to a meeting. Then, encourage members to present problems, issues, and concerns in a firm but respectful and courteous manner. Also encourage members to be open to feedback about what they could do to contribute to, or bring about, the desired changes they are requesting.

During the meeting, seek out and highlight values, concerns, and interests held in common by the group and the individual who has been invited. Do not magnify or highlight differences. Instead, clarify confusing communications and help negotiate an acceptable settlement when conflicts arise, drawing upon the common values and interests that have been uncovered. Help the group and the invited individual to commit themselves to a plan of action to resolve the concerns that are raised, and set a time when progress on reaching the agreed-upon goals can be reviewed.

Between meetings, facilitate communication between group members and key decision-makers. When there is poor communication, group members frequently erroneously conclude that key decision-makers do not care about their needs. For their part, key decision-makers sometimes dismiss the concerns of the elderly. Taking sides will place the group, the practitioner, and key decision-makers in adversarial positions that are often counterproductive. Instead, the most effective approach in most situations is for the practitioner to act as a mediator. Interpret the needs of members to those in a position to respond. Help members to understand the constraints on those in decision making capacities, and how they are planning to respond.

Another approach to establishing linkages is to set up regularly scheduled meetings between designated individuals from the advocacy group and those individuals who make the policy decisions and supervise the personnel that affect the group and its constituency. End such meetings by clarifying how particular issues will be resolved, by specifying commitments, and by designating a time line for their implementation. For example, the cochairs of the previously mentioned residents' council have a regularly scheduled meeting with the facility's administrator in which they share examples of situations needing change and ideas and suggestions made during council meetings for addressing these situations. The cochairs report the results of their meetings with the facility's administrator during the next meeting of the residents' council, and also in a column reserved for this purpose that is part of a newsletter prepared by the facility on a quarterly basis.

A third way to establish linkages is to reach out and gain the attention and support of community leaders, the general public, and the larger constituency served by the group. This tactic is especially useful when cooperation is not forthcoming from key decision-makers who have the power to implement the group's recommendations. Members of advocacy groups can testify at public hearings, meet with and write to civic officials, prepare newspaper releases, appear on radio and television public service programs, engage in networking and coalition building with state and national advocacy groups such as the American Association of Retired Persons, the Grey Panthers, or the National Council on Aging, and, if necessary, engage in picketing and other demonstrations.

As the group develops, practitioners should encourage the fullest possible participation by all members who are represented by an advocacy group. In community settings, this may mean arranging for transportation, scheduling meetings at convenient times and in convenient locations, and helping to protect members from threats, reprisals, and other sanctions they may encounter as a result of their participation in the group. In institutional settings, it may mean reminding members about meetings, helping them to get to meetings, and gaining assurances from administrators that residents can express their opinions without fear of reprisal.

To help advocacy groups achieve their goals during the middle phase, several experts also recommend the use of systematic problem-solving procedures (see, for example, Lowy 1985; Cox 1987; Perlman and Gurin 1971). An effective problem-solving model for advocacy groups includes the following steps: (1) defining the problem to be resolved, (2) gathering information about it, (3) defining alternative action plans, (4) examining each alternative for its strengths and weaknesses, (5) developing an action plan from among the alternatives, (6) planning a strategy for the implementation of the action plan, (7) implementing the action plan, (8) evaluating and monitoring its impact, and (9) revising the plan and reimplementing it as necessary.

To ensure the continued development and effective ongoing functioning of advocacy groups, practitioners should stand ready to help members overcome any obstacles that they may encounter as the group continues to meet. For example, there may be a crisis in leadership when a founding member of the group dies, when the group encounters resistance to its initiatives, when a particular issue causes conflict among members, or when the group finds it needs technical assistance to achieve one of its objectives.

Whatever the obstacle, the support and assistance of a concerned professional can often be invaluable in helping the group to sustain itself through difficult periods in its development.

CASE

The residents' council of the Ann Taylor highrise apartment complex evolved from a previous group. Initially, a group of residents were recruited for a research project evaluating the effects of two different approaches to the use of reminiscence techniques in groups (see Sherman 1987). As the group approached its planned termination date, members expressed interest in continuing to meet. The leader spoke with the research director, mentioning the group's interest and the fact that she could not continue to lead the group. He told her that he knew someone who was interested in leading a group and that, from his perspective, it would be fine to encourage the members to continue meeting. The leader shared this information with group members, and a meeting with the new leader was arranged. The following dialogue took place when the new leader, Ms. F., was introduced to the group.

Ms. P.: I'd like to introduce you to Mrs. F. She has volunteered to facilitate the group after I leave.

[The members smile, greeting Ms. F. cordially.]

Ms. F.: I'm really looking forward to meeting with you! I've talked with Ms. P. about what you've been doing. Ms. P. mentioned that you wanted to do something different from the reminiscing you've been doing, but she said you were rather uncertain about what that might be.

Mr. M.: Well, yes, I guess that's right *[looking around the group]*. I don't want to speak for everybody but I think it's fair to say that we've really enjoyed these meetings, getting to know each other, and the reminiscing has helped us to get closer, to really get to know each other. I don't know if you understand what I mean?

Ms. F.: The sharing of your pasts has helped you get to know each other?

Mr. M.: Right.

Ms. F.: Did you know each other before. I mean, before you came to the group?

Ms. C.: A few of us knew each other. For example, my husband and I, his name is Tom *[turning for a moment to her husband]*, play bridge with Ann and Dave *[smiling at Mr. and Ms. M.]*, and I've known Mrs. Z. for many years. We went to high school together.

Ms. F.: Really! Isn't that something. Small world, isn't it?

Ms. C.: Yes, it really is. But I didn't know anyone else, except to say hello in the hall to a couple [of the members] who live in the same building as me. You see, there are three towers here, and each one has fifteen floors. That's a lot of people.

Ms. F.: Oh, I see. I knew it was a big place, but I didn't know how big. I guess you're going to have to help me learn about what it's like to live here, and about you. *[pause]* Has that been the experience of the rest of you, I mean getting to know each other through the group? *[scanning the group]*

Ms. D.: I didn't know anyone when I came to the first meeting.

Ms. T.: Neither did I. But it sure has been good! I really hope we can continue to meet.

Ms. Y.: So do I.

[Other members nod.]

Ms. F.: Well, I hope so too. So, what would you like to do? Any ideas?

[Silence]

Ms. P.: You know, I've been thinking. There's no residents' council or anything like that in this complex. The management just seems to run things the way they think best.

Ms. B.: That's a laugh. They don't care about us.

Ms. P.: The members have complained from time to time about the building management.

Ms. Y.: That's an understatement if I ever heard one!

[Laughter from the group]

Mr. J.: I sure would like to do something about organizing the residents [of the buildings].

Mr. C.: Mr. J. has been after us to do something for a long while. He's right to. Something has to be done. But nobody knows what to do. Do you know, they just had new elevators put into Tower 2. I don't know if any of you are aware of it. *[to Ms. F.]* They're brand new. But the doors close so fast they're really a problem for the slower residents. Why one women in her eighties was knocked over last week. But, the management doesn't seem to care. I guess they'll wait till someone gets knocked over and breaks a hip!

Ms. P.: Well. I'd like to continue this, but we have some things to finish up.

Ms. F.: Oh, I'm sorry for interrupting. We can talk more about what we're going to do together next week.

Ms. P.: Not at all. It's just that with the research, and all, we have some forms to fill out today.

Ms. F.: Oh yes, I understand.

Ms. P.: Would you like to plan on meeting at this same time? How about it, everybody? *[Members nod or voice their agreement.]* Is that okay with you, Mrs. F.?

Ms. F.: Oh yes, I was hoping that would be the case. I've set aside the time. See you all next week.

Mr. J.: Just one thing.

Ms. P.: What is it, Mr. J.?

Mr. J.: Well, I know of at least one other person who'd like to come. Is that okay now that we're going to end the research part?

Ms. F.: It's okay with me. But why don't we hold off until next week, and see if everybody is comfortable with that. Okay?

[scanning the group]

Mr. J.: Sure.

This first portion of the dialogue illustrates how the group evolved. Notice that the new leader was very positive about the prospects for the group making a transition and about her role in it. Notice also members' frustration and sense of discouragement and futility regarding the building management.

The following week when Ms. F. met with the group, much of the time was spent getting to know members. A number of ideas about how to proceed were also discussed, including turning the group into an arts and crafts group or a service group. Near the end of the following group session, the following dialogue occurred.

Ms. F.: I'm getting the sense that you have some pretty strong feelings about the way Ann Taylor Apartments are run, but you feel frustrated and powerless about what to do about it.

Ms. Y.: I guess you could say that. If you open your mouth and say anything, their response is, if you don't like it here, leave.

Ms. F.: Has anyone actually said that?

Ms. Y.: Oh, yes, Miss T., I heard her myself. But she's not the only one, they're all like that.

Ms. F.: Who is Miss T.?

Ms. Y.: She's one of the girls who sits in the office, collects our rent, reports plumbing problems, you know.

Ms. F.: When you say they're all like that, who in particular are you referring to besides Miss T.?

Ms. C.: Mrs. A. is nice. She's also in the office most of the time. But Mrs. Y. is right about Miss T. She's awful. Acts like she owns the place.

Ms. F.: Who besides Miss T. is a problem?

Mr. J.: I think it's a general attitude, right on down from Mr. B., the director of the complex. For example, if you get sick, they immediately want to get you out of your apartment. They don't want people in wheelchairs or anything, even if it's only temporary. They want to move you to the nursing home across the street.

Ms. F.: Do you know people who have been asked to leave?

Mr. J.: Not personally, but I've heard rumors to that effect.

Mr. C.: They certainly don't seem like they care, I mean the management. They don't ask for our opinion about anything, and when we give it they don't pay any attention to it.

Ms. F.: Is that how you all feel? *[scanning the group]* Then why don't you do something about it? Why not organize a group to speak up on your behalf, a residents' council, where the facts would come out and the residents could decide together what to do about problems that come up? We could start with this group, and invite others to join us.

Ms. B.: They wouldn't like that.

Ms. F.: Who's they?

Ms. B.: Mr. B., Mrs. J., and the rest of the staff.

Ms. F.: Let me see, Mr. B. is the director. Who is Mrs. J.?

Ms. B.: Mrs. J. is the assistant director. *[pause]* Besides, Miss T. could make life really difficult, if she wanted to.

Ms. F.: How?

Ms. B.: Oh, ask you to leave. Raise your rent. Conveniently forget about making repairs when you let her know about a problem. Things like that.

Ms. F.: Are the rest of you afraid of what might happen if you speak up?

Ms. M.: Well, it is nice here. The rent is low. And what's the sense of causing trouble? It won't do any good anyway.

Ms. F.: Pretty pessimistic about the chances of success, eh? *[silence]* What about the rest of you? What do you think about all of this?

Mr. J.: I think we should form a group to stick up for ourselves. It's a good idea. I'm not worried about what they'll do.

Ms. S.: I wonder how the administration would really react? *[pause]* I mean, I wonder if they really would try to get back at us for speaking out?

Ms. Z.: What would it [the residents' council] do? Would you be willing to help us get started? *[looking at Ms. F.]*

Ms. F.: What it would do would be up to you. Generally, a residents' council works with administration to improve living conditions. And, sure, I'd be willing to help you get started. You know several years ago when I was living in Chicago, I worked with a community action group in a poor neighborhood. It was quite effective. We got a lot accomplished. Started a crime watch program, a neighborhood beautification program, and a number of other programs. I can remember when we first met, some of the members were afraid of reprisals from drug dealers, landlords, kids in the neighborhood. But that never materialized. I think they

were surprised when people began to stick up for themselves. And
there's strength in numbers.

Ms. D.: Yes, but you don't know what it's like around here. They won't
care what we say.

Mr. J.: How do we know unless we try?

Ms. D.: Well, that's true.

Ms. F.: I wonder. You know Mrs. D. is right. I don't know what it's like,
and I'm not well known here. How about if I introduce myself to Mr. B.,
Mrs. J., and the staff in the office. Get to know them a little bit, what
they're concerned about, and what they think about the idea of a residents' council. We won't be meeting next week because of the holiday. I
could try to meet with them in the next couple of weeks and report what
happened at our next meeting.

Mr. J.: Good idea.

Mr. C.: I agree.

Ms. F.: What about the rest of you? *[Almost everyone nods in agreement.]*
What about you, Miss B., and you, Mrs. S.?

Ms. B.: I'm all for it.

Ms. S.: You won't mention our names, will you? I mean, what we said
here. I don't trust them.

Ms. F.: I'm glad you brought that up. No. As we agreed at the beginning,
what is said here stays here. Meanwhile, since I'm not well known here,
Mr. J., will you and anyone else who cares to ask around and find out if
other residents have any interest in forming a resident's council? Also,
you can invite the member you mentioned last week to our next meeting. Okay? *[scanning the group]*

[Members nod]

Mr. J.: Be happy to.

Notice that much of the dialogue in this portion of the transcript was
spent helping members to share how they perceived their situation. Ms. F.
dealt directly with members' feelings of helplessness and fears of reprisal.
A number of times she attempted to help members become clearer and
more concrete about vague statements. By offering to meet with the
administrators of the apartment complex, she began the task of establishing
a linkage between the group and those who were in a position to implement
recommended policy changes.

In this situation, it turned out that management was quite supportive of
the idea of the residents' council. When Ms. F. met with Mr. B. and Ms.
J., both expressed their surprise at their supposed lack of interest. They
said that they had been thinking about starting a residents' council but that
they were short-staffed and had never gotten around to attempting to

organize the residents. They said they would welcome the input. For example, they said that they had not heard about the problem with the elevator doors. They also mentioned that this would be a good time to make any changes in the elevators, since they were newly installed in Building 2 and would soon be installed in the other two buildings.

Over the course of the next six months, Ms. F. helped Mr. J. and the other members of the original group to form a residents' council. After four more weekly meetings, and much between-meeting work, an organizational meeting was held. Those who attended (eighteen individuals) decided to meet on a monthly basis. At its first regular meeting, the group elected officers from those who were present, and Mr. J. was selected as the first president. Mr. B. and Ms. J. continued to be supportive of the residents' council. Ms. J. became the liaison to the officers of the group, meeting with them once a month and coming to meetings as requested. Ms. F. continued to provide consultation to the leadership and the membership of the newly formed group.

SUMMARY

This chapter has focused on the skills a practitioner needs to work with service and advocacy groups. Characteristics that distinguish service and advocacy groups from other types of groups of older adults were described in the first portion of the chapter. The second portion of the chapter was focused on tasks associated with facilitating service groups, such as finding worthy service activities and matching volunteers with available service opportunities. The third portion of the chapter then described the particular skills needed to lead advocacy groups, such as how to motivate members, how to work with key decision-makers, and how to help organize and structure meetings. The chapter concluded with a case example illustrating an advocacy group in action.

9

Group Work with Family Caregivers of the Frail Elderly

Because family caregivers play an important role in the lives of frail older persons, the last chapter of this book considers group work methods to support these individuals. Examples of groups to support family caregivers include

- A one-session community forum and educational seminar in which health care and social service providers discuss available community resources and services for the frail elderly and their family caregivers.
- A group for adult children caring for frail parents that is sponsored by a family service agency.
- A group for those who have family members residing in a skilled nursing facility.
- A group for spouses caring for aging veterans that is sponsored by an adult day health care center of a Veterans Administration Hospital.
- A group sponsored by a local chapter of the Alzheimer's Disease and Related Disorders Foundation.

IMPORTANCE OF FAMILY CAREGIVERS

Informal caregiving by family members is by far the most common means of providing community care to frail older persons (U.S. Department of Health and Human Services 1982). Nearly 5.1 million older persons living in the community require assistance with some aspect of personal care or home management in order to maintain independent living (AARP 1986). Nearly three quarters of these individuals rely solely on family and friends to meet their long-term care needs, with most of the remainder relying on a combination of family care and paid help (Doty 1986). The need for care ranges from occasional assistance with specific tasks, such as shopping and household chores, to around-the-clock monitoring of serious health problems.

Frail older persons without family caregivers are much more likely to be found in nursing homes (U.S. Senate Special Committee on Aging 1987, 1988). However, helping to prevent premature institutionalization is only one aspect of the contribution that family caregivers make to the quality of life of the frail elderly. The kind of high-quality, round-the-clock, personalized care provided by loving family members who are intimately familiar with the capacities, needs, and desires of frail family members can't be duplicated even by the most dedicated and skilled of professional caregivers.

Even when the health-care needs of frail family members warrant professional intervention, including hospitalization or placement in a nursing home, family caregivers continue to play an important role in the family member's life, often attending support groups sponsored by the nursing home where their relative is placed. Although most caregiver support groups are offered for those who care for community residing elderly, nursing homes and other institutional settings also frequently offer groups for family members of residents. These groups offer members an opportunity to learn more about the care of their relatives and the operation of the facility. Members are encouraged to discuss their own adjustment and the adjustment of their relative. Also, members can learn how to relate better to their relatives when they visit and how to advocate for their relative when they believe there are deficits in the care that they receive (see, for example, Kilen 1978; Lovegren and Rosenberg 1978; Greenberg 1978).

Despite the superiority of family caregivers in most situations, practitioners should not automatically assume that family caregiving is the best arrangement in all situations. When family relationships are severely strained and there is a long-standing history of interpersonal conflict, older adults may be better off being cared for by professional and paraprofessional caregivers than by family members.

CAREGIVER SUPPORT GROUPS

A number of studies have demonstrated that group intervention is effective for supporting family caregivers (see, for example, Green and Monahan 1987; Lovett and Gallagher 1988; Montgomery and Borgotta 1989; Toseland and Rossiter 1989; Toseland, Rossiter, and Labrecque 1989a, 1989b, 1989c; Zarit, Anthony and Boutselis 1987). There are many ways that caregiver groups can prevent and alleviate the stress that results from caring for a frail family member, including (1) providing caregivers with a respite from caregiving, (2) reducing isolation and loneliness, (3) encouraging the ventilation of pent-up emotions and the sharing of feelings and experiences in a supportive atmosphere, (4) validating, universalizing, and normalizing caregivers' thoughts, feelings, and experiences, (5) instilling hope and affirming the importance of the caregiver's role, (6) educating caregivers about the aging process, the effects of chronic disabilities, and community resources, (7) teaching effective problem-solving and coping strategies, and (8) helping caregivers to identify, develop, and implement effective action plans to resolve pressing problems related to caregiving (Toseland and Rossiter 1989; Toseland, Rossiter, Peak, and Hill in press).

THE NATURE OF FAMILY CAREGIVING

To work effectively with family caregivers, it is important for practitioners to understand who these individuals are and the nature of their needs. The responsibility for the care of a frail elderly relative is rarely shared equally by all family members. Although some degree of shared responsibility is common, there is generally one primary caregiver in a family. The decision about who will provide care follows a "principle of substitution" (Shanas 1968). If a spouse is available, he or she is most likely to provide care. If not, then an adult daughter is most likely to become the primary caregiver. In the absence of an adult daughter, a son or a daughter-in-law is most likely to provide care. If none of these family members are available, other relatives, neighbors, and friends are the next most likely to provide care. Practitioners should be aware that the differential sharing of caregiving responsibilities among family members can cause conflict, particularly among siblings, because the primary caregiver may become angered by the lack of involvement of brothers or sisters in the care of a parent.

Caregiving situations vary considerably depending on the nature, extent, and duration of the disabilities experienced by the care receiver and on each caregiver's unique response to his or her particular caregiving situation. Factors such as the health, marital status, sex, personality, and coping style of the caregiver make a difference, as do such factors as whether the caregiver and the care receiver live together and what the nature of their kin relationship is. For example, adult children tend to be more concerned than spousal caregivers with the involvement of their siblings in the care of a frail parent and with balancing the demands of caregiving with the needs of their own family, whereas spousal caregivers tend to provide more extensive care, and for longer periods of time, than do adult children. Similarly, female caregivers tend to provide more hands-on care than do male caregivers (see, for example, Young and Kahana 1989). Recognition of the variability among caregivers is essential for meeting their individual needs within the group context.

Although every caregiving situation is unique, there are nevertheless some universal issues faced by caregivers. Brody (1985) has suggested that a central issue confronting caregivers is their ability to understand, accept, and meet the dependency needs of care receivers. It can be difficult to care for someone upon whom a caregiver has previously depended. Dependency needs may be perceived as particularly stressful when they are manifested in ways that are unpleasant or pathological. Dealing with a parent's incontinence, for example, is different from dealing with the incontinence of an infant. Also, dependency needs are often made more difficult by the inherently unstable and unpredictable nature of care receivers' physical conditions. Caregivers frequently find it difficult to make plans to enjoy any leisure time they may have because their care receiver's health status can change rapidly. Caregivers are constantly on call. They worry about small changes in the care receiver's health, fearing that these may be precursors of larger declines.

Caregiving produces a heightened awareness of the potential loss of a loved family member and of the caregiver's own potential dependence and death. It is normative for caregivers to experience feelings of loss and of grief as they watch a family member decline (Gallagher 1985). Although grief cannot be completely resolved until some time after the care receiver dies, practitioners can be helpful by validating anticipatory mourning as normative and by facilitating the caregiver's movement through stages of the grieving process.

Grieving processes are most noticeable prior to death when care receivers have chronic illnesses such as Alzheimer's disease, with which there is a long period of decline involving changes to which the caregiver must continually adjust. For example, accepting the initial diagnosis of Alzheimer's disease requires a different type of adaptation than eventually accepting the care receiver as a greatly changed person who will never again be the same. Practitioners should use their knowledge of adaptation to loss and grief when working with groups of family caregivers. It can be helpful to share with group members their knowledge of the grieving process, to help members locate themselves in the process, and to affirm and support caregivers' efforts to adapt to continuously changing caregiving situations.

Caregiving is rewarding to those who take pride in being able to help a loved relative, but it is also extremely demanding. Caregiving often involves a long-term commitment that can severely stress the resources of even the most dedicated family member. Stress from caregiving can have a negative effect on the caregiver's emotional, social, and physical well-being. For example, symptoms of depression and clinically diagnosable depressive disorders have been reported to occur at a much higher rate among family caregivers than the general population (see, for example, Coppel, Burton,

Becker, and Fiore 1985; Gallagher et al. 1989; Myers et al. 1984). Caregivers are also frequently troubled by anxiety, anger, interpersonal sensitivity, hostility, frustration, and excessive guilt and self-blame.

Caregiving can contribute to social and interpersonal problems by restricting leisure and recreational activities. Caregivers frequently feel trapped in their socially isolating situations (Farkas 1980). Conflicts with other family members about caregiving responsibilities are common (Cantor 1983).

Physical problems such as disturbance of normal sleep patterns, problems with appetite, and psychosomatic difficulties are also common among family caregivers (Golodetz, Evans, Heinitz, and Gibson 1969). Lifting, toileting, transporting, and other physical demands of caregiving can be exhausting and can cause back injuries and other problems because many caregivers have little or no prior experience providing for care receivers' physical needs and are not aware of the most effective techniques.

The specific type of assistance provided by family caregivers is a better predictor of stress than the actual amount of effort expended (Horowitz 1985). For example, personal care tasks such a toileting, bathing, lifting, and transferring are often thought to be particularly stressful because they demand great physical stamina from spousal caregivers and an uncomfortable degree of intimacy from adult children.

The type of impairment also makes a difference in the level of stress experienced by caregivers. For example, Horowitz (1985) has suggested that it is "the appearance or worsening of mental, rather than physical, symptomology that is most stressful to families" (215). However, others have pointed out the complex interaction between objective and subjective burden. For example, Montgomery (1989) has suggested that caregiver stress is a function of both the degree and kind of care provided and the caregivers' expectations and resources. Thus, when assessing caregiver needs and how to best support them within the group context, practitioners should consider both the objective demands of the caregiving situation and caregivers' subjective responses to their particular situation.

ESTABLISHING CAREGIVER GROUPS

Because of the different experiences and issues faced by adult children and spousal caregivers, and by male and female caregivers, practitioners should consider developing homogenous groups based on these characteristics (Zarit in press; Zarit and Toseland 1989). Cohesion and intimacy tend to develop more rapidly in homogenous caregiver groups, and members are able to focus on issues that are particularly pertinent to their familial relationship with the care receiver.

Other issues in group composition, such as whether groups should be specific to a disease or heterogeneous and whether the group should have a professional or a peer leader, should be considered prior to recruiting participants. Regarding the issue of disease specificity, there is some preliminary evidence in the literature that caring for those with mental disabilities such as dementia may be more stressful than caring for those with physical disabilities (see, for example, Birkel 1987). Although additional research is needed, if a large enough pool of potential participants is available, clinical experience suggests that it is useful to develop separate groups for caregivers of those with dementia and other mental health problems and for caregivers of those with physical disabilities. Such an approach allows the practitioner to focus the content of the group more specifically and encourages the rapid development of mutual support, mutual empathy, and cohesion. However, the benefits of recruiting homogenous groups of caregivers should be weighed against the practical problems of recruiting a sufficient number of participants to form a viable group.

Regarding the question of professional versus peer leadership, analyses of audiotaped group sessions and empirical data from a recent study on caregiver support groups (Toseland, Rossiter, and Labrecque 1989a,b,c; Toseland, Rossiter, Peak, and Hill in press) revealed that well-supervised peer leaders can lead caregiver support groups as effectively as can professional leaders. However, the study also revealed that professional leaders may be needed to lead more intensive follow-up groups for selected participants who are experiencing severe psychiatric symptoms, and for those who wish to explore long-standing interpersonal conflicts in their relationship with the frail family member for who they are caring.

Making initial contact with a sufficient number of caregivers to begin a group can be difficult. Caregivers tend to be reluctant to ask for help. Most believe that it is their filial responsibility to provide care. Seeking help is sometimes perceived as abandoning their responsibility and the person for whom they are caring. Because many have never had to ask for help before, pride can also be an obstacle. Even for motivated caregivers, resistance to "outside help" by the frail older person, and the bewildering complexity of the social service and health care system, also present obstacles to help seeking.

Active outreach efforts in the form of feature newspaper stories, personal or telephone contacts with social service, health care, and religious organizations that frequently come into contact with frail older persons, public service announcements on radio and television, appearances on local radio and television programs, and educational forums sponsored by community agencies are sometimes needed to engage a sufficiently large group of family caregivers to begin a group. Also, special recruitment efforts may be needed for Hispanic, Afro-American, and Asian minorities, who do not respond well to the recruitment methods just described (Toseland and Rossiter 1989). Extensive personal contact with religious and civic leaders and networking with community organizations trusted in minority communities are particularly effective approaches for reaching this population (Garcia-Preto 1982; Roberts 1987).

In some situations, caregivers seek help only for themselves. They want to learn to cope more effectively, but do not want the care receiver or other family members to know about their planned participation in a group. In such situations, caregivers' wishes should be respected. But, when confidentiality is not a problem, it can be useful for the practitioner to make a direct assessment of the care receiver and other family members. One or more family meetings can give the group worker a more complete understanding of the situation.

For screening purposes, and for preparing caregivers for what to expect in a group, an intake interview is often helpful. During the interview, the practitioner should assess the extent of stress a caregiver is experiencing. When considering treatment options, practitioners should be aware that participation in a caregiver group can be particularly beneficial for socially isolated individuals and for those who need emotional support or better problem-solving and coping skills. For those who are extremely stressed or who have mental health problems, individual counseling is the treatment of choice (Toseland, Rossiter, Peak, and Smith in press).

During the intake interview, the worker should carefully listen to what potential members would like to get out of the group and should prepare them for what to expect. In addition to describing any previous groups the worker has facilitated, it can be useful to show a brief film of a caregiver support group in action.[1]

LEADING CAREGIVER GROUPS

There are many different types of support group programs for family caregivers. Some are time-limited whereas others are long-term. Some have closed membership policies whereas others are open to whomever comes to group meetings. Many use a combination of education and discussion in an empathic and supportive atmosphere that emphasizes mutual sharing and mutual help, but some are more psychoeducationally oriented,

1. Two excellent films are *Time to Care,* which can be obtained by writing the New York State Office for the Aging, 2 Empire State Plaza, Albany, New York 12223; and *In Care Of: Families and Their Elders,* which can be obtained by writing the Brookdale Center on Aging of Hunter College, 425 East 25th Street, New York, New York 10010.

focusing on the acquisition of specific problem-solving and coping skills (Toseland and Rossiter 1989).

The following topics are frequently addressed in caregiver support groups: (1) understanding the elderly relatives for whom members are caring, (2) helping caregivers make better use of informal and formal social supports, (3) improving caregivers' coping abilities, (4) helping caregivers take better care of themselves by balancing the needs of others with their own needs, (5) helping caregivers improve problematic relationships with the care receiver and other family members, and (6) improving caregivers' home-care and behavior-management skills.

During group meetings, caregivers can gain valuable information about the processes of aging and the progression of specific ailments. Understanding disease processes helps caregivers to anticipate and plan for future caregiving demands. Also, it can help them to improve their relationship with the frail relative for whom they are caring. Learning more about what the care receiver is going through, both physically and emotionally, can help caregivers become more tolerant of the care receiver's behavior. It can help them to attribute the care receiver's problematic behavior to the situation rather than to deliberate malice (Smith and Sperbeck 1980). Also, caregivers become less likely to take care receivers' emotional outbursts and negative interactions personally and are able to react with increased empathy and understanding.

Caregivers can become overwhelmed when they do not get enough help from siblings and other family members in sharing the responsibilities of caregiving. In some situations, family members are simply not willing to share the responsibilities of caregiving. However, in other situations, it is caregivers' reluctance to ask for help, rather than the reticence of family members, that results in the failure to share greater responsibility. Therefore, during group meetings it is important to help caregivers accurately assess their need for assistance and explore the reasons for their reluctance to ask for help from other family members. The group interaction that results from such an inquiry can motivate members to make specific requests of brothers, sisters, and other family members. Experience with many different caregiver groups suggests that when these requests are clearly focused and specific, they often meet with success.

Caregivers also frequently lack information about formal sources of support and about whether their frail relatives are eligible to receive particular services. In groups, caregivers can learn together about what resources are available and about how to access them. Also, they can learn about the benefits and drawbacks of using particular resources directly from the experiences shared by their fellow group members.

Caregivers frequently need help to develop more effective coping strategies. Many different coping strategies are used by family caregivers (Quayhagen and Quayhagen 1988), but all are not equally effective. For example, passivity, fantasizing, and self-blame are associated with health and mental health problems whereas active problem solving, information seeking, and logical analysis are associated with emotional and physical well-being (Haley, Levine, Brown, and Bartolucci 1987; Pratt, Schmall, Wright, and Cleland 1985). Coping skills training can be effective in changing patterns of adaptation, thereby reducing stress and improving caregivers' emotional and physical well-being (Toseland and Smith in press). Experience suggests that relatively simple techniques such as paced, deep breathing and positive self-talk can be very effective for helping caregivers cope with the stress of caregiving.

Caregivers also need encouragement to take better care of themselves and to balance their own needs with the needs of others. Caregivers frequently neglect their own needs to fulfill their caregiving, family, and work responsibilities. Even small, regularly scheduled respites from caregiving can do much to maintain a caregiver's physical and emotional stamina. Therefore, it can be helpful to remind caregivers of the importance of their own health and well-being, both to themselves and to all those who depend upon them. In a group, caregivers can be encouraged to set aside regularly scheduled time for themselves. Sometimes, this means helping members of the group to set limits by informing the person for whom they are caring, and other relatives, that they will not be available for caregiving activities during certain times of the week. The resistance that some caregivers display to the idea of taking time out for themselves is often greatly diminished, or completely eliminated, by the enthusiastic response the idea receives from other group members who have set aside a regularly scheduled time for themselves and have found this to be helpful in coping with the relentless demands of caregiving.

Caregivers also frequently need help improving their home-care and behavior-management skills. Practitioners can be helpful by suggesting ways that the home environment can be better adapted to persons with physical or cognitive impairments. For example, telephones with large numerals can aid the visually impaired, amplifiers connected to telephones can make it easier for the hearing impaired, and rearranging the household to minimize the need to climb stairs can make it easier for the physically impaired to be mobile.

Practitioners can also be helpful by demonstrating specific home-care techniques that caregivers can use with frail relatives. For example, there are right and wrong ways of lifting a bedridden person, but some caregivers do not know how to do so without risking injury to themselves or to their frail relative. If the practitioner is not familiar with these techniques, a community health nurse or other health care professional can be invited to the group for a guest presentation. Also, because dementia and other physical and psychological problems can create behavioral disturbances, family caregivers frequently can benefit from training in behavior-management skills such as those described by Pinkston, Linsk, and Young (1988).

CASE

To illustrate the therapeutic benefit of support groups for caregivers, a group led by a professional social worker who had over five years of clinical experience working with individuals and family members with chronic disabilities will be described. The group relied heavily on supportive interventions that included (1) ventilation of stressful experiences in an understanding and supportive environment, (2) validation and confirmation of similar caregiving experiences, (3) affirmation of members' ability to cope with their situations, (4) praise for providing care, and (5) support and understanding when struggling with difficult situations.

In addition to support, the group utilized a semistructured approach relying on education and problem-solving. The educational component focused on a different topic each week: (1) session 1 provided an introduction to the support group, (2) session 2 focused on caregivers' emotions and feelings, (3) session 3 focused on care receivers' reactions to illness, (4) session 4 focused on the caregiver taking care of himself or herself and doing positive things with his or her frail parent, (5) session 5 focused on communication between the caregiver and care receiver and between the caregiver and other family members, (6) session 6 focused on community resources, (7) session 7 focused on medical needs, pharmacology issues, and the nursing home placement process, and (8) session 8 focused on how to manage within the home and on group termination.[2] Participants were encouraged to ask questions, to share information, and to discuss issues that were related to the weekly topic presented by the leader.

The problem-solving component was introduced during the first group session as a device to help members move beyond ventilation of experi-

2. There are a number of excellent manuals available that suggest topics for caregiver support group meetings and provide useful background material. Three of these include *Caregivers' Support Group Facilitator's Manual,* which can be obtained by writing Department of Veterans Affairs, Central Office, Social Work Service (122), 810 Vermont Avenue NW, Washington, D.C. 20420; Montgomery, R., ed. *Helping Families Help.* Washington: University of Washington Press, 1985; and *Practical Help: Guide for Course Leaders,* which can be obtained by writing the New York State Office for the Aging, 2 Empire State Plaza, Albany, New York 12223.

ences and emotional reactions to methods for improving their coping skills. Each week participants were encouraged to work on their individual concerns using a problem-solving model that was similar to the one that has already been described in chapter 6 of this text. As is common in caregiver support groups, because the members had a tremendous need to ventilate pent-up emotions and to share their experiences and concerns with each other, the problem-solving model was not always carried out in a linear, step-by-step fashion. Still, by using it, the leader was able to help all the participants address at least one pressing problem during the course of the eight-week group, and many participants addressed several problems.

During the first session, members shared information about themselves. The leader, Ms. T., spoke first. She modeled what was an appropriate level of self-disclosure for a beginning discussion. She described her professional experience, her own caregiving experience, some of the positive experiences she had had in previous caregiver groups, and what she hoped would be some of the beneficial outcomes of participating in the group. Next, members introduced themselves one by one in a group go-round, sharing the following information about the person for whom they were caring:

Ms. K.: Ms. K.'s mother, age eighty-one, lives alone, has diabetes, is extremely overweight, has been widowed twice, and is depressed. Although married and working fulltime, Ms. K. still manages to see her mother twice a day. She does her mother's shopping and supervises her mother's medication.

Ms. M.: Ms. M cares for her mother-in-law, age eighty-three, who came to live in her home seven years ago after a small stroke. Three years ago, Ms. M.'s husband died. Since his death, her mother-in-law, who is also a diabetic, has been totally dependent on Ms. M. and is home alone all day while Ms. M. works as a legal secretary.

Ms. S.: Ms. S. is caring for her mother, who is bedridden. Ms. S.'s mother has cancer, heart disease, and Parkinson's disease, and has lived with her and her husband for five years. An aide comes in three times a week for four hours a day, but the remaining burden of care is left to Ms. S.

Ms. D.: Ms. D's mother, Bertha, age seventy-six, had lived alone until she suffered a stroke six months prior to the first group meeting. She now lives next door to Ms. D. in a duplex that Ms. D. bought with the help of her mother.

Ms. J.: Ms. J.'s father, age eighty-seven, has lived with her for ten years. Ms. J. is an only child, divorced, with no children. Her father has a heart condition and arthritis, wears a hearing aid, and is very argumentative. Ms. J. finds it very difficult to live with her father and wants to learn how to cope with her impatience with him.

Ms. Y.: Ms. Y.'s mother, age ninety-three, has Alzheimer's disease and diabetes. Ms. Y.'s husband resents his mother-in-law's presence and would like Ms. Y. to take steps to place her in a nursing home.

Ms. R.: Ms. R. has been taking care of her mother for thirteen years since her father died. Her mother, age seventy-four, lives next door. Ms. R.'s own health is poor due to open-heart surgery three years ago and arthritis in her legs.

Ms. N.: Ms. N.'s mother, age seventy-seven, lived alone until four years ago, when she had a series of strokes. Her physician did not feel she should be home alone when released from the hospital. She has been living in Ms. N.'s home ever since.

Ms. W.: Ms. W. is caring for her 71-year-old mother, who is suffering from manic depression and high blood pressure. Ms. W.'s mother has been in this country for forty-five years and has lived in Ms. W.'s home since Ms. W. and her husband were married twenty-five years ago. Ms. W.'s mother worked as a cleaning lady and is now retired. She has had mental health problems for many years and has been in and out of the psychiatric units of local hospitals. She takes medication to control her psychiatric symptoms and her high blood pressure.

After the introductions, norms for group participation were discussed and agreed to by all members. Emphasis was placed upon the confidential nature of the group discussions. Since problem-solving was a major focus of the group, the previously described eight-step problem-solving model was described in some detail by Ms. T. Also, there was an effort made by Ms. T. to incorporate problem-solving into each of the weekly educational topics. For example, when discussing feelings that caregivers typically experienced, the focus was not just on group sharing of particular emotions such as anger or guilt but also on reinforcing problem-solving techniques that could help members to cope better with these feelings outside of the group.

The following dialogue is taken from session 3 of the group.

Ms. W: My husband has had it with my mother. I can understand his feelings. She is hard to live with. But, I'm caught in the middle. I'm the only daughter she has.

Ms. Y.: I'm in the same situation. You know, my mother has Alzheimer's disease. In the past two years it's gotten a lot worse. My husband says I should find a good place to put mom, a nursing home, but I just can't bring myself to do it!

Ms. W.: *[looking at Ms. T.]* What can I do?

Ms. T.: Both of you are in a difficult situation. *[looking at Ms. W.]* Is there one thing that your mother does that is particularly bothersome?

Ms. W.: *[pause]* When mom refuses to take her medication, her mood swings really get out of hand. At that point, even I have trouble with her.

Ms. T.: Is there any pattern to your mom's refusal to take her medication?

Ms. W.: It seems she does it when we try to get away for the weekend. We have a camp on Lake Thompson. *[pause]* We've been going up there for years. It's only been the past few years when mom has gotten so frail that it [going to camp] has become a real problem. We have a lovely person from church, a neighbor, look after her when we go now, but I think she resents us leaving her alone.

[Ms. T. asks Ms. W. to elaborate on her relationship with her mother. After gathering additional information, several possible solutions to the problem are suggested by members.]

Ms. Y.: Why don't you take her with you?

Ms. W.: We've tried that. The trip is just too much for her. She gets exhausted. Besides, she really doesn't like it up there. You know, it's a pretty primitive camp. No TV, radio reception isn't very good, and the place is small, only three rooms. That's the way they are up there.

Ms. J.: Maybe you could put the medication in her favorite beverage and leave them in individual containers in the refrigerator.

Ms. W.: I don't think that will work. My mother insists on taking her own medication.

Ms. D.: How about using that respite service up at St. Peter's? We used it and it was good. They could give her her medications.

Ms. W.: Mother would never go for that.

Ms. T.: Remember about step 2 of the problem-solving model *[pointing to the board where it is posted]. [to Ms. W.]* Don't judge the solutions before hearing what everyone has to say. Okay?

Ms. W.: Oh, yes. I forgot.

Ms. D.: What does her psychiatrist say? Why don't you ask him what to do?

Ms. N.: What about having a home health aide come in when you're gone?

Ms. T.: Anybody else have any suggestions?

Ms. R.: You have a brother, don't you?

Ms. W.: Yes, two of them.

Ms. R.: What about asking one of them to take your mother or to sit with her when you want to go away?

Ms. T.: Anybody else? *[scanning the group for suggestions]* Okay, then, let me go over what has been suggested.

Ms. T. recaps the suggestions. Ms. W. says that asking the psychiatrist is the suggestion she is most comfortable with. Ms. W. describes what she will ask the psychiatrist, and the group helps her figure out how she will respond if he does not address her questions appropriately. Ms. W. also says she might ask one of her brothers to help out. She explains that she has not wanted to trouble her brothers, who "are both very busy with their own families." However, she also explains that one lives close by, and both have offered to help out in the past.

At each of the subsequent sessions, Ms. T. tries to reinforce problem-solving skills and to focus group discussion in that direction. For example, at the next session, in response to Ms. T's query, Ms. Y. says, "I feel better than I did before coming here. The situation hasn't become any easier, but I've begun thinking about various alternatives [for mom]." Ms. Y. goes on to say that group members "really understand what I'm going through deciding if it's time to place her [mother]."

The following dialogue, taken from the fourth group session, illustrates that it is possible for more than one person to derive benefit from a group discussion of a particular topic.

Ms. T.: Does anybody feel manipulated in their caregiving situation?

Ms. J.: I think manipulation gains advantage.

Ms. T.: I don't understand quite what you mean. Why don't you give us an example?

Ms. J.: When my father says he really doesn't feel well tonight, I think he is really telling me not to go out and leave him. I feel manipulated, like my life is out of my control. If I leave him, and something happened while I was out, I would feel terribly guilty for not being there, but when I stay home I really resent having to give up my plans.

Ms. T.: Maybe he needs to be reassured that he's still as important to you as you are to him.

Ms. W.: You know this need for reassurance could explain my mother too.

Ms. T.: Do you see a connection between your mother's medication problem and feeling manipulated?

Ms. W.: Well, yes, when she doesn't take her medicine she becomes the center of attention. It's almost like she believes it will distract us from going to our camp without her on weekends.

Ms. J.: Your mother won't take her pills just to feel that you still love her and will not abandon her?

Ms. W.: It sounds as if it could be, don't you think? *[to Ms. T.]*

Ms. T.: What do you think? *[scanning the group]*

Ms. Y.: Even if it's true, what can she do about it?

Ms. T.: You know, I found it helps to let them know you know they are manipulating you. Sometimes if you lay your cards on the table, you can be in a better position to prevent the manipulation.

Ms. M.: That doesn't sound so easy to do. My mother-in-law would just say I was overreacting.

Ms. R.: You have to remember that you have rights, too. You have to stand up for yourself.

[Ms. T. asks Ms. W. if she has any other thoughts. Ms. W. brings up her worries about vacation plans for the upcoming summer season.]

Ms. W.: If my husband and I can't handle her [her mother's] intrusion into our weekend trips, what would she do if we tried to go on a longer vacation? I thought I was going to enjoy myself once he [her husband] retired. Even having company over is a problem. Mental illness is not like physical illness.

Group members respond empathically. They agree that mental illness is potentially more embarrassing because of the unpredictable nature of some psychiatric symptoms.

Ms. W.: And you know, I'm darn tried of hearing, "I don't know how you do it" from family and friends. I'm not looking for meaningless praise.

Ms. Y.: I know exactly what you mean. Occasionally, I'd like to hear an offer of help, rather than praise.

During session 5, Ms. T. brings up the issue of group termination. She mentions that another group she conducted had continued to meet. She also mentions that group members could be a resource to each other by keeping in regular phone contact. This leads to a general discussion by group members about the benefits of the support group.

Ms. R.: On the way over here tonight I was worrying about what I would do when the group ended. You know, friends don't really understand. They mean well, but unless they are doing it too [caregiving], they just don't know what it's like to be tied down like this and not know when it's going to end. Sometimes I think my mother will go on forever and I will die first.

Ms. S.: You're right. How many friends can you discuss the differences between Depends and Attends [different brands of adult diapers], which one you use, and which store has the best prices?

Ms. N.: Yeah, even if you have a good friend, you think you'll drive her away if you talk about what's really on your mind. Can you tell your friend you think about what it would be like if your mother died? Your friend will think you're a monster and tell you you should be grateful your mother is still alive. I don't know what I would do without the group.

Ms. W.: You know, ever since I started coming here I've been much more patient with my mother because I know I can let it all out here. I really

look forward to coming here because I know you all understand what I'm going through.

Ms. T.: I take it, then, from all your comments that you're not sure if you want to end. Why don't you all give it some thought and we'll talk about it again at the next session?

During the next group session, Ms. W. admits to still feeling manipulated.

Ms. W.: I'm playing her game, playing into her hands, and I can't take it anymore. I finally got a chance to speak to Dr. L. about my mother's medication. He mentioned a supported apartment program, run by the county mental health center.

Ms. T.: Mrs. W., how do you feel about the suggestion from the doctor?

Ms. W.: Terrible. I can't bring myself to dial the phone numbers that are necessary to make the arrangements.

Ms. K. and Ms. J. both advise Ms. W. that even if she feels uncomfortable considering this move, still she has come a long way from the first session. However, other members confront Ms. W. and remind her that it takes two to continue this manipulative pattern.

Ms. M.: Nobody can manipulate you unless you let them.

Ms. N.: That's right. It takes two, you know. You must be cooperating with her or she wouldn't be able to do it.

Ms. T.: Mrs. W., by not going [on weekends], you give your mother a tremendous sense of power and control.

Ms. W.: But even her psychiatrist says he never dealt with someone like her before.

Ms. N.: Do you find that reassuring?

Ms. W.: Yeah, wouldn't you?

Ms. T.: Just remember, Mrs. W., you are the one who is responsible for your own happiness, not Anna [her mother]. It's up to you to take control of this situation, and you can do it.

Ms. W.: I know I have to do it; I have to do something.

During the seventh group session the following dialogue occurred.

Ms. W.: I have some good news. I finally got up the courage to ask my brother. He spoke to Dan [her other brother], and they agreed to team up and help out. They said they would take care of mom anytime we went away, as long as we let them know in advance, and that's not a problem. Jack [her husband] was real happy about that, so he hasn't bothered me one bit about mom being in our house recently. In fact, he's been a big help lately.

Ms. T.: That's wonderful.

[Members nod and there is a pause.]

Ms. Y.: I've been thinking maybe it's time to find a place [nursing home] for mom. But, every time I do I get to feeling so guilty.

Ms. T.: *[speaking to Ms. Y. and the entire group]* Remember the self-talk coping skills we learned earlier. Part of guilt is what you tell yourself. Give yourself credit for time served, look at what you have done and have tried to do already.

During the eighth group meeting, the members decided to continue to meet once a month and to stay in contact with each other by telephone between meetings.

During a follow-up meeting almost one year after the eight weekly group meetings, Ms. Y. reported the following news.

Ms. Y.: As some of you already know, mom is now at East Shore [a skilled nursing facility]. She took a turn for the worse about a month ago. It happened right after our last group meeting. She was up at St. Peter's [hospital] for over a week. I didn't know what to do *[pause]* about taking her back I mean. She was so bad she didn't even recognize me anymore. I thought about what you [members of the group] had said to me during the meetings, how much I had done for mother over the years, and how I shouldn't feel guilty when it was time to have her go to a home. It meant a lot to me.

Ms. T.: You've meant a lot to us.

Ms. Y.: I just couldn't keep taking care of her. I had to watch her every minute, afraid she'd burn down the house or something. I had lunch with Kay [Ms. N.] while my mother was in the hospital, and Julie and Sadie [Ms. W. and Ms. K.] called. That helped give me the courage to go ahead with what I had to do. You know, without the support of the group, I think I would have fallen apart.

SUMMARY

This chapter has focused on the skills necessary to work with family caregivers of the frail elderly in groups. I began with a brief description of family caregivers, the impact that caregiving has upon them, and the value of support groups for this population. Next, the special skills that are needed to establish and lead caregiver support groups were delineated. Emphasis was placed on caregivers' needs for support and education, as well as their needs for coping skills and home-care skills training. The chapter concluded with a case example of a caregiver support group in action.

References

Altman, K. 1983. Psychodrama with the institutionalized elderly: A method for role re-engagement. *Journal of Group Psychotherapy, Psychodrama & Sociometry* 36 (3):87–94.

American Association of Retired Persons. 1986. *A profile of older persons.* Washington, D.C. American Association of Retired Persons.

American Psychiatric Association. 1980. *Diagnostic and statistical manual of mental disorders.* 3d ed. Washington, D.C. American Psychiatric Association.

Antonucci, T. C. 1985. Personal characteristics, social support, and social behavior. In R. H. Binstock and E. Shanas, eds., *Handbook of aging and the social sciences* (2d ed.), 94–128. New York: Van Nostrand Reinhold.

Atchley, R. 1983. *Aging: Continuity and change.* Belmont, Calif.: Wadsworth.

Atchley, R. C. 1982. The process of retirement: Comparing women and men. In M. Szinovacz, ed., *Women's retirement: Policy implications of recent research,* 153–68. Beverly Hills, Calif.: Sage.

———. 1989. A continuity theory of normal aging. *Gerontologist* 29 (2):183–90.

Atlas, L., and M. Morris. 1971. Resident government: An instrument for change in a public institution for indigent elderly. *Gerontologist* 11:209–12.

Bales, R. 1950. *Interaction process analysis: A method for the study of small groups.* Reading, Mass.: Addison-Wesley.

———. 1955. How people interact in conference. *Scientific American* 192:31–35.

Bednar, K., and T. Kaul. 1978. Experimental group research: Current perspectives. In A. Garfield and A. Bergen, eds., *Handbook of psychotherapy and behavior change* (2d ed.), 769–816. New York: John Wiley & Sons.

Beisgon, B. 1989. *Life enhancing activities for the mentally impaired elderly.* New York: Springer.

Bengtson, V. L., M. N. Reedy, and C. Gordon. 1985. Aging and self-conceptions: Personality processes and social contexts. In J. E. Birren and K. W. Schaie, eds., *Handbook of the psychology of aging* (2d ed.), 544–93. New York: Van Nostrand Reinhold.

Berman, J. S., and N. C. Norton. 1985. Does professional training make a therapist more effective? *Psychological Bulletin* 98:401–7.

Bernstein, D., and T. Borkovec. 1973. *Progressive relaxation training: A manual for the helping professions.* Champaign, Ill.: Research Press.

Bertcher, H., and F. Maple. 1974. Elements and issues in group composition. In P. Glasser, R. Sarri, and R. Vinter, eds., *Individual change through small groups,* 186–208. New York: Free Press.

———. 1977. *Creating groups.* Beverly Hills, Calif.: Sage.

Bienenfeld, D. 1988. Group psychotherapy with the elderly in the state hospital. In B. MacLennan, S. Saul, and M. Weiner, eds., *Group therapies for the elderly*, (177–88). Madison, Conn.: International Universities Press.

Birkel, R. 1987. Toward a social psychology of the home-care household. *Psychology and Aging* 2:294–301.

Birren, J., and K. Schaie. 1985. *Handbook of the psychology of aging*. New York: Van Nostrand Reinhold.

Birren, J., and R. Sloane, eds. 1980. *Handbook of mental health and aging*. Englewood Cliffs, N.J.: Prentice Hall.

Blatner, H. 1973. *Acting-In*. New York: Springer.

Bloom, B., and L. Broder. 1950. *Problem-solving processes of college students*. Chicago: University of Chicago Press.

Booth. H. 1986. Dance/Movement therapy. In I. Burnside, ed., *Working with the elderly: Group processes and techniques* (2d ed.), 211–24. Boston, Mass.: Jones and Bartlett.

Brody, E. M. 1985. Parent care as a normative family stress. *Gerontologist* 25 (1):19–29.

Brookfield, S. D. 1986. *Understanding and facilitating adult learning*. San Francisco: Jossey-Bass.

Buchanan, D. 1981. Psychodrama: A humanistic approach to psychiatric treatment for the elderly. *Hospital & Community Psychiatry* 33:220–23.

Burnside, I. 1969. Communication problems in groupwork with the disabled. *American Nurses Association, clinical conference*, 125–31. New York: Appleton-Century-Crofts.

———. 1970. Loss: A constant theme in group work with older persons. *Hospital and Community Psychiatry* 21 (6):21–25.

———. 1986. *Working with the elderly: Group process and techniques*. 2d ed. Boston: Jones and Bartlett.

Butler, R. 1963. The life review: An interpretation of reminiscence in the aged. *Psychiatry* 26 (1):65–76.

———. 1974. Successful aging. *Mental Health* 58 (3):6–12.

Butler, R., and M. Lewis. 1982. *Aging and mental health: Positive psychosocial and biomedical approaches*. 3d. ed. Columbus, Ohio: Merrill.

Cantor, M. H. 1983. Strain among caregivers: A study of experience in the United States. *Gerontologist* 23:597–604.

Chen, Y. 1985. Economic status of the aging. In R. H. Binstock and E. Shanas, eds., *Handbook of aging and the social sciences* (2nd ed.), 641–65. New York: Van Nostrand Reinhold.

Clark, P., and N. J. Osgood. 1985. *Seniors on stage: The impact of applied theatre techniques on the elderly*. New York: Praeger.

Cohen, C. I., and H. Rajkowski. 1982. What's in a friend? Substantive and theoretical issues. *Gerontologist* 22:261–66.

Coppell, D. B., C. Burton, J. Becker, and J. Fiore. 1985. Relationships of cognitions associated with coping reactions to depression in spousal caregivers of Alzheimer's Disease patients. *Cognitive Therapy and Research* 9:253–66.

Coppola, M., and R. Rivas. 1986. The task-action group technique: A case study of

empowering the elderly. In M. Parnes, ed., *Innovations in social group work*, 133–47. New York: Haworth Press.

Cox, E. 1988. Empowerment of the low income elderly through group work. *Social Work with Groups* 11 (4):111–19.

Cox, F. 1987. Community problem solving: A guide to practice with comments. In F. Cox, J. Erlich, J. Rothman, and J. Tropman, eds., *Strategies of Community Organization* (4th ed.), 150–67. Itasca, Ill.: Peacock.

Critchley, M., and R. Henson. 1977. *Music and the brain.* Springfield, Ill.: Thomas.

Davis, F., and N. Lohr. 1971. Special problems with the use of co-therapists in group psychotherapy. *International Journal of Group Psychotherapy* 21:143–58.

Debor, L., D. Gallagher, and E. Lesher. 1983. Group counseling with bereaving elderly. *Clinical Gerontologist* 1 (3):81–90.

Delbecq, A., A. Van de Ven, and D. Gustafson. 1975. *Group techniques for program planning: A guide to nominal group and delphi processes.* Glenview, Ill.: Scott, Foresman.

Devitt, M., and B. Checkoway. 1982. Participation in nursing home resident councils: Promise and practice. *Gerontologist* 22 (1):49–53.

Doty, P. 1986. Family care of the elderly: The role of public policy. *Milbank Quarterly* 64:34–75.

Durlack, J. A. 1979. Comparative effectiveness of paraprofessional and professional helpers. *Psychological Bulletin* 86:80–92.

———. 1981. Evaluating comparative studies of paraprofessional. *Psychological Bulletin* 89:566–69.

Egan, G. 1982. *Skilled helper: model skills, and methods for effective helping.* 2d ed. Monterey, Calif.: Brooks/Cole.

Eissler, K. 1977. On the possible effects of aging and the practice of psychoanalysis. *Psychoanalytic Quarterly* 46 (1):182–83.

Emerick, D., L. Lasser, and M. Edwards. 1977. Nonprofessional peers as therapeutic agents. In A. Gurman and A. Razan, eds., *Effective psychotherapy: A handbook of research*, 120–61. New York: Pergamon Press.

Erikson, E. K., J. M. Erikson, and H. Q. Kirmick. 1986. *Vital involvement in old age.* New York: W. W. Norton.

Farkas, S. 1980. Impact of chronic illness on the patient's spouse. *Health and Social Work* 5:39–46.

Feil, N. 1982. *V/F Validation the Feil method: How to help disoriented old-old.* Cleveland: Edward Feil Productions.

———. 1983. Group work with disoriented nursing home residents. In S. Saul, ed., *Group work with frail elderly*, 57–65. New York: Haworth Press.

Feldman, R., and H. Wodarski. 1975. *Contemporary approaches to group treatment: Traditional, behavior modification and group-centered.* San Francisco, Calif.: Jossey-Bass.

Felton, B., S. Lehmann, A. Adler, and M. Burgio. 1977. Social supports and life satisfaction among old and young. Paper presented at the meeting of the Gerontological Society, November, at San Francisco.

Fisher, P. 1989. *Creative movement for older adults.* New York: Human Sciences Press.

Flatten, K., B. Wilhite, and E. Reyes-Watson. 1987a. *Exercise activities for the elderly.* New York: Springer.

——. 1987b. *Recreation activities for the elderly.* New York: Springer.

Folsom, J. 1968. Reality orientation for the elderly mental patient. *Journal of Geriatric Psychiatry* 1 (2):291–307.

Ford, C., and R. Sbordone. 1980. Attitudes of psychiatrists toward elderly patients. *American Journal of Psychiatry* 137 (5):571–77.

Foster, J., and R. Foster. 1983. Group psychotherapy with the old and aged. In H. Kaplan and B. Sadock, eds., *Comprehensive Group Psychotherapy,* 269–77. Baltimore Md.: Williams & Wilkins.

Foster, P., ed. 1983. *Activities and the "well elderly."* New York: Haworth Press.

Fry, P. 1983. Structured and unstructured reminiscence training and depression among the elderly. *Clinical Gerontologist* 1 (13):15–37.

Galinsky, M., and J. Schopler. 1977. Warning: Groups may be dangerous. *Social Work with Groups* 22 (2):89–94.

Gallagher, D., J. Rose, P. Rivera, S. Lovett, and L. Thompson. 1989. Prevalence of depression in family caregivers. *Gerontologist* 29 (4):449–56.

Gallagher, D. E. 1985. Intervention strategies to assist caregivers of frail elders: Current research status and future research directions. In C. Eisdorfer, M. P. Lawton, and G. Maddox, eds., *Annual review of gerontology and geriatrics,* Vol. 5, 249–82). New York: Springer.

Garcia-Preto, D. 1982. Puerto Rican families. In M. McGoldrick, J. Pearce, and J. Giordino, eds., *Ethnicity and family therapy,* 164–86. New York: Guilford.

Garland, J., H. Jones, and R. Kolodny. 1976. A model of stages of group development in social work groups. In S. Bernstein, ed., *Explorations in group work,* 17–71. Boston: Charles River.

Gaylord, S., and W. Zung. 1987. Affective disorders among the aging. In L. L. Carstensen and B. A. Edelstein, eds., *Handbook of clinical gerontology,* 76–95. New York: Pergamon Press.

Getzel, J. 1983. Resident councils and social action. In G. Getzel and J. Mellor, eds., *Gerontological social work practice in long-term care.* 179–85. New York: Haworth Press.

Ginsberg, B. 1988. Structuring your retirement leisure time. *Parks and Recreation* 23 (5):46–49.

Gitterman, A., and L. Shulman, eds. 1986. *Mutual aid groups and the life cycle.* Itasca, Ill.: Peacock.

Goldfarb, A. 1971. Group therapy with the old and aged. In H. Kaplan and B. Sadock, eds., *Comprehensive Group Psycychotherapy,* 623–42. Baltimore: William & Wilkins.

Golodetz, A., R. Evans, G. Heinritz, and C. Gibson. 1969. The care of chronic illness: The responsor role. *Medical Care* 7:385–94.

Green, V. L., and D. J. Monahan. 1987. The effect of professionally guided caregiver support and education group on institutionalization of care receivers. *Gerontologist* 27:716–21.

Greenberg, L. 1978. Improving communication: Educating families. *Journal of American Health Care Association* 4 (1):21–28.

Griffin, M., and M. Waller. 1985. Group therapy for the elderly: One approach to coping. *Clinical Social Work Journal* 13 (3):261–71.

Group for the Advancement of Psychiatry, Committee on Aging. 1971. *The aged and community mental health.* New York: Group for the Advancement of Psychiatry, Committee on Aging.

Hagestad, G. O., and B. L. Neugarten. 1985. Age and the life course. In R. H. Binstock and E. Shanas, eds., *Handbook of aging and the social sciences* (2d ed.), 35–61. New York: Van Nostrand Reinhold.

Haley, W. E., E. G. Levine, S. C. Brown, and A. A. Bartolucci. 1987. Stress appraisal coping and social support as predictors of adaptational outcome among dementia caregivers. *Psychology and Aging* 2:323–30.

Hartford, M. 1962. *The social group worker and group formation.* Ph.D. diss., University of Chicago, School of Social Service Administration.

———. 1985. Group work with older adults. In A. Monk, ed., *Handbook of gerontological services,* 169–83. New York: Van Nostrand Reinhold.

Hastings, L. 1981. *Complete handbook of activities and recreational programs for nursing homes.* Englewood Cliffs, N.J.: Prentice Hall.

Hattie, J., C. Sharpley, and H. Rogers. 1984. Comparative effectiveness of professional and paraprofessional helpers. *Psychological Bulletin* 95:534–41.

Heap, K. 1979. *Process and action in work with groups.* Elmsford, N.Y.: Pergamon Press.

Helgeson, E., and S. Willis, eds. 1987. *Handbook of group activities for impaired older adults.* New York: Haworth Press.

Hennessey, M. 1986. Music therapy. In I. Burnside, ed., *Working with the elderly: Group processes and techniques* (2d ed.), 198–210. Boston, Mass.: Jones and Bartlett.

Hiemstra, R. P. 1972. Continuing education for the aged: A survey of needs and interests of older people. *Adult Education* 22 (2):100–9.

Hill, W. 1977. Hill interaction matrix (HIM): The conceptual framework, derived rating scales, and an updated bibliography. *Small Group Behavior* 8 (3): 251–68.

Horn, L., and E. Griesel. 1977. *Nursing Homes: A citizen's action guide.* Boston: Beacon Press.

Horowitz, A. 1976. Indications and contraindications for group psychotherapy. *Bulletin of the Menninger Clinic* 40:505–7.

———. 1985. Family caregiving to the frail elderly. *Annual Review of Gerontology and Geriatrics* 5:194–245.

Hunter, W. 1951. A proposed activity center for older people. *Geriatrics* 2:121–28.

Hurley, O. 1987. *Safe therapeutic exercise for the frail elderly: An introduction.* Albany, N.Y.: Center for the Study of Aging.

Ingersoll, B., and L. Goodman. 1983. A reminiscence group for institutionalized elderly. In M. Rosenbaum, ed., *Handbook of short-term therapy groups,* 247–69. New York: McGraw Hill.

Ingersoll, B., and A. Silverman. 1978. Comparative group psychotherapy for the aged. *Gerontologist* 18 (2):201–6.

Kamin, J. 1984. How older adults use books and the public library: A review of the literature. Occasional papers no. 165 (Eric Document Reproduction Service No. ED 247954). Champaign, Ill.: University of Illinois.

Kane, R., and P. Kane. 1981. *Assessing the elderly: A practical guide to measurement.* Lexington, Mass.: Lexington Books.

Kaplan, J. 1953. *A social program for older people.* Minneapolis: University of Minnesota Press.

Kart, G., E. Metress, and J. Metress. 1978. *Aging and health.* Reading, Mass.: Addison-Wesley.

Kastenbaum, 1963. The reluctant therapist. *Geriatrics* 18:296–301.

Katz, R., and B. Genevay. 1987. Older people, dying and countertransference. *Generations* 11:28–32.

Kilen, E. B. 1978. Family discussion group meetings. *Journal of American Health Care Association* 4 (1):5–6,8,10.

Killeffer, E., R. Bennett, and G. Gruen. 1985. *Handbook of innovative programs for the impaired elderly.* New York: Haworth Press.

King, K. 1982. Reminiscing psychotherapy with aging people. *Journal of Psychosocial Nursing and Mental Health Services* 20 (2):21–25.

Klein, A. 1970. *Social work through group process.* Albany, N.Y.: School of Social Welfare, State University of New York at Albany.

———. 1972. *Effective group work.* New York: Association Press.

Kline, D. W., and F. Schieber. 1985. Vision and Aging. In J. E. Birren and K. W. Schaie, eds., *Handbook of the psychology of aging* (2nd ed.), 296–331. New York: Van Nostrand Reinhold.

Knight, B. 1986. *Psychotherapy with older adults.* Beverly Hills, Calif.: Sage.

Knox, A. B. 1986. *Helping adults learn.* San Francisco: Jossey-Bass.

Konopka, G. 1954. Social group work in institutions for the aged. In G. Konopka, ed., *Group work in the institution: A modern challenge,* 276–85. New York: Whiteside & Morrow.

Kosberg, J., and H. Audrey. 1978. Attitudes toward elderly clients. *Health & Social Work* 3, (3):67–90.

Krasner, I. 1952. Factors associated with status in a recreational program for the aged. *Journal of Jewish Communal Service* 28 (3):290–301.

Kubie, S., and G. Landau. 1953. *Group work with the aged.* New York: International Universities Press.

Kubler-Ross, E. 1969. *On death and dying.* New York: MacMillan.

Lakin, M. 1982. A note on the old and young in helping groups. *Psychotherapy: Theory, Research and Practice* 19 (4):444–52.

———. 1988. Group therapies with the elderly: Issues and prospects. In B. MacLennan, S. Saul, and M. Weiner, eds., *Group therapies for the elderly,* 43–56. Madison, Conn.: International Universities Press.

Lakin, M., B. Openheimer, and J. Bremer. 1982. A note on old and young in helping groups. *Psychotherapy: Theory, Research, and Practice* 19:444–52.

Lamb, H. R., and M. Mills. 1986. Needed changes in law and procedure for the chronically mentally ill. *Hospital and Community Psychiatry* 37:475–80.

Lang, N. 1972. A broad range model of practice in the social work group. *Social Service Review* 46 (1):76–84.

La Rue, A., C. Dessonville, and L. F. Jarvik. 1985. Aging and mental disorders. In J. E. Birren and K. W. Schaie, eds., *Handbook of the psychology of aging* (2d ed.), 664–702. New York: Van Nostrand Reinhold.

Lazarus, L., ed. 1984. *Clinical approaches to psychotherapy with the elderly.* Washington, D.C.: American Psychiatric Press.

Lazarus, L., L. Groves, N. Newton, D. L. Gutmann, H. Ripeckyj, R. Frankel, J. Grunes, and S. Havasy-Galloway. 1984. Brief psychotherapy with the elderly: A review and preliminary study of process and outcome. In L. Lazarus, ed., *Clinical approaches to psychotherapy with the elderly,* 15–35. Washington, D.C.: American Psychiatric Press.

Lazarus, R., and S. Folkman. 1984. *Stress, appraisal, and coping.* New York: Springer.

Lebowitz, B. 1978. Old age and family functioning. *Journal of Gerontological Social Work* 1 (2):111–18.

Lee, J. 1983. The group: A chance at human connection for the mentally impaired older person. *Social Work with Groups* 5 (2):43–56.

Lesser, J., L. Lazarus, R. Frankel, and S. Havasy. 1981. Reminiscence group therapy with psychotic geriatric in-patients. *Gerontologist* 21 (3):291–96.

Leszcz, M. 1987. Group psychotherapy with the elderly. In J. Sadavoy and M. Leszcz, eds., *Treating the elderly with psychotherapy: The scope for change in later life,* 325–49. Madison, Conn.: International Universities Press.

Levine, B. 1980. Co-leadership approach to learning group work. *Social Work with Groups.* 3:35–38.

Lewis, M., and R. Butler. 1974. Life review therapy: Putting memories to work in individual and group psychotherapy. *Geriatrics* 29 (11):165–73.

Lieberman, M. A., and N. Bliwise. 1985. Comparisons among peer and professionally directed groups for the elderly: Implications for the development of self-help groups. *International Journal of Group Psychotherapy* 35 (2):155–75.

Lieberman, M. A., L. D. Borman, and associates. 1979. *Self-help groups for coping with crisis.* San Francisco: Josey-Bass.

Lieberman, M. A., and S. S. Tobin. 1983. *The experience of old age: Stress, coping and survival.* New York: Basic Books.

Lieberman, M., I. Yalom, and M. Miles. 1973. *Encounter groups: First facts.* New York: Basic Books.

Linden, M. 1953. Group psychotherapy with institutionalized senile women: Study in gerontologic human relations. *International Journal of Group Psychotherapy* 3:150–70.

Lovergren, J., and S. Rosenberg. 1978. Experiences in nine patient/family education workshops. *Journal of American Health Care Association* 4 (1):18–21.

Lovett, S., and D. Gallagher. 1988. Psychoeducational interventions for family caregivers: Preliminary efficacy data. *Behavior Therapy* 19:321–30.

Lowy, L. 1955. Group work with older adults. In L. Lowy, ed., *Adult education and group work,* 164–204. New York: Whiteside Morrow.

———. 1985. *Social work with the aging.* New York: Harper & Row.

Luborsky L., B. Singer, and L. Luborsky. 1975. Comparative studies of psychotherapies. *Archives of General Psychiatry* 32:995–1008.

McCormack, D., and A. Whitehead. 1981. The effect of providing recreational activities on the engagement level of long-stay geriatric patients. *Age and Aging* 10:287–91.

McDermott, C. 1989. Empowering the elderly nursing home resident: The resident rights campaign. *Social Work* 34 (2):155–57.

McGuire, F., and D. Dottavio. 1986–1987. Outdoor recreation participation across the lifespan: Abandonment, continuity, or liberation. *International Journal of Aging and Human Development* 24 (2):87–100.

Macheath, J. 1984. *Activity, health and fitness in old age.* New York: St. Martin's.

McMorde, W., and S. Blom. 1979. Life review therapy: Psychotherapy for the elderly. *Perspectives in Psychiatric Care* 17:292–98.

Madera, E. J., and A. Meese. 1986. *The self-help sourcebook: Finding and forming mutual and self-help groups.* Denville, N. J.: Selfhelp Clearinghouse.

Maier, N. 1963. *Problem-solving discussions and conferences: Leadership methods and skills.* New York: McGraw-Hill.

Maisler, J., and K. Solomon. 1976. Therapeutic group process with the institutionalized elderly. *Journal of the American Geriatrics Society* 2:412,542–46.

Mangen, D. J., and W. A. Peterson. 1982. *Research instruments in social gerontology,* vol. 2. Minneapolis: University of Minnesota Press.

Maxwell, J. M. 1952. *Centers for older people: A project report.* New York: National Council on the Aging.

Middleman, R. 1968. *The non-verbal method in working with groups.* New York: Association Press.

———. 1978. Returning group process to group work. *Social Work with Groups* 1:15–26.

Montgomery, R., and E. Borgotta. 1989. The effects of alternative support strategies on family caregiving. *Gerontologist* 29 (4):457–64.

Montgomery, R. J. V. 1989. Investigating caregiver burden. In K. S. Markides and C. L. Cooper, eds., *Aging stress and health,* 201–18. New York: John Wiley and Sons.

Morris, R., and S. A. Bass, eds. 1988. *Retirement reconsidered.* New York: Springer.

Munzer, J., and H. Greenwald. 1957. Interaction process analysis of a therapy group. *International Journal of Group Psychotherapy* 7:175–90.

Myers, J. K., M. M. Weissman, G. L. Tischler, C. E. Holzer, P. J. Leaf, H. Orvaschel, J. C. Anthony, J. H. Boyd, J. D. Burke, Jr., M. Kramer, and R. Stoltzman. 1984. Six-month prevalence of psychiatric disorders in three communities. *Archives of General Psychiatry* 41:959–67.

Neugarten, B. 1987. Older people: A profile. In G. Smith and S. Tobin, eds., *Sociocultural and service issues in working with the elderly,* 3–13. Albany, N.Y.: Resource Guide Series, School of Social Welfare, Professional Development Program.

Newmark, L. 1963. The development of a resident's council in a home for the aged. *Gerontologist* 3:22–25.

Nietzel, N., and S. Fisher. 1981. Effectiveness of professional and paraprofessional helpers: A comment on Durlack. *Psychological Bulletin* 89:555–65.

Olmsted, M. 1959. *The small group.* New York: Random House.

Olsho, L. W., S. W. Harkins, and M. L. Lenhardt. 1985. Aging and the auditory system. In J. E. Birren and K. W. Schaie, eds., *Handbook of the psychology of aging* (2d ed.), 332–77. New York: Van Nostrand Reinhold.

Orr, A. 1986. Dealing with the death of a group member: Visually impaired elderly in the community. In A. Gitterman and L. Shulman, eds., *Mutual aid groups and the life cycle*, 315–32. Itasca, Ill.: Peacock.

Papell, C., and B. Rothman. 1980. Social group work models: Possession and heritage. In A. Alissi, ed., *Perspectives on social group work practice*, 116–32. New York: Free Press.

Parham, I., M. Priddy, T. McGovern, and C. Richman. 1982. Group psychotherapy with the elderly: Problems and prospects. *Psychotherapy: Theory Research and Practice* 19:437–43.

Parloff M., and R. Dies. 1977. Group psychotherapy research 1966–1975. *International Journal of Group Psychotherapy* 27:281–319.

Pepitone, A., and G. Reichling. 1955. Group cohesiveness and the expression of hostility. *Human Relations* 8:327–37.

Perlman, R., and A. Gurin. 1971. *Community organization and social planning*. New York: Wiley.

Pernell, R. 1986. Empowerment and social group work. In M. Parnes, ed., *Innovations in social group work*, 107–18. New York: Haworth Press.

Petty, B., T. Moeller, and R. Campbell. 1976. Support groups for elderly persons in the community. *Gerontologist* 15:522–28.

Pfeiffer, E., and E. Busse. 1973. Mental disorders in later life—Affective disorders; paranoid, neurotic, and situational reactions. In E. Busse and E. Pfeiffer, eds., *Mental illness in later life*, 109–44. Washington, D.C.: American Psychiatric Association.

Pfeiffer, J. W., and J. E. Jones. (1972–1981). *Annual handbook for group facilitators*. 1st–10th eds. LaJolla, Calif.: University Associates.

Pinkston, E. M., and N. L. Linsk. 1984. *Care of the elderly: A family approach*. Elmsford, N.Y.: Pergamon Press.

Pinkston, E. M., N. L. Linsk, and R. N. Young. 1988. Home-based behavioral family treatment of the impaired elderly. *Behavioral Therapy* 19:331–44.

Poggi, R. G., and D. I. Berland. 1985. The therapist's reactions to the elderly. *Gerontologist* 25 (5):508–13.

Powell, T. J. 1987. *Self-help organizations and professional practice*. Silver Spring, Md.: National Association of Social Workers.

Pratt, C. C., V. C. Schmall, S. Wright, and M. Cleland. 1985. Burden and coping strategies of caregivers to Alzheimer's patients. *Family Relations* 34:27–33.

Quayhagen, M. P., and M. Quayhagen. 1988. Alzheimer's stress: Coping with the caregiving role. *Gerontologist* 28:391–96.

Ragheb, M. G., and C. Griffith. 1982. The contribution of leisure participation and leisure satisfaction to life satisfaction of older persons. *Journal of Leisure Research* 14 (4):295–306.

Ray, D., M. Raciti, and C. Ford. 1985. Ageism in psychiatrists: Associates with gender, certification and theoretical orientation. *Gerontologist* 25:496–500.

Reid, W., and P. Hanrahan. 1982. Recent evaluations of social work: Grounds for optimism. *Social Work* 27 (4):328–40.

Roberts, R. 1987. The epidemiology of depression in minorities. In P. Meuhrer, ed., *Research perspectives on depression and suicide in minorities.* Washington, D.C.: Department of Health and Human Services, National Institute of Mental Health.

Robinson, P. K., S. Coberly, and C. E. Paul. 1985. Work and retirement. In R. H. Binstock and E. Shanas, eds., *Handbook of aging and the social sciences* (2d ed.), 503–27. New York: Van Nostrand Reinhold.

Rose, S. 1989. *Working with adults in groups.* San Francisco: Jossey Bass.

Rosen, C., and S. Rosen. 1982. Evaluating an intervention program for the elderly. *Community Mental Health Journal* 18 (1):21–33.

Rosow, I. 1974. *Socialization to old age.* Berkeley: University of California Press.

Salamon, M. 1986. *A basic guide to working with elders.* New York: Springer.

Salamon, M., and A. Nichol. 1982. Rx for recreation. *Aging* 333/334:18–22.

Salthouse, T. A. 1985. Speed of behavior and its implications for cognition. In J. E. Birren and K. W. Schaie, eds., *Handbook of the psychology of aging* (2d ed.), 400–26. New York: Van Nostrand Reinhold.

Schlenger, G. 1988. *Come and sit by me: Discussion programs for activity specialists.* Owings Mills, Md.: National Health Publishing.

Schloss, G. 1988. Growing old and growing: Psychodrama and the elderly. In B. MacLennan, S. Saul, and M. Weiner, eds., *Group therapies for the elderly,* 89–104. Madison, Conn.: International Universities Press.

Schwartz, W. 1961. The social worker in the group. In *New Perspectives on Services to Groups: Theory, Organization and Practice,* 7–34. New York: National Association of Social Workers Press.

Seashore, S. 1954. *Group cohesiveness in the industrial work group.* Ann Arbor, Mich.: Survey Research Center, Institute for Social Research, University of Michigan.

Shanas, E. 1968. *Old people in three industrial societies.* New York: Atherton Press.

Shanas, E., and G. L. Maddox. 1985. Health, health resources, and the utilization of care. In R. H. Binstock and E. Shanas, eds., *Handbook of aging and the social sciences* (2d ed.), 696–726. New York: Van Nostrand Reinhold.

Shapiro, S. 1954. The old cronies. *Group* 16 (3):3–12; 21–22.

Shere, E. 1964. Group therapy with the very old. In R. Kastenbaum, ed., *New thoughts about old age,* 146–48). New York: Springer.

Sherman, E. 1987. Reminiscence groups for the community elderly. *Gerontologist* 27 (5):569–72.

———. In press. Experiential reminiscence and life review therapy. In G. Lietaer, J. Rombauts, and R. Van Balen, eds., *Client-centered and experiential psychotherapy in the nineties.* Leuven: Leuven University Press.

Shock, N., and A. Norris. 1970. Neuromuscular coordination as a factor in changes in muscular exercise. In D. Brunner and E. Jokl, eds., *Physical activity and Aging,* 92–99. New York: Karger.

Shock, N. W. 1977. Biological theories of aging. In J. E. Birren and K. W. Schaie, eds., *Handbook of the Pscyhology of Aging,* 103–15. New York: Van Nostrand Reinhold.

Shore, H. 1952. Group work program development in homes for the aged. *Social Service Review* 26 (2):181–94.

Shulman, L. 1984. *The skills of helping individuals and groups.* 2d ed. Itasca, Ill.: Peacock.

Shulman, L., and A. Gitterman. 1986. *Mutual aid groups and the life cycle.* Itasca, Ill.: F. E. Peacock.

Silver, A. 1950. Group psychotherapy with senile psychiatric patients. *Geriatrics* 5:147.

Simpson, G. M., and P. R. A. May. 1982. Schizophrenic disorders. In J. H. Greist, J. W. Jefferson, and R. L. Spitzer, eds., *Treatment of mental disorders,* 143–83. New York: Oxford Press.

Smith, G. C., and D J. Sperbeck. 1980. *Attributing causality in aging families: Theoretical and practical implications of a social-psychological perspective.* Paper presented at the annual meeting of the Gerontological Society, San Diego, Calif.

Smith, M., G. Glass, and T. Miller. 1980. *The benefits of psychotherapy.* Baltimore, Md.: Johns Hopkins Press.

Sprung, G. 1989. Transferential issues in working with older adults. *Social Casework* 70 (10):597–602.

Sterns, H. L., G. V. Barrett, and R. A. Alexander. 1985. Accidents and the aging individual. In J. E. Birren and K. W. Schaie, eds., *Handbook of the psychology of aging* (2d ed.), 703–24. New York: Van Nostrand Reinhold.

Steuer, J., J. Mintz, C. L. Hammen, M. A. Hill, L. F. Jarvik, T. McCarley, P. Motoike, and R. Rosen. 1984. Cognitive-behavioral and psychodynamic group psychotherapy in treatment of geriatric depression. *Journal of Consulting and Clinical Psychology* 52 (2):180–89.

Sturgis, E., J. Dolce, and P. Dickerson. 1987. Pain management in the elderly. In L. L. Carstensen and B. A. Edelstern, eds., *Handbook of clinical gerontology,* 190–203. New York: Pergamon Press.

Sussman, M. B. 1979. *Social economic supports and family environments for the elderly.* Final report. Washington, D.C.: Administration on Aging.

Taulbee, L. 1986. Reality orientation and clinical practice. In I. Burnside, ed., *Working with the elderly: Group processes and techniques* (2d ed.), 177–86. Boston, Mass.: Jones and Bartlett.

Thurman, J., and C. Piggins. 1982. *Drama activities with older adults.* New York: Haworth Press.

Tobin, S. S. 1985. Psychological adaptation to stress by the aged. In B. B. Davis and W. G. Wood, eds., *Homeostatic function and aging,* 181–95. New York: Raven Press.

Tobin, S. S., J. W. Ellor, and S. Anderson-Ray. 1986. *Enabling the elderly: Religious institutions within the service system.* Albany, N.Y.: State University of New York Press.

Tobin, S. S., and J. Gustafson. 1987. What do we do differently with elderly clients? *Journal of Gerontological Social Work* 10 (3/4):107–21.

Tobin, S. S., and M. A. Lieberman. 1976. *Last home for the aged: Critical implications of institutionalization.* San Francisco: Jossey-Bass.

Toseland, R. 1977. A problem solving group workshop for older persons. *Social Work* 22 (4):325–26.

————. 1981. Increasing access: Outreach methods in social work practice. *Social Casework* 62 (4):227–34.

Toseland, R., and M. Coppola. 1985. A task centered approach to group work with the elderly. In A. Fortune, ed., *Task centered practice with families and groups*, 101–14. New York: Springer.

Toseland, R., J. Decker, and J. Bliesner. 1979. A community outreach program for socially isolated older persons. *Journal of Gerontological Social Work* 1 (3): 211–24.

Toseland, R., A. Derico, and M. Owen. 1984. Alzheimer's Disease and related disorders: Assessment and intervention. *Health and Social Work* 9 (3):212–28.

Toseland, R., and L. Hacker. 1982. Self-help groups and professional involvement. *Social Work* 27 (4):341–47.

————. 1985. Social worker's use of self-help groups as a resource for clients. *Social Work* 30 (3):232–39.

Toseland, R., A. Krebs, and J. Vahsen. 1978. Changing group interaction patterns. *Social Service Research* 2 (2):219–32.

Toseland, R., and W. Reid. 1985. Using rapid assessment instruments in a family service agency. *Social Casework* 66:547–55.

Toseland, R., and R. F. Rivas. 1984. *An introduction to group work practice*. New York: Macmillan.

Toseland, R., and S. Rose. 1978. Evaluating social skills training for older adults in groups. *Social Work Research and Abstracts* 14 (1):25–33.

Toseland, R., and C. Rossiter. 1989. Group intervention to support caregivers: A review and analysis. *Gerontologist* 29 (4):438–48.

Toseland, R., C. Rossiter, and M. Labrecque. 1989a. The effectiveness of three group intervention strategies to support caregivers. *American Journal of Orthopsychiatry* 59 (3):420–29.

————. 1989b. The effectiveness of peer-led and professionally-led groups to support family caregivers. *Gerontologist* 29 (4):465–71.

————. 1989c. The effectiveness of two kinds of support groups for caregivers. *Social Service Review* 63 (3):415–32.

Toseland, R., C. Rossiter, T. Peak, and P. Hill. In press. Therapeutic processes in peer-led and professionally-led support groups for caregivers. *International Journal of Group Psychotherapy* 40 (3).

Toseland, R., C. Rossiter, T. Peak, and G. Smith. In press. The comparative effectiveness of individual and group interventions to support family caregivers. *Social Work*.

Toseland, R., E. Sherman, and S. Bliven. 1981. The comparative effectiveness of two group work approaches for the evaluation of mutual support group among the elderly. *Social Work with Groups* 4 (1/2):137–53.

Toseland, R., and M. Siporin. 1986. When to recommend group treatment: A review of the clinical and the research literature. *The International Journal of Group Psychotherapy* 36 (2):171–201.

Toseland, R., and G. Smith. In press. The effectiveness of individual counseling for family caregivers of the elderly. *Psychology and Aging*.

Tropp, E. 1976. A developmental theory. In R. Roberts and N. Northern, eds.,

Theories of social work with groups, 198–237. New York: Columbia University Press.

Tross, S., and J. Blum. 1988. A review of group therapy with the older adult: Practice and research. In B. MacLennan, S. Saul, and M. Weiner, eds., *Group therapies for the elderly,* 3–32. Madison, Conn.: International Universities Press.

Tuckman, B. W. 1965. Development sequences in small groups. *Psychological Bulletin* 63:384–99.

U.S. Bureau of the Census. 1989. *Statistical abstract of the United States: 1989.* 109th ed. Washington D.C.: U.S. Government Printing Office.

U.S. Department of Health and Human Services. Assistant Secretary for Planning and Evaluation. 1982. Working papers on long-term care prepared for the 1980 Undersecretary's Task Force on Long-Term Care. Washington, D.C. U.S. Department of Health and Human Services.

U.S. Senate Special Committee on Aging (1987–1988). *Aging in America: Trends and projections.* Washington, D.C.: U.S. Senate Special Committee on Aging.

Vickery, F. 1952. A place in the sun for the aged: Group work activities for older people with an emphasis on club programs. *Group* 14 (2):3–8;23–24.

Waller, M., and M. Griffin. 1984. Group therapy for depressed elders. *Geriatric Nursing* 5 (7):309–11.

Weinberg, J. 1975. *The action approach.* New York: New American Library.

Weiner, M., A. Brok, and A. Snadowsky. 1987. *Working with the aged.* 2nd ed. East Norwalk, Conn.: Appleton-Century-Crofts.

Weisman, C. B., and P. Schwartz. 1989. Worker expectations in group work with the frail elderly: Modifying the models for a better fit. *Social work with groups* 12 (3):47–55.

Whitbourne, S. K. 1985. The psychological construction of the life span. In J. E. Birren and K. W. Schaie, eds., *Handbook of the psychology of aging* (2d ed.), 594–618. New York: Van Nostrand Reinhold.

Wills, T. 1978. Perceptions of clients by professional helpers. *Psychological Bulletin* 85:968–1000.

Wilson, G., and G. Ryland. 1949. The Friendship Club. In G. Wilson and G. Ryland, *Social group work practice: The creative use of the social process,* 514–29. Boston: Houghton Mifflin.

Wilson, M. 1977. Enhancing the lives of aged in a retirement center through a program of reading. *Educational Gerontology* 4 (3):245–51.

Wolcott, A. 1986. Art therapy: An experimental group. In I. Burnside, ed., *Working with the elderly: Group process and techniques,* 292–310. Noth Scituate, Mass.: Duxbury Press.

Wolk, R., and R. Wolk, 1971. Professional workers' attitudes toward the aged. *Journal of the American Geriatrics Society* 19:67–90.

Woods, J. 1953. *Helping older people enjoy life.* New York: Harper.

Yalom, I. 1983. *Inpatient group psychotherapy.* New York: Basic Books.

———. 1985. *The theory and practice of group psychotherapy.* 3d ed. New York: Basic Books.

Yesavage, J., and T. Karasu. 1982. Psychotherapy with elderly patients. *American Journal of Psychotherapy* 36:41–55.

Yost, E., L. Beutler, M. Corbishley, and J. Allender. 1986. *Cognitive group therapy: A treatment approach for depressed older adults*. New York: Pergamon Press.

Young, R., and E. Kahana. 1989. Specifying caregiver outcomes: Gender and relationship aspects of caregiving strain. *Gerontologist* 29 (5):660–66.

Zarit, S. 1983. *Aging and mental disorders*. Rev. ed. New York: Free Press.

————. In press. Interventions with frail elders and their families: Are they effective and why? In M. Stephens, J. Crowther, S. Hobfoll, and D. Tennenbaum, eds. *Stress and coping in later life families*. Washington, D.C.: Hemisphere.

Zarit, S., C. Anthony, and M. Boutselis. 1987. Interventions with caregivers of dementia patients: A comparison of two approaches. *Psychology and Aging* 2:225–34.

Zarit, S., and R. W. Toseland. 1989. Current and future directions in caregiving research. *Gerontologist* 29 (4):481–83.

Author Index

213

Subject Index

About the Author

RONALD W. TOSELAND is a practicing clinician at Catholic Family Services, Albany, New York, and a faculty member at the School of Social Welfare, State University of New York at Albany.